INDIA
BY RAIL

Royston Ellis

BRADT PUBLICATIONS, UK
HUNTER PUBLISHING, USA

For V. Keshav Raj
– an officer and a gentleman –
whose friendship and encouragement
helped me complete over 35,000 km of train rides
to research this guide.

First published in 1989 by Bradt Publications, 41 Nortoft Road, Chalfont St Peter, Bucks, SL9 0LA, England. Distributed in the U.S.A. by Hunter Publishing Inc., Raritan Center Parkway, CN94, Edison NJ 08818

British Library Cataloguing in Publication Data
Ellis, Royston
   India by rail.
   1. India (Republic) Visitors' guides
   I. Title
   915.4'0452

   ISBN 0-946983-30-5

Maps and plans by Hans van Well
Cover photographs: Front – The ubiquitous passenger locomotive of India (WP/733) built in 1949 photographed at Dalang on the branch line to Puri, Orissa (photo by Anthony Lambert).
Back – The Shatabdi Express (photo courtesy of Mr Rajagopalachari, General Manager, Northern Railway, New Delhi (India)).

Typeset by Acorn Bookwork, Salisbury, Wiltshire
Printed and bound in Hong Kong by Colorcraft Ltd.

THE AUTHOR

Royston Ellis, born in England, left school age 16 determined to be a writer. He quickly won fame as a poet, pop biographer and youth chronicler before leaving England, age 20, for a life of travel.

Under the pen name of Richard Tresillian, he has written many best selling novels, including *The Bondmaster*. He is a contributor of travel articles to magazines and newspapers world wide, including *Business Traveller*, *Asia Pacific* and *The Sunday Times*, and is the author of Bradt Publications' *Guide to Mauritius*.

Royston Ellis first visited India in 1963, and has had a home in the Indian sub-continent since 1980. He has travelled extensively in India by rail.

The author, sketched by train driver B. S. Gill; on the Kalka/Shimla railway.

ACKNOWLEDGEMENTS

Indian Railways must be one of the friendliest railways in the world: every railwayman I approached during the research for this guide, from train cleaners to general managers, was exceptionally helpful. I am grateful to them all.

To my old friend, John Burley, my thanks for introducing me to a seasoned rail traveller, Jeremy Sleeman, who sent me to his railway guru, the remarkable Dr Dandapani who is the GSA for Indrail Pass in the UK. Without the help of Dr Dandapani and of Mr R. Mathur, then Member Traffic, Railway Board, and his successor, Mr K.V. Balakrishnan, collecting information for this guide would have been impossible.

On my travels, I was sometimes accompanied by railwaymen and I am grateful for their encouragement, especially to Mr G. Chitti Babu of Southern Railway and to Mr D.R. Sharma of Northern Railway. Mr Leigh Pinero of Southern Railway was another stalwart and Mr L.S. Gaikwad of Central Railway was particularly helpful, as were Mr A. Chaturvedi, the Supervisor of the ITB, and Mr D.V. Sharma of the Railway Board Directorate of Tourism, who both coped patiently with my ever-changing itineraries.

All rail travellers in India have a person at every station to whom they can turn for advice and assistance: the Station Superintendent. Mr B. Jeyachandran, SS of Coimbatore and Mr M. Radhakrishnan, SS of 'Ooty' are among the many to whom I am indebted. To new railway friends, Mr G. Gurumurthy and Mr S. Radhakrishnan of the NV restaurant at Coimbatore station and to 'VIP bearer' Mr T. Vijayan of Ernakulam, my special thanks for making me feel at home. To B.S. Gill, a diesel locomotive driver on the Kalka/Shimla line who is also a renowned artist, my gratitude for his sketches.

I am especially grateful to Mr A.P. Muthuramalingam, Chief Commercial Inspector, Tiruchchirappalli for checking parts of my text, and to Alexander John of Trivandrum who took time from his studies to join me on journeys checking facts in 1989.

Off the rails, Ian and Deidre Wilson in Calcutta, Deepak Seth in Delhi and Arunesh Maiyar in Bombay were gracious hosts, and Guman Singh in Jaiselmer, Kishar Arya in Ranchi and Rodney Henricus of Air Lanka were helpful at the right moments. My thanks too to my manager in Sri Lanka, K.P. Neel Jayantha and my assistant Tissa Samarsekera.

In England, Hugh Ballantyne kindly provided photos, help and the section on steam locomotives. Anthony Lambert likewise provided advice and photos.

Royston Ellis
Bentota, Sri Lanka
1989

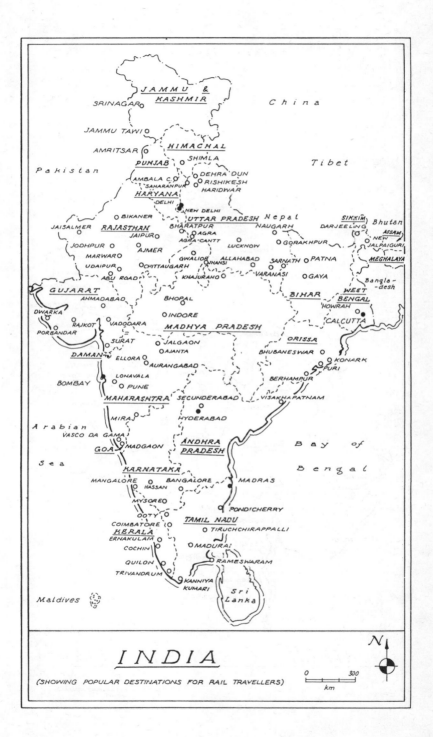

INDIA

(SHOWING POPULAR DESTINATIONS FOR RAIL TRAVELLERS)

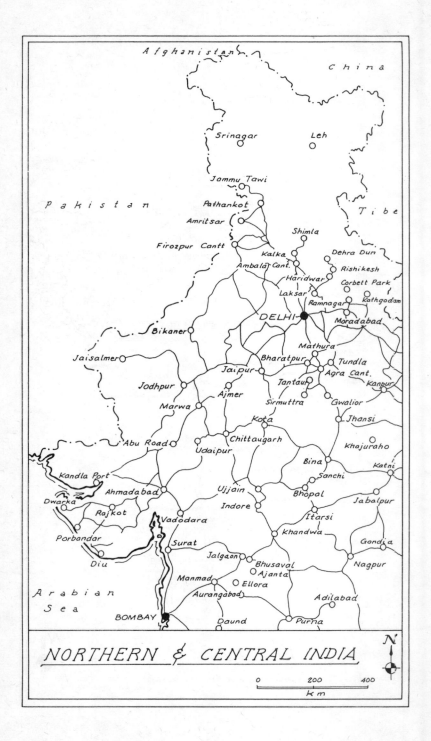

NORTHERN & CENTRAL INDIA

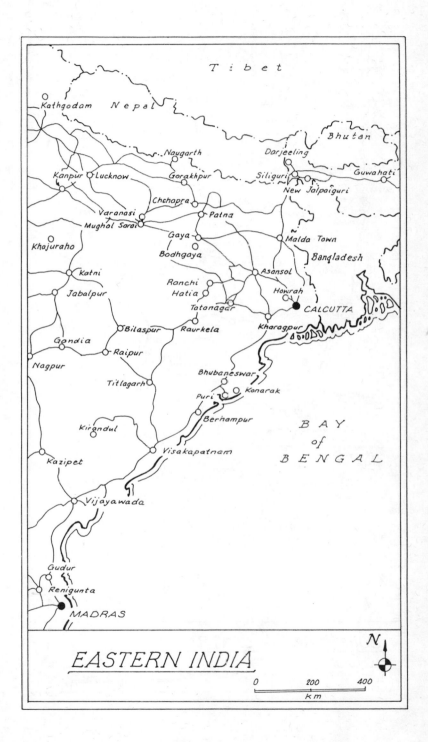

EASTERN INDIA

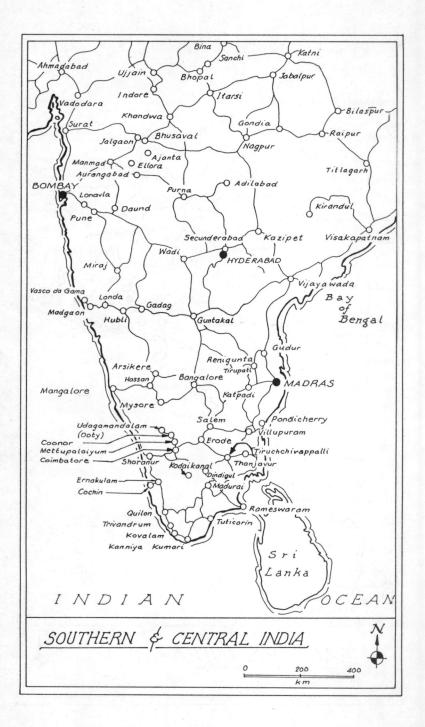

SOUTHERN & CENTRAL INDIA

0   200   400
km

Contents

Chapter 1

Discovering India by Rail

Whether you are a first time visitor to India, or an experienced traveller there, you'll find the best way to know India is to travel her length and breadth by train. It's an adventure that will teach you a lot about yourself as well as about India, and it's no hardship since trains in India are efficient, fast, frequent and fun.

Fly in a group or tour by coach and you'll be safely isolated from prolonged contact with India. Travel by local bus and you'll certainly see more than a tourist would, but you'll be uncomfortable and will end up hating the country simply because you feel awful.

Only train travel provides a comfortable berth for you to sleep on, meals at your seat, on-board toilets (some with a shower), travelling companions as diverse as the whole of India, and an aisle along which you can walk to stretch your legs or to meet new people. All that while travelling a network so extensive it has direct trains linking stations over 3,000 km apart.

The facilities are not just for the 1st Class passenger, all classes have bunks and bearer (waiter) service of meals, snacks and soft or hot drinks to your seat. On top of that, train travel is so inexpensive, you can travel in air-conditioned (AC) luxury (if that's your style) at less than a penny a kilometre.

When you travel by train you are taking part in contemporary Indian culture. It is a learning experience as well as a means of getting from, say, Madras to Bangalore. Indian fellow travellers will be kind and tolerant, talking to you if you wish, or respecting your need for solitude if you make it plain you want to be left alone. Put yourself in the right frame of mind, a positive one, and you will get far more out of discovering India by rail than a cheap train ride.

The beauty of all this is that there has never been a better time to travel in India by train. Within recent months rail travel has been transformed until it has become an experience foreigners, as well as Indians, find convenient and pleasurable.

It hasn't always been so. Yet now you can forget those horror stories about four hours spent in a queue to make reservations, about dreadful food, over-crowded compartments and rude railway officials.

1

The word is out in railwayland to help foreign tourists. It's easy to understand why. There is a nationwide drive to increase the number of tourists who visit India each year. (A target figure is 2.5 million by 1990.) They bring foreign currency which the country, and Indian Railways, needs. Tourism generates at least 10 per cent of India's foreign currency earnings without exporting any of the country's valuable material resources. Each new hotel room generates 12 new jobs.

The total of tourist arrivals rose to 1,163,774 in 1987. Brits topped the list with 166,590 visitors, with US citizens in second place with 134,876. About 80 per cent of the Indrail Passes sold each year are bought by Britons. The newly opened (1987) International Tourist Bureau (ITB) at New Delhi station handled over 76,400 rail bookings by foreign tourists in its first year of operation.

Improved services

It's not just because Indian Railways wants foreign tourists that services have improved. Computers have revolutionized the reservations process, benefiting every rail traveller. Meals and drinks are served more hygienically in covered foil casseroles and disposable cups. And for the foreign tourist there is a special quota of seats reserved on many trains, so a foreigner need not join the general queue to purchase tickets.

Actually, not all of India's over 7,000 stations pamper foreign tourists as a matter of course. Many of the stations I've visited are off the tourist track. I discovered, though, that by following the procedures set out in this guide, travel problems will be few.

Facilities for foreigners

First, a word of explanation for my use of the term 'foreign tourist'. A foreign passport holder who visits India for business or leisure is termed a 'foreign tourist' by Indian Railways, as opposed to an Indian who is touring by rail. I share the dismay of those who don't like to be called 'tourists' especially as we are clearly a different breed from the average 'package tourist'. But that's the way it is!

Foreign tourists, through the special quota, can make advance reservations for berths on busy trains when an Indian might only be wait-listed. 'Foreigners are our guests,' an official said when I queried the reason for giving foreigners priority over nationals. The real reason might be commercial: foreign currency makes foreigners valuable. I mention this to salve the conscience of sensitive travellers who have qualms about being treated to special privileges. Of course, if you want to join a long line and try to make your reservation from the general quota, and travel in the cheapest 2nd Class accommodation, you can. But, remember, you are thereby depriving an Indian, who can only afford the cheapest ticket, of a place in that queue and on that train.

By using the facilities developed for foreigners (such as priority bookings, travel in upper class carriages) the traveller is not only contributing much-needed foreign exchange but easing the pressure for the ordinary Indian rail passenger as well.

Don't worry about missing anything through making your reservation from the foreign tourist quota, or through the station superintendent's influence, you will still see (and smell and feel) the real India. You can't escape it when travelling by train.

Home on the rails

You can confidently make your home on the train, or simply take a train for a short trip, such as on India's 'bullet train', the Shatabdi Express which takes only 115 minutes for the 119 km run from New Delhi to Agra. The Shatabdi Express is a symbol of the changes taking place in Indian Railways. The best train to Agra used to be the Taj Express but that takes 90 minutes longer in non AC discomfort. The new train is all air conditioned with a pantry in each coach and meals included in the fare (see Chapter 11).

However, because of the distance between important stations, most train journeys in India involve overnight travel. An advantage in travelling overnight is that it saves time and the cost of hotel accommodation. Some tourists plan their itineraries around overnight trains, making the train their home. If there is a daylight alternative, you might like to take it so you can watch India passing by the window. Despite the improved comfort of train travel (the wooden seats in 2nd Class have recently been cushioned), it does require stamina and a certain kind of personality to spend several days and nights on a train.

Station amenities

As always with Indian Railways, there is a solution to every difficulty. A long journey can be broken at stations *en route* for a shower (most stations have them either in bathrooms attached to waiting rooms or in a separate building) or for a motionless night on *terra firma* at a railway retiring room.

Retiring rooms are one of Indian Railways' best kept secrets which few foreigners bother to discover. They are private guest rooms with attached bathrooms available at stations for rent by ticket (and Indrail Pass) holders for any period of 24 hours. They are perfect, secure bases from which to explore a town, or to recover from several nights on the rails. The station restaurants are close by and sometimes room service is provided.

Retiring rooms are usually the cheapest or the best value in town. If you only need a bed and don't worry about privacy, some stations also have dormitories, with lockers, showers and toilets (see Chapter 7).

Other facilities available depend on a station's importance. The major ones have closed circuit television (CCTV) showing US panel games, wrestling and Hindi movies chopped up between live station announcements. There could also be a chemist and curio shops, a book kiosk with US and UK best-selling paperbacks, a fruit stall, and drinking water either from coolers or dispensed by formidable ladies with ladles. All stations will have food and tea vendors, and waiting rooms.

Password
If you have several train journeys in mind, it can be more economical, and certainly much easier, to travel on an Indrail Pass (see Chapter 3).

Rail facts
Indian Railways is the second largest railway system on earth under a single management.

Origin:	1853 with 34 km of track, Bombay/Thane.
Network:	61,976 route kilometres.
Services:	7,000 passenger services operated daily.
Passengers:	10.38 million every day.
Stations:	7,084
Locomotives:	9,161 with 3,298 diesel, 4,427 steam and 1,436 electric traction.
Rolling Stock:	30,474 passenger coaches and 346,844 goods wagons.
Track:	Broad Gauge (BG): 1.67 m wide, most of the main line trunk routes: 33,831 km.
	Metre Gauge (MG): 1.00 m wide, mostly as feeder lines: 23,898 km.
	Narrow Gauge (NG): 0.762 m or 0.610 m wide, on limited sections of difficult terrain: 4,247 km.
Overall average speed, including halts:	Express/Mail trains: 47.1 kph (BG), 36.9 kph (MG).
	Pasenger trains: 27.2 kph (BG), 26.1 kph (MG).
Bridges:	114,260
Level crossings:	37,101
Regular employees:	1,617,600 plus 200,000 casual workers.
Average wage:	Rs 24,808 p.a.
Retiring rooms:	1,970 beds at 385 stations.
Dormitories:	1,214 beds at 156 stations.
Catering:	Available at 2,987 stations and on 87 pairs of trains.

(Statistics supplied by Indian Railways, as at March 31 1988.)

Administration
Nine railways: Northern, North Eastern, Northeast Frontier, Eastern, Central, South Central, South Eastern, Western and Southern.

If you start your train journey from New Delhi, your first experience will probably be of Northern Railway, the busiest and most crowded. Bombay is served by Central and Western, and Calcutta by Eastern and South Eastern. Madras is the HQ of Southern Railway.

The railways are run by the Ministry of Railways through the Railway Board. According to the Board's yearbook, 'The economic, agricultural and industrial development of India is inextricably interwoven with Indian Railways' development and fortunes.'

Railwayland in India is really a country within a country. It has its own electricity service, telephone system, hospitals, colleges, bureaucracy. It is so self-sufficient it stands apart from the normal life of India, yet without the railways there would be no normal life.

Steam and special trains

You will catch glimpses of steam engines, usually shunting, throughout India, but hurry if you want to ride a steam train. They are being phased out rapidly with 523 steam engines condemned in 1987/88. In ten years they will all have gone (see Chapter 6).

In the meantime, though, there is a chance to ride not only steam engines, but also the lorry-like rail car from Kalka to Shimla, the rack-and-pinion steam train to 'Ooty' with its wooden carriages like something from an Agatha Christie movie, and the famous, but painfully slow, toy train to Darjeeling, when it is operating. In addition a train created out of carriages that used to belong to maharajas, the Palace on Wheels, steams through Rajasthan once a week. More modern marvels are the superfast Rajdhani Expresses serving New Delhi, Calcutta and Bombay, the Shatabdi Express between New Delhi and Jhansi and the commuter specials like the double-deckers from Bombay and the newly-opened Calcutta metro. Or you can travel in your own private coach on special tours (see Chapter 11).

Chapter 2

Planning the Trip

PRELIMINARIES

Advance planning is essential to get the most out of travelling by train in India. Foreigners who expect a train service run the way it is at home will be annoyed to find they can't buy a ticket to travel overnight at a moment's notice. Reservations have to be made on certain day-time trains and on all overnight trains. It is to your advantage to do so as far in advance as possible.

When planning the trip, set aside at least one day after your arrival in India to make reservations. At the gateway cities of New Delhi, Bombay, Calcutta and Madras, there are special bureaux dealing with foreign rail tourist bookings as well as counters at the airports. When you buy an Indrail Pass outside India, reservations can be done at the same time but you will need to confirm them on arrival (see Chapter 3).

Maps

The first requirement for planning your trip is a map of India on which to locate the places you want to visit. Maps of India are available from good bookshops and, in England, from Edward Stanford Ltd, 12/14 Long Acre, London WC2E 9LP. Tel: 01 836 1321. In the USA, try The Complete Traveler at 199 Madison Avenue, New York, NY 10016. Tel: 212 685 9007 or Forsyth Travel Library Inc., PO Box 2975, 9154 West 57 St, Shawnee Mission, KS 66201-1357. Tel: 913 384 3440.

Free maps and lots of city and state information, as well as a leaflet about rail travel, are available from the Government of India tourist offices.

On your map, mark the places you want to visit so you can choose the most convenient airport. The typical first-time visitor to India usually wants to visit Agra and Kashmir with a side trip to Nepal, in which case Delhi is the gateway city. As the rail booking facilities at the International Tourist Bureau (ITB) at New Delhi station are the best in India, it's the ideal place for starting any rail journey.

6

Government of India Tourist Offices

AUSTRALIA
Sydney: 9th Floor, Carlton Centre, 55 Elizabeth Street, Sydney NSW 2000. Tel: 02-232-1600/1796.

AUSTRIA
Vienna: Opernring 1/E/11, 1010 Vienna. Tel: 5871462.

CANADA
Toronto: 60 Bloor Street, West Suite No. 1003, Ontario M4W 3B8. Tel: 416962 3787/88.

FRANCE
Paris: 8 Boulevard de la Madeleine, 75009 Paris 9. Tel: 4265-83-86.

ITALY
Milan: Via Albricci 9, 21022 Milan. Tel: 804952.

JAPAN
Tokyo: Pearl Building, 9–18 Ginza, 7-Chome, Chuo-ku, Tokyo 104. Tel: (03) 571-5062/63.

KUWAIT
Kuwait: Saadoum-Al-Jassim Bldg, Fahad Al-Salem Street, 13048 Safat. Tel: 2426099/88.

MALAYSIA
Kuala Lumpur: 2nd Fl. Wisma HLA, Lot No. 203, Jalan Raja Chulan 50200. Tel: 2425301/285.

SINGAPORE
Singapore: 5th Floor Podium Block, Ming Court Hotel, Tanglin Road, Singapore 1024. Tel: 2355737.

SWEDEN
Stockholm: Sveavagen 9-11, S-11157 Stockholm. Tel: 08-215081.

SWITZERLAND
Geneva: 1–3 Rue de Chantepoulet, 1201 Geneva. Tel: 022-321813.

THAILAND
Bangkok: Singapore Airlines Bldg, 3rd Floor, 62/5 Thaniya Road, Bangkok. Tel: 2352585.

UAE
Dubai: PO Box 12856, DNATA, Dubai. Tel: 695398.

UNITED KINGDOM
London: 7 Cork Street, London W1X 2AB. Tel: 01-437-3677/78.

USA
Chicago: 230 North Michigan Avenue, Chicago IL 60601. Tel: 312-236-6899/7869.

Los Angeles: 3550 Wilshire Boulevard, Suite 204, Los Angeles CA 90010. Tel: 213-380-8855.

New York: 30, Rockefeller Plaza, Room 15, North Mezzanine, New York NY 10020. Tel: 212-586-4901/2/3.

WEST GERMANY
Frankfurt: Kaiserstrasse 77-111, 6000 Frankfurt Main-1. Tel: 235423/24.

TIMETABLES

A rail timetable is useful so you can see how long it takes to travel
between cities, but if you don't have one, measure the distance on the
map between the major cities you want to visit. For every 50 km, allow
one hour of train time. For example, the distance between Delhi and
Jammu Tawi (the station for Kashmir) is about 550 km which means a
journey of 11 hours. From the journey time chart on page 159,
Chapter 9, you can see that the fastest journey time between those
cities is actually 10 hrs 10 mins. Other trains take from 11 to 15 hours.

The best timetable readily available outside India is the Thomas
Cook Overseas Timetable which contains 30 pages devoted to India
showing, in easy to understand format, the times of all important trains
and the classes available. There is also a route map which is useful for
planning the trip since all rail lines are shown. The timetable is
published six times a year and is available from the Timetable
Publishing Office, Thomas Cook Ltd, Thorpe Wood, Peterborough
PE3 6SB, England. Tel: 0733 502568.

Indian Railways publish a timetable called *Trains At A Glance*
(TAG) twice a year (May and November) which is available outside
India for US$3 through the GSAs for the Indrail Pass (see Chapter 3).
In India it costs Rs6. It contains most of the train times and
information a visitor will need. Codes by each station entry indicate
the facilities available.

The TAG has a station index although it does not give the page
number of every reference to each station. Also, there is no indication
of what classes of accommodation are available on each train, nor all
the stops the train makes.

More detailed timetables which include all the halts made by slow
passenger trains are published by each of the nine railway zones,
covering the services operated by each zone. They are only available in
India, at the station bookstalls within their area. These timetables cost
Rs5 each. Unfortunately, they are not always accurate about what
classes are available.

There is a publication that combines all the zone timetables in one,
thick volume, with an index showing every station. Called *Newman's
Indian Bradshaw* it is published monthly and costs Rs20. It is
sometimes difficult to obtain in India although its cover lists 70
stations, including Howrah and Sealdah in Calcutta, Delhi (but not
New Delhi) and Bombay (VT but not Central) where it can be bought.
It is not sold in Madras. The overseas agents for this excellent if
crudely-printed volume are Wm Dawson & Sons Ltd, Cannon House,
Folkestone, Kent, England.

Midnight is indicated as 2400 hrs for train arrivals, and 0000 hrs for
departures.

How long?

The ideal length for a holiday in India is at least three weeks, but with careful planning you can see a lot by train in just one week. I've suggested some itineraries in Chapter 9. A three week visit allows sufficient time to recover from the flight, get used to the heat, the clamour, the food, and to feel at ease. You'll be able to see enough different parts of India in three weeks to whet your appetite for further visits when you can concentrate on the areas you most enjoyed.

Planning the itinerary

It is a common error of first-time travellers to try to include too much on their itinerary. It is difficult to imagine the distances involved, or the effect on a newcomer to India of a lot of train travelling. For instance, from Delhi to Madras is 2194 km (1362 miles), the same distance as the crow flies from Paris to Leningrad. So allow time in your itinerary not just for the train journey but for extras such as delays, waiting time, and also for recovery, relaxation, a chance to see the sights, and to let things happen.

Unfortunately, the sheer volume of traffic makes delays almost inevitable. Many routes are single track only so a train has to wait on a double track section for any oncoming trains. This is known as 'crossing' and explains why a train stops in the middle of nowhere. The late running of one train extends to the train behind it and can affect the train coming towards it too.

If you are on a train that seems bound to arrive late, don't worry about missing the connection since that could be late as well. Also, because of 'cushion time' in rail schedules, even as much as an hour's delay could have been allowed for. This gives an opportunity for the train to make up time on the last lap of its journey and arrive on schedule.

Just in case, allow at least an hour to make connections unless there are plenty of alternative trains should you actually miss the one you want. Stations in India are always interesting places to wait; if you tire of watching the other passengers you could have a meal, a shower or take a walk into town. If you have to hang around a station during the night, check into a retiring room and sleep; the attendant will wake you on request (see Chapter 7).

As well as train delays, there are likely to be unexpected frustrations when you do arrive at your destination, such as a local holiday or a strike, or it could even be something nice that makes you want to stay longer. Build plenty of 'cushion time' into your own itinerary with days of nothing planned so that you have some spare days if you need them.

Plan your route to save on time. Once you've left your originating city, it makes sense not to return there unless you have to. Avoid backtracking; trains in India go across country too, not just via Delhi or the main cities. For instance, you can go from Agra to Lucknow without having to change at Delhi.

If timetables bore you, work out basically where you want to go and leave it to the Indrail Pass GSA (see next chapter) or, in India, the rail tourist guide at one of the Foreign Tourist Bureaux to suggest an itinerary. They will know the main trains but you may have to curb their enthusiasm to book you on trains leaving or arriving at impossible times.

Avoid trains that bring you to your destination late at night, especially if you've never been there before. Also trains leaving before 0600 should be resisted. Not only does that mean early rising but the passengers already on the train will be sleeping and that will make settling in difficult.

The ideal departure time is about 1000 with 1800 hours the latest for overnight journeys so you have time to size up the other occupants of the compartment before bedding down for the night. Lower berths, incidentally, are only supposed to be occupied as berths from 2100 to 0600. They are used as seats for all occupants during the day.

Not all trains have 1st or AC class, although all do have 2nd class of some sort. Some trains over certain routes are better than others over the same route; it's worth finding out which are faster, more convenient and have a pantry car.

Most important trains run daily but there are some superfast long distance expresses which run only once a week. You will need to study the timetables carefully, and all the little notes too, to find the best trains. I've listed some of them in Chapter 12.

When to go

The most popular time for rail tourists is November to February which is the peak of the usual tourist season of September to March. April, May and June should be avoided, not because the weather is unbearably hot (which it is), but because that's the domestic tourist season. All India takes to the tracks then to visit relatives, attend weddings, go home, make a pilgrimage or simply to ride a train because everyone else is doing it. 85 per cent of Indians on holiday travel by rail. The trains are packed, reservations are impossible to get, and it's hell on wheels.

July and August is the monsoon season and a favourite time for foreigners to take the train to Jammu Tawi on the way to Kashmir, or to head for Shimla. If you can only visit India during April to August, plan on staying in the cooler hill areas and make sure you have train and hotel reservations secured.

Although in July and August you'll be drenched with perspiration in Delhi (humidity can reach 90 per cent) in December and January the capital can be cold. If you're starting a trip from Delhi, the spring (February and March) and autumn (October and November) are best.

How to go

The four international airports of Delhi, Bombay, Calcutta and Madras are accessible by frequent direct flights from Europe and Asia. From other continents, a break in journey is usually necessary.

Flights to Delhi from London take nine hours nonstop and up to 15 hours via other points. Return fares range from £2,124 1st Class and £1,286 Business Class down to £507 for a special Economy Class fare. The same fares apply for Bombay; Calcutta and Madras are a few pounds more. There are cheaper fares available. For instance, the travel organization, Wexas International (45 Brompton Road, Knightsbridge, London SW3 1DE, England; membership enquiries: Tel: 01 581 0349) quotes about £455 return to any of the gateway airports.

Trailfinders Travel Centre at 46/48 Earls Court Road, London W8 6EJ, England. Tel: 01 938 3366 offers a complete service for the independent traveller, and no membership is required. They have fares by many airlines between £400 and £500 depending on the season, and can also offer great discounts on top hotels. They have an immunization centre, a travel insurance service and a library for their clients, as well as a travel bookshop. Reduced rate tickets can be bought by cash or credit card and issued on the spot.

Student and independent travellers can make their arrangements through STA. Their main UK office is at 74/86 Old Brompton Road, London SW7 3LQ. Tel: 01 581 1022, for intercontinental enquiries. They also have offices in Bristol, Cambridge and Oxford and at many campus cities in the USA. Their fares are competitive with the best and their staff are experienced travellers.

A novel way of flying to India is to go to Goa or Trivandrum. Inspirations East Ltd, P.O. Box 990, Windsor, Berks SL4 3WW. Tel: 0753 830883, sell a special flight/rail package throughout the season (October to April) from Gatwick to Goa and Trivandrum. They have no agents and you can only book directly with them. Return fares start at £550 and include basic accommodation for four nights on arrival, a 15 day Indrail Pass (1st Class) and three nights accommodation before departure. Since Goa and Trivandrum are much pleasanter airports to arrive at than any of the 'big four' this seems an attractive deal. For the dedicated rail traveller, Trivandrum is preferable to Goa since there are many lines and sights within easy reach, whereas from Goa there is only one way out (see Chapter 10).

Access to Trivandrum is also possible from Colombo, Sri Lanka, by Air Lanka (recommended) and Indian Airways as are the airports of Tiruchchirappalli (not as efficient as Trivandrum), Bombay and Madras. Sea travel by ferry from Sri Lanka to Rameswaram is temporarily suspended. Travel overland from Nepal is possible to link up with a rail connection to Gorakhpur or Patna where onward reservations can be made.

If you arrive at Trivandrum, Goa or Tiruchchirappalli, or overland from Nepal, allow at least a day to make rail reservations since there are no special Foreign Tourist Bureaux at those stations. When buying a rail ticket in Nepal, make it for the short journey to the first major station in India where you can buy an onward ticket. Otherwise you can get ripped off, paying more for the ticket in Nepal than you would in India and not getting the reservations you think you've got (see Chapter 10: Gorakhpur).

Where to go

In addition to the cities of Delhi (the top favourite), Bombay, Calcutta and Madras, the most popular destinations for foreign rail travellers are:

Agra (Taj Mahal)
Aurangabad (for Ellora caves)
Bangalore (a Raj resort)
Bhubaneswar (Temple City)
Goa (via Vasco da Gama station)
Gorakhpur (for Nepal)
Jaipur (Pink City)
Jaiselmer (desert fort)
Jalgaon (for the caves at Ajanta)
Jammu Tawi (for bus to Kashmir)
Jhansi (for Khajuraho carvings)
Jodhpur (for Rajasthan)
Madurai (Tamil culture)
New Jalpaiguri (for Darjeeling)
Ooty (Udagamandalam, for hill railway and resort)
Puri (for Konark sun temple and sea)
Quilon (for Kerala backwaters)
Rameswaram (for Sri Lanka ferry, when operating)
Shima (hill resort)
Varanasi (Benares, ancient holy city)

Some other places worth visiting are Udaipur, the Venice of the East; Mysore, for its charm and sandalwood; Cochin, (via Ernakulam), for its maritime heritage; and the Land's End of India, Kanniya Kumari, with its sun and moon rising over three seas.

How to get to these destinations by train is detailed in Chapter 9, and what facilities you'll find at these and some other popular stations is shown in Chapter 10.

What to take

As little as possible. Even a flight bag weighing only 5 kg can be a strain to carry in extreme heat. You really do not need half the things you feel you should take. Anyway, if you do find you've left something behind, you can usually buy a replacement in India.

By reducing your belongings to the minimum essentials, you can probably pack everything in a bag small enough to carry on the plane with you. A duffle bag is good because its flexible shape allows it to be stuffed away or used as a pillow, but be careful of storing valuables in it since it can be ripped open. If you will be trecking or hiking, a backpack is best. It should have an internal frame as an external one can break easily and sticks into people and things. Keep it as light as possible.

A small suitcase, made of a lightweight, durable shell, gives you mobility, stores neatly under a train seat and is more secure because it can be locked. If you take a lot of luggage, it could be worthwhile storing it while you are travelling by train, and buying a cheap case in India (at about £4.00/$7.00) to take only what you need on your rail trip.

Books are usually the heaviest and bulkiest item in a traveller's luggage. Fortunately, you won't need many. Railway bookstalls (Wheelers in the north and Higginbothams in the south) are excellent, with a vast range of popular, and classical, paperbacks in English. If you need to keep in touch with the world, a miniature portable radio that receives BBC World Service is useful. Some travellers are inseparable from their Walkmans; it seems a shame to block your ears to India like that.

Prepare yourself for train travel in the same way that you would for a long-haul flight. Take an eyeshade and ear plugs so you can sleep if the compartment light is on and people are talking late into the night.

For sleeping on trains, a cotton sleeping bag liner from the YHA can be useful, with a blanket bought in India instead of taking a sleeping bag. If you intend visiting chilly hill stations, then a sweater and even a jacket, scarf and woolly hat could be needed.

Whatever clothes you take should be lightweight and quick drying. Cotton underwear (as long as it's loose) is the best, with a spare set for when you're washing the dirty ones. Shirts with lots of deep pockets with buttons or zips are a good idea. A cotton money belt is favoured by experienced travellers and is especially useful for keeping valuables close to your body when you're asleep.

Safari-type shirts can be made up from jazzy cotton material for about £3 each in 24 hours. A tailor will be willing to copy your favourite garments so you need not take spares but have them made there.

The light cotton shirts and pyjama-like trousers worn by Indian travellers are ideal for male and female foreigners and can be bought cheaply. A *lungi*, a floor length piece of cloth wrapped around the waist, is good for nightwear or for hiding under when you're changing clothes in a crowded carriage.

Most garments sold in Europe for wear in the tropics are a disappointment, either too hot or too fashionable to be practical. An exception are the trousers (bags) produced by Rohan Designs plc, 30 Maryland Road, Tongwell, Milton Keynes, MK15 8HN, England. Tel: 0908 618888. Rohan bags have large zippered pockets everywhere, including one that curls inside the back thigh, useful for keeping an emergency stash of toilet paper. Dark colours are best since light shades quickly show the grime from train travel. One pair is enough since you can be certain they'll dry overnight in a retiring room bathroom but they're so lightweight, you could take two in case of a special occasion. My bags were admired by fashion-conscious Bombayites and by diplomats at a cocktail party in Calcutta. Other rail travellers I met wearing them swore by them too.

A pair of sandals is essential for wearing in train toilets. Cheap plastic ones (from Rs10) can be bought at street markets. These, and a stout pair of walking shoes or good trainers, will be sufficient footwear. Socks should be cotton.

A small pocket torch is necessary for night travel, and a padlock or two, and a pocket knife for peeling fruit. You may like an air-filled pillow but this can be bought at main stations for about £1.50/$2.60 which includes an attractive woven cotton pillow case. The neck support pillows marketed worldwide have synthetic material covers and cause too much sweating in the heat. They're expensive too compared with full size pillows in India.

Take a plastic container for your special toiletries. Toothpaste and soap can be purchased everywhere but imported eau de colognes are expensive. You will need toilet paper; although it can be bought in India, it's in small rolls and you will have to hunt for it. A large plastic bag is always useful, especially when you take a shower on a train (see Chapter 5).

You will need a small towel, although bath towels are provided in railway retiring rooms, for drying your hands when you wash them before and after eating a meal with your fingers. No handtowel, or paper, is provided in train toilets but the bedroll you can rent at night does have a handtowel in it. A handkerchief will do in an emergency although it will soon smell of curry unless you wash it out frequently. Wet wipes or similar could help then.

An essential item is a water bottle and you can buy them at most stations. Outdoor equipment shops in Europe and the USA sell tougher ones designed for hikers. These are ideal. Carry a crown bottle opener too or, more versatile, a Swiss Army knife, for opening soft drinks and beer bottles.

It is worthwhile taking your full quota of liquor into India since imported spirits are very expensive. Take film as well. You can buy notebooks and pens in India. Take, or buy, your own cup into which enough tea or coffee can be poured by station vendors. You pay

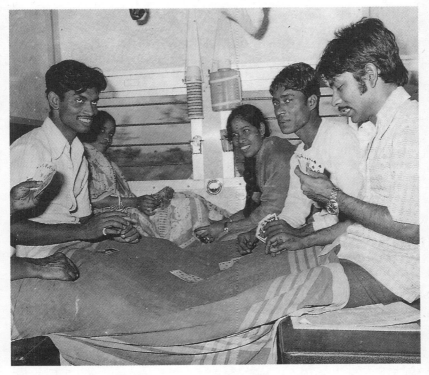

Bring a pack of cards, and you can make friends anywhere!

according to the measure. The tea is delicious, milky and with cinnamon or ginger flavour.

HEALTH

I was advised to take all sorts of medical preparations but I threw out most of the ointments and pills soon after arrival when I discovered I could buy them locally. However, take your favourite headache and diarrhoea remedies and any prescription medicines you need, anti-malaria pills and water purifying tablets (available from Boots). Sometimes brand name medicines available in India are out of date.

Unless a visitor arrives in India from a yellow fever area, no vaccinations are required for entry. However, they are recommended.

Cholera: If you are going from India to a country that imposes restrictions on arrivals from India because of cholera, then you need to have an inoculation and a certificate to prove it. In any case, a cholera jab is a good thing to have before you go. It is effective for six months.

Yellow fever: Do not arrive in India without a certificate of vaccination against yellow fever within six months of departing from a declared yellow fever area, such as Kenya, or by an aircraft that's transitted such areas; you'll find yourself isolated in quarantine for six days. The vaccination is effective for ten years.

Malaria: There is a risk of malaria throughout the year, so be prepared. The British Airways medical service advises Paludrin (no prescription); two tablets a day starting one day before arrival. Nivoquine (no prescription) should also be taken; two tablets weekly, starting one week before travel. The tablets should also be taken for four weeks after leaving India. In the UK, advice on malaria precautions is available by taped message on telephone number 01 636 7921.

Diarrhoea: Non-prescription remedies are limited in variety in the UK, but don't worry, you can easily buy prescription pills (such as Lomotil) to stabilize yourself from station pharmacies in India. Take Imodium with you, just in case. The Indian Railways' medical service is excellent so if you are suffering, a railway doctor could fix you up. Since water is a cause of gippy tummy, carry purifying tablets (Iodine) to use in it if there is absolutely nothing else to drink. A water filter is even more effective, and may be purchased from MASTA (Medical Advisory Services for Travellers Abroad), Keppel St, London WC1E 7HT. Tel: 01 631 4408. MASTA can also sell you a Concise Health Brief containing up to date medical information for India.

SAFETY

Keep your passport with you (in a deep, zippered pocket, or body belt) all the time. Not just for security but to show whenever it's asked for by officials.

Do not display large amounts of money. Keep enough for the day's expenses in your wallet or purse and hide the rest somewhere else. Resist all temptation to exchange foreign currency other than with licensed dealers. It's illegal and you stand a very good chance of being ripped off.

Leave your most valued possessions at home; they could get lost or stolen. Leave your address book and Filofax behind too, and only bring copies of the addresses and information you need. Keep a record of your credit card and passport numbers at home together with a photocopy of your airline ticket and insurance policy in case of emergency.

A padlock is useful, either for locking your luggage to the chain provided under the seats of newer carriages, or to lock the retiring room, locker or compartment door when you're absent. A combination padlock removes the risk of losing the key. There is a combination padlock with a metre of steel wire (it's called a 'Travellers Lock Away') that is ideal for securing luggage to a carriage fixture when you're sleeping or leave it unattended.

Keep travellers cheques, money and tickets close to you. When sleeping on trains, have them on your body somewhere (in the pocket of your pants or stuffed in your body belt but not under the pillow). Keep the numbers of everything important in a separate place so if you do lose anything you have the details. Insure to cover loss of possessions as well as for accident and illness.

Sooner or later when you tell people you are planning to travel in India by train, someone will ask 'Are you sure it's safe?' It is, as long as you are sensible. Train travel itself has generally a good standard of safety, especially when the volume of passengers travelling every day is taken into consideration. For security while on a train see Chapter 5.

MONEY

Take your money in US dollar or pound sterling travellers cheques. Many travellers find the changing process is time-consuming at city banks. The solution is to change money at the airport on arrival, or at the cashier's desk of major hotels. (You don't necessarily have to stay there but would need to be using one of their public rooms such as the coffee shop.)

You can also use travellers cheques to buy rail tickets at the ITB in New Delhi and the Foreign Tourist Bureaux elsewhere and receive the change in rupees (see Chapter 3). Tickets and reservations from the foreign tourist quota have to be paid in foreign currency or travellers cheques anyway. Credit cards can be used in hotels and shops but not for buying rail tickets.

If you don't have an onward or return ticket, make certain you have access to enough funds to leave India when you want to. Better to bring the money in some form (travellers cheques, credit cards) since having funds sent from overseas can take ages. Don't expect your consul to send you home if you get destitute.

The usual safeguard of being able to cash a home country personal cheque guaranteed by a banker's card (at your consul) or credit card, when you need money in an emergency, cannot be relied on in India because of exchange controls. If you do run out of money, you may have to borrow from friends or check into a good hotel and sign the bills until funds arrive from home.

The **currency** of India is the rupee (Rs) and there are a 100 paise (P) to one rupee. Coins are in denominations of 5, 10, 25, 50 paise and 1, 2 and 5 rupees. There are 2, 5, 10, 20, 50, 100 and 500 rupee notes.

Finding change isn't the problem it used to be. However, save coins and low denomination notes to pay the correct amount to platform vendors; the train could pull out before you get your change.

What will it cost?

It depends on you. If you intend to buy your air ticket to leave India and your rail tickets while there, then allow sufficient for those in your budgeting. The cost of Indrail Passes and train tickets are in the next chapter.

While you are on a train, expenses are easy to control: meals, drinks (no alcohol), reading matter and a bedroll for the night are all. Expenses increase when you get off the train although if you stay in station retiring rooms and eat in railway restaurants, these will still be low.

Getting to and from what you've come to see, the cost of souvenirs, medicines, laundry, beers, nights in hotels and occasional extravagance will demand a larger budget.

The cost of a day on a train and a night at a railway station, could work out as follows:

MEDIUM BUDGET			LOW BUDGET		
Meals					
Nonveg b/fast	Rs	7.00	Veg b/fast	Rs	5.00
Special NV lunch		15.00	Veg lunch		7.00
Std NV dinner		9.00	Std NV dinner		9.00
Snacks/fruit		15.00	Snacks/fruit		5.00
Drinks					
Tea/soft drinks			Tea (and tap water)		7.00
Mineral water		25.00			
Reading					
News magazine		10.00	Newspaper		2.00
Night					
Bed in twin bedded			Dormitory bed		15.00
room		30.00			
		Rs 111.00			Rs 50.00
(Approximately £4.22/US$7.40)			(£1.90/US$3.33)		

If you go off the rails, expect your expenses to double or triple. Allow plenty for those nights in luxury hotels (at £25/$44 to £65/$115) when you want pampering.

RED TAPE

Visa

Citizens of all countries, including the Commonwealth, require visas to enter India. A multiple entry visa will be needed if you intend to visit Nepal or Sri Lanka from India and then return home via India. Incidentally, a multiple entry visa is not valid for re-entry if you actually return to your home country, or go on further than neighbouring countries, and then try to use it to get back into India. You need a new visa then.

A Tourist Visa, whether single or multiple entry, is valid for three months stay in India from the date of the first entry. It can be extended for a further three months by applying to the Foreigners' Registration offices in New Delhi, Bombay, Calcutta or Madras. There are also Entry Visas and Transit Visas but the Tourist Visa is the one rail travellers on holiday need.

An application form, obtainable from travel agents, tourist offices or the Indian High Commission or Embassy, requires personal particulars including Father's/Husband's name. Three passport size photographs have to be submitted with the completed form. Personal applications are usually approved for the next working day while postal applications take two to three weeks.

The Visa Shop in London's Charing Cross Shopping Arcade (part of the underground station), Tel: 01 379 0419/0376, can handle visa applications for a fee of £10. Visa fees vary from time to time. In January, 1989, the fee was £23 (single entry) or £34.50 (two or three entries) for British citizens. US citizens and Commonwealth citizens paid £3 or £4 for a visa, while European Community citizens (other than British) paid £2.50.

Restricted, Protected Areas, Long Term or Research Project Visas take 10 to 12 weeks. If you are not a UK resident but apply in London, the time to get the visa can extend to three or more weeks.

The High Commission of India is at India House, Aldwych, London WC2. Tel: 01 836 8434/0990. In Birmingham, it is at 86 New Street, Birmingham B2. Tel: 021 6430829. In Ireland, the Embassy of India is at 6 Leeson Park, Dublin 6. Tel: 970843/970806.

Tourists must arrive in India within six months of the date of issue of the visa. The form asks you to state the port of landing but if you change you mind and fly to Madras instead of Delhi, it won't matter. No proof of return air ticket is required, nor evidence of funds available.

As well as the visa, a special permit is required to visit Darjeeling town by train. This is obtainable from the Foreigners' Registration offices in Calcutta, Delhi, Bombay or Madras, or from any Indian mission abroad. The northern districts of West Bengal (Darjeeling, Cooch Behar, Malda, Jalpaiguri and West Dinapur) are restricted areas, as are the states of Assam, Maghalaya and Tripura.

A permit is also needed to visit Punjab but not for travelling by rail from Delhi to Jammu Tawi or Shimla via Punjab.

Photographs
Permits are required to photograph locomotives, trains and loco sheds. If you are planning extensive and serious photography, make sure you

have one before you go so you can ward off the rare official who may want to hinder you. Apply to your nearest Indian High Commission or Embassy at least 90 days in advance to make sure of getting the necessary piece of paper. On the other hand, for casual photography (as long as no notice is displayed specifically prohibiting it) you can snap away without a permit.

Arrival

On the flight to India you will be given a card to fill in for immigration. A classic misprint on this seems to be asking for the name of your father's husband. Fill the card in accurately and be prepared for a long wait at the Immigration desk since your passport and the card will be scrutinized by two sets of officials in different offices.

There are red and green channels in customs but you'll be stopped, even in the green channel. Importation of personal jewellery, camera, tape recorder, binoculars, transistor radio, professional equipment, etc., is permitted duty free provided all items are taken out with you when you leave.

200 cigarettes or 50 cigars or 250 g of tobacco and alcoholic liquor up to 0.95 litres (you'll have to drink some of it if you have a full litre bottle) are permitted duty free. The interrogation can be either searching or casual; don't try to be clever.

There is no restriction on the amount of foreign currency that may be taken into India. However, more than US$1,000, or its equivalent, should be declared on a currency declaration form. This helps if you want to take it out again. No Indian currency may be taken in.

You can change travellers cheques and cash at the airport exchange counters (open 24 hours a day). Keep the receipt of the transaction since you will need this when you try to pay a hotel bill in rupees, to prove you bought rupees with foreign currency. Don't change all your foreign currency as you might need it to buy rail tickets (see Chapter 3). Your exchange receipts will be needed if you want to exchange rupees back to foreign currency.

Departure

By the time you leave India, you will be used to queuing, but make sure you join the right queue when checking in for your flight; you might have to queue to pay the embarkation tax first. The foreign travel tax, as it's called, was raised in 1989 to Rs 150 for passengers departing for Sri Lanka, Nepal, Maldives, Pakistan, Afghanistan, Bangladesh, Bhutan and Burma. Departure for other overseas destinations costs Rs 300 in tax, payable in rupees.

Exit permits are not required by holders of tourist visas who have stayed less than 90 days. If you've stayed over 90 days you'll need an income tax clearance certificate. You are not supposed to take Indian rupees out of the country.

You will be given a departure card to fill in before joining the long wait at Immigration. Duty free goods such as cameras brought into India may have to be produced to customs; be prepared for questions. There will be several security searches before you eventually board the plane.

SOLO AND GROUP TRAVEL

The success of a decision to go alone, with friends or in a group ultimately depends on your own personality. Whatever you decide, you'll see the same India but your experience will be more intense if you're alone. You'll probably be adopted by friendly fellow passengers but it can be lonely too. If you travel with a companion, you'll have someone with whom to share everything, the bad as well as the good and also the luggage-minding duties.

It's only natural to want to travel with a companion in a country as extraordinary as India. However, the pairs of travellers I've met never seemed to be enjoying themselves as much as I was. They sat together, played cards, talked, ate and slept as an exclusive group of two, making no effort to speak to their fellow passengers unless to demand some information.

While there are obvious advantages in travelling with a friend, there are snags which only become apparent once you're on the train. If you don't know your companion very well, little quirks of behaviour could ruin your own enjoyment of the trip. Trains are not the place for the honeymoon stage of any relationship. Also, when travelling with companions, you may have to defer to their wishes, and thus miss sights and experiences. My personal choice is to travel alone. As a solo traveller, you will feel more at ease, especially at night, in an AC 2 tier coach or 1st Class than in a claustrophobic 72 berth 2nd Class carriage.

Children

Couples whom I met travelling with children seemed happy enough. Most western children adore rail travel and can spend hours train spotting or wandering around stations. Obviously, very young children will be a problem because of the extra care and attention they need. It is not always possible for families to be accommodated in the same sleeping compartment at night, so parents may have to make a special request to the conductor to see that their daughter is assigned a berth with at least one of them, and not separately.

Women travellers

Women travellers, alone or in pairs, face the usual problems, often through western insensitivity to Indian mores; modest dress and behaviour can help prevent misunderstandings. There is safety in numbers so women may feel more secure in a four berth cabin than in

THE THOMAS COOK OVERSEAS TIMETABLE

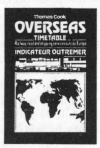

RAIL SERVICES

ROAD SERVICES

SHIPPING SERVICES

MAPS ★ TOWN PLANS

CLIMATIC INFORMATION

PASSPORTS ★ VISAS

HEALTH REGULATIONS

GENERAL TRAVEL INFORMATION

Probably the most adventurous timetable ever published, the Thomas Cook Overseas Timetable brings together in one book surface travel timetables (rail, road and shipping) for virtually all countries outside Europe. With the help of a valued worldwide network of correspondents, it includes much information not readily available in any other form. Its pages contain maps and town plans, comprehensive travel information on the countries covered (passports & visas, health regulations, currency, clock times, languages, post and tele-communications, driving regulations and tourist assistance) as well as thousands of time-tables.

The INDIAN section devotes over 20 pages to timetables of Indian Railways and is laid out in a simple-to-follow format. A two-page key map enables the user to find the required tables quickly and easily. All main lines and most minor ones (particularly those of tourist interest) are included.

There is a table of principle bus services, especially useful in areas of the North West and North East not served by rail; long-distance bus services in other parts of the country are also featured. There are tables of the shipping services along the West Coast and those linking the Lakshadweep, Andaman and Nicobar Islands to the Mainland.

Town plans include Bombay, Calcutta, Delhi and Madras, and the Indian entry in the Travel Information section offers up-to-date notes on entry requirements and a wealth of useful things to know while in the country. Published every two months.

THE THOMAS COOK RAILPASS GUIDE

Published annually around Easter, the Thomas Cook Railpass Guide brings together in one 32-page booklet a wide range of international, national and local travel offers, including national bus/motor coach passes, regional rover tickets and many city runabout tickets and transport passes. The INDIAN entry gives full details of the Indrail pass with prices and how to obtain it.

The Overseas Timetable and the Railpass Guide are obtainable from all Thomas Cook UK Travel Shops, or by post from Thomas Cook Publications (TPO/1), P.O. Box 36, Thorpe Wood, PETERBOROUGH PE3 6SB, U.K.

RAILWAY MAP OF INDIA

The official Railway Map of India in 1:3 500 000 scale, showing track gauges, single/double line and electricification. The various states and railway administrations are shown in separate colours for easy identification.

Measuring approximately 1150 × 900mm, this splendid map is a must for anyone planning to travel by rail in India.

Obtainable by post from Thomas Cook Publications (TPO/1), P.O. Box 36, Thorpe Wood, PETERBOROUGH PE3 6SB, U.K.

a two berth coupe. In a carriage with 45 or 71 other passengers, there would be no privacy for outright assault and other passengers would intervene at overt unpleasantness. The story about a foreign woman being raped on the roof of a moving train has become part of the rail travellers folk lore. The moral is to keep off the roof!

All trains have a separate, unreserved coach for lady passengers, usually part of, or next to, the guard's brake van. This coach has SYLR painted on it, meaning Second Class Ladies' Luggage Room coach. On trains involving a night journey, government railway police will be posted to travel in the coach. Failing that, women may feel more comfortable in the AC 2 tier carriages which are not so cramped as 2nd Class, are brighter lit and have attendants on duty and, being more expensive, have a different type of passenger.

There are separate Ladies Only waiting rooms at most stations. Some also have separate counters (and thus special queues) for ladies to buy rail tickets or to make reservations, but these are not found everywhere. The AC sleeper carriages have Ladies Only toilets.

Disabled travellers

Disabled travellers should be warned that the steps into and out of carriages (especially onto low platforms) are so steep that even for able-bodied passengers they can be hazardous. Wheelchairs are available at some stations for the (temporarily?) disabled with plenty of willing assistance from porters (for a tip) and from railway staff in an emergency. Rail travel for a disabled foreigner alone would be very difficult.

Group travel

The major long haul tour operators, through their High Street retailers, offer package holidays in India which include some rail travel. For the novice, this is a hassle-free way of sampling an Indian train but it is likely to be much more expensive than travelling independently. There are also specialist travel agents who arrange tours for dedicated rail enthusiasts, among them: Dorridge Travel Service Ltd, 7 Station Approach, Dorridge, Solihull, West Midlands, B93 8JA, England. Tel: 05645 776252; and Rail Travel & Photography, 83 Baswich Lane, Stafford, ST17 0BN, England. Tel: 0785 40352. International Railtours, 60 Cable Rd, Whitehead, Co. Antrim, BT38 9PZ. Tel: 09603 72446. One couple, Jane and Ashley Butterfield, charter their own carriage and have it attached to different trains for groups to tour India (see page 217).

IN INDIA

Public Holidays

Festivals, dry days, special events . . . there seems to be no end to disruptions to normal life, and the traveller will often arrive in a

SOUTH CENTRAL RAILWAY APPEALS
DO NOT DETAIN TRAINS

RAIL ROKO & RASTA ROKO are resorted to by organisors of agitations to press their demands.

SOME INSTANCES

1. "DATE: 15.7.88 PLACE: ONGOLE. Severe dislocation of rail traffic caused by agitators squatting on the track ... to highlight the grievances of Cotton Growers of Prakasam District!

2. "DATE: 27.7.88   PLACE: SECUNDERABAD.   VIJAYAWADA, NANDYAL Trade Union Organisations squatted on track as part of RASTA ROKO.. to press withdrawal of proposed changes in Industrial Disputes Act. etc.,

"PLEASE   DO   NOT   DETAIN TRAINS"

* Detained trains set off "CHAIN REACTION" by causing other trains to be detained.
* Thousands of passengers get detained at locations far away from their homes.
* Goods trains carrying essential commodities such as foodgrains, coal can not reach destinations affecting the Public Distribution System, power generation etc.

ISSUED IN PUBLIC INTEREST
BY
SOUTH CENTRAL RAILWAY

strange town when everything is closed. Further inconvenience comes from strikes, parades and demonstrations.

However carefully you plan, you will probably arrive somewhere when it's a local dry day. If it is and you are desperate for a drink, an experienced bicycle- or auto-rickshaw taxi driver should know a place where you can buy a bottle.

I tried it once. It wasn't a religious holiday but some sort of strike. We found the wine shop heavily shuttered. The rickshaw driver took my money, looked up and down the road, then banged on the shutters. A panel at the bottom of the door opened at pavement level and a hand shot out for the money. The panel closed only to open seconds later and the hand emerged holding a bottle of chilled beer.

National public holidays are January 26, Republic Day; August 15, Independence Day; October 2, Mahatma Gandhi's birthday; December 25, Christmas Day.

Time

Indian Standard Time is 5½ hours ahead of GMT, 4½ hours behind Australian Eastern Time and 10½ hours ahead of Eastern Standard Time in the USA. It's the same time in Sri Lanka and Nepal, and half an hour ahead of time in the Maldives.

Train times are listed on the 24 hour clock in timetables and at most stations, although you will occasionally see notices referring to 12.00 am, meaning 12 noon. In timetables, midnight is shown as 2400 hours for arrivals and 0000 hours for departures.

Business hours

Hours of business vary from region to region. Banks are generally open Monday to Friday from 1000 to 1400 hours and 1000 to 1230 on Saturdays. Post offices operate from 1000 to 1700, Monday to Friday and on Saturday mornings. Offices function from 0930 to 1700 and some Saturdays. Shops generally open from 0930 to 1800, except Sundays.

Reservation offices at stations have their own habits but they are generally open between 0900 and 1800. Avoid the period between 1230 and 1400 as they'll close for lunch sometime during that time, regardless of the people queuing for tickets.

Important stations are open 24 hours a day with ordinary tickets on sale, but some booking offices close 30 minutes before the departure of a train. The Station Superintendent's office is usually open 1000 to 1800; his duties are undertaken by his deputy outside those hours.

Electricity

Voltage in most places is 220 volts AC, 50 cycles, with some areas also having DC supplies. Check the voltage before using electrical appliances. Socket sizes vary, they're usually round pin.

Station retiring rooms are nearly all dimly lit so if you intend reading in bed, your own 100 watt light bulb would help. Rooms with air conditioning units often have huge boxes like disco equipment as part of their control system. Some retiring rooms have electrically-heated hot water in their showers.

Drinking water

All stations have water for drinking at several points along the platform, either from standpipes, cold water dispensers or from water carts. This is drawn from the local supply so its potability is the same as that of the water drunk by the area's residents. A visitor will not have the immunity of locals so if you intend to drink it, collect it in a water bottle and dissolve a purifying tablet in it or filter it first. Like most travellers I never drink tap water, nor do I have ice in my drinks. In India, I buy bottled mineral water which costs from Rs 7 to Rs 20. Bisleri *Aqua Minerale* is the most widely found. It's not generally on sale at stations, though, except those frequented by foreign tourists, since Indians prefer sweet drinks.

Alcohol

'English wine shops' are to be found close to stations; they don't sell English or any kind of wine, only Indian-made spirits and beer. Alcohol is not sold at any station or on any train (except the tourist-oriented Palace on Wheels).

Officially, drinking alcohol is illegal on trains which only encourages passengers to fill their thermos flasks with whisky and ice instead of tea. Unofficially, if you need a beer, an amenable bearer might produce a cold one when the train stops long enough at a station with a wine shop close by.

Indian beers have extraordinary names such as Knock Out, He-Man 9000 and Bullet. My favourites are Haywards 5000, Rosy Pelican and the more common Black Label and Kingfisher brands. They cost around Rs 20 for a 650 ml bottle. In Goa, Arlem beer is half that price. Indian whisky is sweeter than Scotch; the rum is very good.

Indian wine is not up to much, except for the notable exception of Indian 'champagne'. The Indage group with technical help from Piper-Heidsieck, produces a splendid sparkling wine under the Marquise de Pompadour label (also sold as Omar Khayham), by the *methode champenoise* from grapes grown near Bombay. It is superb but unfortunately it is only available for export. The Oberoi Hotels actually re-import it to sell for their guests. I've also had it at Fariyas Holiday Resort (near Lonavla station). It's well worth trying; a pity the wine isn't as good.

Smoking

Smoking on trains without the consent of fellow passengers is a punishable offence. It is not allowed in the AC sleeper carriages, nor on local/suburban trains. Very few 2nd Class carriages are exclusively designated 'Non Smoking'.

Food

Meals cooked in railway kitchens will be prepared from fresh ingredients since supplies are bought daily to meet the huge demand. Kitchens are run by the railway zone catering division or by licensees and there is an army of catering inspectors and plenty of guidelines on standards to ensure quality.

There are usually two restaurants at stations: the vegetarian, abbreviated in conversation to 'veg' (V) and non-vegetarian, referred to as 'non-veg' (NV). Sometimes they will be the same restaurant with a door at one end for V and an NV door at the other, although with separate kitchens. Prices are standardized throughout the railway zone, and clearly displayed.

The meals served on trains are according to a limited standardized menu. Usually they are prepared at a base kitchen and put onto the train for serving at meal times to your seat. Simple items such as breakfast and snacks will be prepared in the pantry car, if there is one.

You will be asked if you want a veg or non-veg meal when ordering lunch or dinner. Although a vegetarian meal has vegetables with the rice and lentils, a non-veg meal actually has no vegetables at all, with curried eggs as a substitute. To get a balanced meal I sometimes order a veg lunch with curried chicken.

On an increasing number of trains, meals are served in foil casseroles, with individual items wrapped in polythene bags. Other trains still use the chrome *thali* plates with compartments for different sauces around the rice. Drinks are served in disposable plastic cups although the disposable, clay teacups of old are still sometimes used by platform vendors.

The variety of railway food, while well prepared and well cooked, is not very exciting unless you can get the pantry chef to cook something special. Actually, some of the best meals I've had on trains were the curries prepared for the staff which I persuaded them to let me try. For a more varied sampling of Indian food, you will have to eat outside railwayland.

Tipping

Railway employees do not expect to be tipped. However, a bearer (the railway name for a waiter or steward) will look after a passenger extra well if there is the likelihood of a tip. Since the bearer rides the train for its entire journey, your welfare will be in his hands throughout a long trip, so it will suit you both to establish a friendly relationship from the outset.

If you haven't been paying after each meal, the bill for all meals, tea, soft drinks etc. will be presented just before you reach your destination, so you can tip them if you want to; ten per cent or more according to how much extra the bearer's done for you.

The attendant who brings the bedroll might hover for a tip, especially if he actually makes up the bed. It's not necessary. Sometimes you'll encounter an urchin who sweeps out the carriage and comes for a tip afterwards. That's really the coach attendant's job and the urchin shouldn't be on the train anyway. The Government of India tourist brochure says: 'Don't encourage beggars by giving them money.'

Porters, who are supposed to carry your bag for Rs 2 to Rs 4, for a head load of 40 kg depending on the station rates, will always want a tip. In hotels and restaurants a service charge is sometimes added but tip if you feel it's worth it. Retiring room attendants only deserve a tip if they have looked after you, your luggage and the room properly. But it's not essential.

Communications

Many stations have post offices within their premises or close by. For an extra fee, letters can be posted on some trains for delivery at the train's destination. Letters can be sent to passengers at railway stations and will be deposited in a glass-fronted cabinet outside the office of the station superintendent (the SS) for collection, but the system is not reliable since anyone can remove the letter.

Telegrams can be sent from Railway Licensed Telegraph Offices to passengers travelling by train in any class. The name of the station where the train stops (it must be for at least ten minutes) and the number or name of the train should be included in the address. Inland telegrams can be sent from stations. The rates are low.

It is possible to telephone from major stations, either locally or long distance. Sometimes the telephones are run by attendants who are handicapped, with their booth being sponsored by the local Rotary or Lions Club.

Language

Signs at stations are supposed to be in three languages: Hindi, English and the state language. Some stations have signs hanging above a platform and as you walk down its length they all seem to be in Hindi. Turn around and walk back and they are all in English, since the signs are double sided.

English is understood throughout India and you will get involved in some deep discussions in English with fellow passengers. The SS speaks English as do other senior station staff. In the south, English will be more readily understood among ordinary people than in the north. If you are stuck, someone will usually be around who can help translate.

Useful phrases in Hindi

Good morning/evening/day/night	*Namaste*
Goodbye/see you	*Phir milenge*
How are you?	*Aap kaise hain?*
Good	*Acha*
Bad	*Kharab*
Please	*Kripaya*
Thank you	*Dhanyavad*
Yes	*Han*
No	*Nahi*
What is your name?	*Aap ka naam kya hai?*
How much is . . . ?	*Kitne ka hai?*
Too much	*Bahut zyada hai*
Come here	*Idhar aaiye*
Go away	*Chale jaaiye*
Water	*Paani*
Cold	*Tanda*
Hot	*Garam*
Big	*Bada*
Small	*Chota*
Where is the . . . ?	*Kahan hai?*
Train	*Rail gadi*
Retiring room	*Vishramgarh*
Restaurant	*Dhaba*

Chapter 3

Ticket to Ride

'What I can't understand,' said the tall Dutchman who boarded the train at Bhubaneswar and sat opposite me, 'is how to buy a ticket to travel by train.'

The Dutchman was a professor in his forties, passionately interested in medieval temples which is what had drawn him to Bhubaneswar. He explained the reason for his question.

'I have a ticket but I don't understand how I got it. I came to the station yesterday and told a clerk I wanted to travel on this train. I filled in the form he gave me then he told me to join a queue.

'I waited an hour but when I was almost at the counter, the clerk said he was going for lunch. I was very angry and left my form there and went to lunch too. When I returned, I'd lost my place in the queue so I went up to another window where no one was queuing. The clerk looked at me, took my money and gave me a ticket.'

The Dutch professor looked bemused. 'How did it happen? How did the second clerk know where I wanted to go? He didn't ask me.'

The professor's experience illustrates the good and the bad of the ticket buying process. He was frustrated by queuing at a counter that closed just as he was about to reach it, so he lost his temper and made a fuss.

Being tall and fair he was easily recognisable so when he returned, even though he went to another ticket window, the clerk knew what he wanted and helped him.

There is a policy in Indian Railways to help foreign tourists to make their reservations. However, most foreigners would rather join a line and wait their turn than demand special treatment because they are foreigners.

Indian tourists who feel themselves to be important will not hesitate to ask the Chief Reservations Supervisor (CRS) or the Station Superintendent (SS) for help if they need it. On Indian Railways, foreigners are regarded as important and are actually expected to approach officials for help.

Where to buy a ticket
Unless you have an Indrail Pass (see page 38) you will need to buy a ticket for the journey. This means a visit to the railway station. The

first rule is not to join any queue until you are absolutely certain it is the right one, and don't join it near closing time.

If in doubt start at the Enquiry counter. Alternatively, a polite request to the Chief Reservation Supervisor (CRS) for help can work wonders so don't be shy to approach him. Tickets should only be purchased from station counters or from official sources. There are touts at the major stations who will take advantage of a foreigner's confusion (or frustration) to offer tickets on trains that are fully booked, or even cut-price tickets. Avoid them since trouble and complications are bound to result. These touts are not always immediately recognisable. Many railway officials dress in white. When I was approached at New Delhi station by a gentleman in white shirt and trousers who asked if I was looking for the ITB, I assumed he was an official. I was busy at the time and didn't stop to talk. Later I saw him with two foreigners in the ITB offering to change money for them. He was not a railway employee at all and quickly left when the ITB Supervisor questioned him.

Rail Travellers' Service Agents have been appointed in some areas to purchase tickets and secure reservations on behalf of passengers. They are authorized to charge a fee of not more than Rs 15 for upperclass bookings and Rs 8 for other classes.

Single journey ticket

At most stations, the ticket purchasing and reservations procedure has been combined (see *Making a reservation*). Tickets to travel without a reserved seat or in 2nd Class non-reserved carriages can be purchased from the booking office window labelled for the class you intend to travel, usually up to the time the train departs. The booking counters will normally be found in the station lobby, not with the counters issuing journey-cum-reservation tickets.

A passenger who has no reservation and who buys a ticket and boards the train and finds a seat may still have to pay a reservation fee if that seat is normally subject to a reservation charge (see page 48). This can be the only way of getting a seat on some trains if the unreservable seats, usually in a 2nd Class carriage at the end of the train, are all occupied to overflowing.

A passenger who intends to travel in the unreserved 2nd Class coach of a superfast train must purchase a supplementary charge ticket (for Rs 2) before boarding the train. Otherwise there is a penalty of Rs 10 payable on the train as well as the supplementary charge.

It is possible at some stations to buy an unreserved single journey 2nd Classs ticket a day in advance of travelling, to save queuing on the actual day of travel. The day of travel will be endorsed on the ticket which will only be valid until midnight on that day.

Tickets are cardboard and coloured according to class:

White: AC 1st Class
Green: 1st Class (Mail, Express or Ordinary) and AC Sleeper (2
            Tier) Class
Orange: AC Chair Car
Drab: 2nd Class (Mail or Express)
Yellow: 2nd Class (Ordinary)

Where printed tickets are not available, you will be issued with a
coupon on which the ticket details are entered by hand.

Platform tickets

In theory, only people holding tickets are allowed on station
platforms. Platform tickets are obtainable from a separate ticket
window. They cost Rs 1.50 and are valid for two hours.

   If you are trying to buy a ticket at the last minute and can't get one in
time because the queue at the window is too long, buy a platform
ticket instead. Before boarding the train present the platform ticket to
the guard. He will issue a guard's certificate and charge you the full
fare for the journey. A passenger trying to travel on a platform ticket
without the guard's certificate will be treated as a ticketless traveller.

Ticketless travel

The penalties for travelling without a ticket are high and can include
jail. Some stations have a magistrate's court within their premises for
dealing with ticketless travellers and other offenders.

   Travelling without a ticket is almost a tradition in India, originating
during the British days when passengers did it to harm an alien ruler.
After partition it was done to express a grievance against the
government. The motive now, unless part of an organized protest, is
simply to cheat the railways.

   In the north of India especially, ticketless passengers add to the
problem of over-crowding in the cheaper carriages where checks aren't
so rigorous. Another problem in northern areas are those passengers
who don't recognize that some carriages are for those who have paid
more for the privilege of an upper class seat. They want to sit there
too, regardless of what class of travel they have actually paid for. If a
passenger with a 2nd Class ticket is caught in a 1st Class seat, not only
must the full 1st Class fare be paid but a penalty too. However, it is
possible for a 2nd Class ticket holder to upgrade to 1st Class by paying
the difference in fares. Permission must be obtained from the guard
before the passenger occupies the higher class of seat.

Ticket inspection

A passenger must have a ticket, even if it is only a platform ticket with
a guard's certificate. Travelling ticket examiners (TTEs) check tickets,
even on trains that don't have a vestibule. TTEs are sometimes in plain

clothes but carry identification to show when requested. On long distance trains, few passengers are ticketless except for those hitching a lift between rural stops.

Tickets are sometimes inspected at the entrance to platforms and they will be collected at the exits after a journey. Tickets are required by people wanting to use the waiting and retiring rooms, to prove that they are genuine passengers.

Lost tickets and refunds

If you buy a ticket and lose it, there is no chance of a refund although you can get a duplicate ticket if it was for reserved travel (see later). Refunds are possible on unused tickets without reservations if presented within three hours after the departure of the train. A fee of Rs 2.00 per ticket is deducted as clerkage from the full refund. This can apply if you've bought a ticket but don't use it because you can't get a reservation or seat on the train.

Travel restrictions

Some trains have restrictions on carrying passengers over short distances. These are usually the major expresses and will not carry passengers making journeys of less than 160 km and in some case not less than 600 km, according to the train. Indrail Pass holders escape these restrictions. The small print of the timetables reveal other restrictions too. For instance, passengers are not allowed to carry milk in cans or bottles on the 352 Bhusaval passenger train between Kalyan and Bombay.

Breaking the journey

Passengers are allowed to make a break on a single journey ticket of more than 400 km after the first 300 km has been travelled. A break can be at any station *en route* at the rate of one day for every 200 km or part of 200 km in addition to the time occupied by the journey. The ticket should be endorsed by the Station Master (SM) where the break occurs with the station code, the date and the SM's initials. Foreign tourists travelling on an Indrail Pass can break their journey anywhere en route without the distance restriction.

Fare extras: superfast trains

There is a supplement payable for travel on certain superfast expresses and mail trains. A list of the trains appears in Chapter 12. It includes the popular Taj and Pink City Expresses. The supplements are paid at the time of reservation/ticket purchase and are the same for children and adults. Indrail Pass holders pay nothing extra. The rates are:

AC Class	Rs 25
AC Sleeper	12
1st Class	12
AC Chair Car	12
2nd Class Sleeper	6
2nd Class sitting	2

Sleeper charge

In 2nd Class there is a surcharge for sleeper accommodation levied according to the distance of a passenger's journey:

Up to 500 km   Rs 10
More than 500 km   15

Indrail Pass holders are exempt from this surcharge; the sleeper fee is included in 1st and AC Class reservation fee.

FARES

Carrying passengers is not lucrative for Indian Railways, according to a DRM who told me that it is a public, not a profitable, service. He seemed to regard passengers as a necessary evil. The carrying of freight was his main interest since that is profit generating and actually subsidizes the passenger services. Attempts to raise fares are resisted by the travelling public who consider they pay enough already. At the lower end of the scale, fares are cheap; at the upper end – for Indians – they are not. The top fare on the Rajdhani Express in AC Class is Rs 1295 (about $86) for the 1384 km overnight ride from New Delhi to Bombay which is not much lower than the air fare. By contrast, the lowest fare by mail or express train in 2nd Class sleeper on the same route is a tenth of that.

Throughout the Indian Railways' network, fares are calculated on a fixed price per kilometre from station of origin to destination, according to the class travelled. The timetables show the kilometres between stations so it is possible to work out the approximate cost by reference to the fare table produced in the zonal timetables and in TAG. Examples of standard fares between stations cannot be quoted with complete accuracy because every fare depends on the route taken. For instance, there are four different routes between Delhi and Calcutta and three between Delhi and Jammu Tawi, all with different fares. In addition, there are various supplements according to the train actually travelled on, as well as reservation and sleeper fees.

The minimum cost of travel by train is Rs 1.50 (US 10 cents) which buys up to 10 km of train ride in ordinary 2nd Class. The most expensive minimum cost is Rs 84 (US $5.60) which will give 15 km of air conditioned 1st Class travel. A sample of fares from 1 to 5000 km (in force in 1989) appears in the accompanying chart.

Discounts

Even though 2nd Class fares are low for foreigners they can represent an obstacle to rail travel for low income or no-income Indians. Concessions are made to certain groups with reductions up to 75 per cent on fares for 1st or 2nd Class travel. The list of groups includes sportsmen, professional entertaining parties, students up to 25 years old on studies, articled clerks, research scholars, blind or deaf and dumb people; TB, cancer and leprosy sufferers; the orthopaedically handicapped; nurses, midwives and war and police widows.

	AC 1st class		AC Sleeper		1st class		AC Chaircar		2nd class Mail/ Express		Passenger	
Km	Rs	$	Rs	$	Rs	$	Rs	$	Rs	$	Rs	$
1	84	5.60	64	4.26	17	1.13	18	1.20	5	0.33	1.50	0.10
50	85	5.66	69	4.60	38	2.53	26	1.73	8	0.53	4.00	0.26
100	136	9.06	93	6.20	59	3.93	36	2.40	14	0.93	9.00	0.60
200	206	13.73	135	9.00	95	6.33	58	3.86	28	1.86	16	1.06
300	290	19.33	181	12.06	134	8.93	82	5.46	37	2.46	22	1.46
500	439	29.26	257	17.13	201	13.40	119	7.93	55	3.66	32	2.13
1000	750	50.00	432	28.80	344	22.93	190	12.66	91	6.06	53	3.53
2000	1262	84.13	692	46.13	575	38.33	310	20.66	141	9.40	87	5.80
2500	1509	100.60	795	53.00	688	45.86	366	24.40	165	11.00	103	6.86
5000	2744	182.93	1304	86.93	1248	83.20	644	42.93	287	19.13	186	12.40
per 50km block over 5000	28	1.86	12	0.80	14	0.93	7	0.46	4	0.26	2	0.13

Fares in Indian rupees, converted at Rs 15 to US $1.00.

The only discount for foreigners is the Indrail Pass. However, foreign students under 25 who are resident in India (and therefore not eligible for the Indrail Pass) can qualify for a 50 per cent reduction on 2nd Class fares for approved journeys, such as to attend a Government organized seminar or to visit places of historical or other importance during vacations.

Children between five and 12 years of age travel at half fare but are subject to the same minimum fares as for an adult. Children age five and under travel free.

Kilometre distance
As with air fares, the price per kilometre drops the further a passenger travels. To help arrive at an estimate of what it might cost, the following is a list of the kilometre distance between selected stations. However, different distances may be used in fare construction.

New Delhi to	Madras Central	2188 km
	Howrah (Calcutta)	1441
	Bombay Central (with WR)	1384
	Bombay VT (via Bhusaval)	1538
	Trivandrum	3054
	Agra Cantt	195
	Bangalore City	2491
	Jammu Tawi	589
	Patna	992
Howrah to	Bombay VT	1968
	Jammu Tawi	1967
	Madras Central	1662
Bombay VT	Madras Central	1279

Sample fares

The sample fares below are taken from the tariff issued by Southern
Railway for fares between Madras Central and the stations listed.

	Rupees				
Km Madras to:	AC 1st	AC Sleeper	1st	AC Chair	2nd Sleeper
Agra Cantt					
1992	1262	692	575	310	141
Bangalore					
358	338	211	156	93	44
Bombay VT					
1279	915	530	418	232	106
Howrah					
1662	1104	624	500	273	125
Hyderabad					
790	627	370	286	163	79
Jammu Tawi					
2776	1656	856	755	400	179
New Delhi					
2188	1360	733	620	333	150
Trivandrum					
906	701	411	321	179	85

Adjusted fares

The fares to many destinations are posted on the walls of station
booking halls. They are the basic fares without the addition of
supplements, reservation fees and sleeper surcharges.

On some routes, the fare per kilometre is adjusted in order,
according to one official source, 'to avoid losses at the cost of
construction and maintenance on certain sections is considerably
heavy.' These routes provide spectacular journeys which are often
undertaken by tourists. They are listed below.

RAILWAY	CHARGEABLE DISTANCE
Neral–Matheran	63 km
Khandwa–Hingoli	Distance plus 33⅓ per cent
Ambala–Kalka	1⅓ times distance
Kalka–Shimla	3 times distance
Pathankot–Jogindar Nagar	1½ times distance
Mettupalaiyam–Wellington	2¾ times distance
Wellington–Udagmandalam	Twice actual distance
Kottavalasa–Kirandul	1½ times distance
Fatehpur Shekhawati–Churu	Twice actual distance
Udaipur–Himatnagar	1⅓ times distance

THE INDRAIL PASS

If you intend making more than two trips by train, consider buying an Indrail Pass: it may not always save you money but there are other advantages, mainly of convenience. Here are some of them, compared with the purchase of several single journey tickets.

Indrail Pass	Single journey tickets
Unlimited kilometres	Distance restriction
Network freedom	Travel restricted
Separate ticket purchase not required	Ticket must be purchased for every journey
All reservations can be made at the same time	Separate reservations must be made for every journey
Reservations can be made by mail through home country GSA	Reservations must be made at stations in person
Reservations can be made 360 days in advance	Reservations can only be made 60 days, or less, in advance
Reservation priority	No priority
Eligible for foreign tourist quota	Only eligible for foreign tourist quota at some stations if pay in foreign currency
No restrictions in travelling short distances on any train	Restrictions
Can break journey anywhere	Restrictions
Can use waiting and retiring rooms anywhere any time	Can only use rooms if holding day's ticket
No supplements payable	Supplements payable
No surcharges payable	Surcharges payable
No reservation fees payable	Reservation fees payable
No sleeper charges payable	Sleeper charges payable
No minimum distance charge	Minimum distance charge
No need for platform ticket	Platform ticket needed for platform visit if not travelling
Can board any train	Must buy a ticket before boarding any train
Recognized as a Very Important Traveller	No special recognition
Reduced queuing	Frequent queuing

The Indrail Pass can be bought in India or abroad from GSAs (General Sales Agents). The cost is calculated in US dollars and payment in foreign currency is based on the dollar price. Passes purchased in India must be paid for in dollars or pound sterling; credit cards are not accepted.

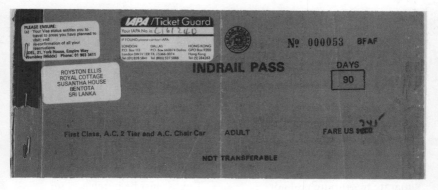

Where to buy the Indrail Pass: outside India

	Telephone	Telex
Australia		
Adventure World, 37 York Street, Sydney.	2903222	22680
Penthouse Travel, 5th level,		
72 Pitt Street, Sydney, 2000 NSW.	2311455	10718892
Canada		
Hariworld Travels Inc,	3662000	062 3918
Royal York Hotel, 100 Front Street West,		
Arcade Level, Toronto, Ont M5J 1E3.		
Denmark		
D.S.B Travel Agency Divn,	(01) 140400	19936
Reventlowsgade 10,		
DK 1651, Kobenhavn V.		
Finland		
Intia Keskua Ltd		
Tarkk Amopujankatu, 8A		
00150 Helsinki 9.		
France		
Le Monde de L'Inde et de L'Asie,	46340320	202221
15 Rue Des Ecoles, Paris 75005.		
Germany		
Asra Orient, Kaiserstrasse 50,	(069) 253098	413451
D-6000, Frankfurt M1.		
Japan		
Japan Travel Bureau,	81-(031) 284-7391	28648
Overseas Travel Division,		
1-6-4 Marunouchi		
Chiyoda KU, Tokyo-100		
Mauritius		
Mauritius Travel & Tourist Bureau		
Sir W. Newton & Royal Rd,		
Port Louis.		

	Telephone	Telex
Thailand		
S S Travel Service,	2367188	87450
10/12–13 S.S. Building,		
Convent Road, Bangkok 10500		
UK		
S.D. Enterprises Ltd,	01 903 3411	94012027
21 York House, Empire Way,	& 01 200 9549	
Wembley, Middlesex, England HA9 0PA		
USA		
Hariworld Travels Inc,	212 957 3000	4952383
30 Rockefeller Plaza,		
Shop 21, North Mezzanine,		
New York, NY 10112.		

In India

Indrail Passes can be bought at the following stations: Ahmadabad, Ajmer, Agra Cantt, Amritsar, Aurangabad, Bangalore City, Bombay, Calcutta, Chandigarh, Gorakhpur, Hyderabad, Jaipur, Madras, New Delhi, Rameswaram, Secunderabad, Trivandrum, Vasco de Gama, Vadodara, Varanasi.

Indrail passes are also available at Delhi, Bombay and Madras airports and from some travel agents.

The ticket doctor

If you can get to London during the planning stage of your trip, there is a remarkable man who will answer all your questions and help plan the itinerary. He is Dr S. Dandapani who has his office on the first floor of the building (York House) next to the Wembley Conference Centre (nearest station is Wembley Park on the underground Metropolitan and Jubilee lines). The full address is: S.D. Enterprises Ltd, 21, York House, Empire Way, Wembley, Middlesex HA9 0PA, England. Tel: 01 903 3411, telex: 94012027 SDEL G. Dr Dandapani is the GSA in Britain for the Indrail Pass but he does much more than that.

'Selling a ticket is child's play', he told me. 'I'm preparing people to visit a great country and come back happy.' Dr Dandapani overflows with sound advice, not just on places to visit, but how to make the most of the trip and even what underwear is best (cotton; jockey shorts for men).

He is a medical doctor, a sociologist who worked for Indian Railways for 25 years and for 15 years as a UN adviser, as well as being an author of more than a dozen books on business management.

Anyone who wants to buy an Indrail Pass will be treated to free advice on what to take, how or where to go and on how to get what you want in India.

This is my second visit to India.
The first time travel was a real
problem. This time with the
Indrail Pass and your reservations
everything has gone smoothly!
Only hitch so far has been
the Darjeeling NG train - which
isn't running due to 'the
agitation'. But I suppose
this is one thing beyond your
control!

    With very many thanks,

Archaeological Survey of India भारतीय पुरातत्त्व सर्वेक्षण

तटीय मंदिर, महाबलीपुरम्, (7वीं शताब्दी)
Shore Temple, Mahabalipuram, (7th Cent.)

MBP 8
75 Paise
Thomson

S.D. Enterprises Ltd.,
21 York House,
Empire Way,
Wembley, Middx.,
HA9 0PA, U.K.

2.00   भारत INDIA   2.00   INDIA

If you have a specific reason for wanting to visit India, tell Dr Dandapani. It's amazing what he can arrange. The parents of a friend of mine wanted to visit a small town named after my friend's grandfather who had lived in India. Dr Dandapani not only plotted the whole rail itinerary, he also arranged for the station superintendent to greet the couple on arrival and for a surprise civic reception for them.

Should you have doubts about travelling by train, even after reading this book, discuss them with Dr Dandapani. His desire is for passengers to be satisfied with their train travels and he has thousands of letters of appreciation to prove they are. He likes to say that he has two million railwaymen working with him and when he promises something, you can depend on him.

'Everything is possible with Indian Railways,' he once told me, 'but you must allow adequate time.'

Dr Dandapani sells more Indrail Passes than anyone else in the world. If you can't visit him, give him a call or write with your itinerary and purchase the pass by post since he mails them wherever required.

In the USA, the pass is available through New York travel agency, Hariworld Travels, in Rockefeller Plaza. They also have a branch in Toronto, Canada.

In 1987, over 8,000 Indrail Passes were sold worldwide. British travellers formed the vast majority of purchasers followed by French, Australian, Japanese and German. The most popular was the 30-day 1st Class pass which also permits travel in AC Sleeper. Next in demand came 21-day and 15-day 1st Class passes.

Pass details

The pass looks like an airline ticket and is issued for three different classes of train travel:

1) Blue Ticket   AC 1st Class
2) Green Ticket   AC Sleeper (2 tier), 1st Class, AC Chair Car
3) Orange/Yellow Ticket   2nd Class

The front cover bears the pass number and indicates its total validity period: 7, 15, 30, 60 or 90 days. There is also a 24 hour pass which is mentioned below. The pass is valid for one year from the date of issue and its validity period starts from the day the first journey begins to midnight on the final day.

The terms and conditions, kept very simple, are outlined inside the front cover. Journey and reservation particulars are noted by carbon duplicate on what is called the 'passenger foil'. There are two of these with the second one forming the back cover of the ticket. The GSA keeps the original of the ticket's 'foils' on which he has entered the passenger details. Also recorded on the foil are the passenger's name, nationality, passport number, fare paid, signature and stamp of the GSA, and the date of issue. The validity of the ticket showing the first and last day of usage is noted in a space at the foot of the ticket. There is space on the rest of the ticket for endorsements showing the train number, date, from/to and remarks concerning every train trip included on the itinerary.

Armed with this you have a permit to travel 'wherever you like, whenever you like and by whatever train you like' within the period of its validity. The words are those of Indian Railways: a remarkable concession. However the pass does not guarantee reserved accommodation, unless you confirm all your arrangements with the GSA at the time of purchase. Even so, onward reservations should be confirmed in India by verifying them at the reservation office on arrival at each destination.

The Indrail Pass can be purchased up to 360 days before travel, and reservations can be made at the same time. Reservations by local travellers within India can only be made up to 60 days in advance, so a foreigner requesting a reservation between 61 and 360 days before a journey, is competing only with other foreigners for a seat or berth. Even within the 60 day period before travel, a foreigner booking from overseas gets priority. The reservation (for which there is no charge) will be confirmed by telex to the GSA within seven days.

In India, the process of making a reservation is greatly simplified by the pass. It entitles you to berths from the foreign tourist quota, and will also bring out the best in station staff willing to help. There are none of the reservation charges, supplements or sleeper surcharges that are levied on single journey tickets.

The Indrail Pass can be bought by foreign nationals who are not resident in India and by Indians residing outside India. A foreign national resident in India is regarded as Indian for the purpose of train travel and is not entitled to reservations from the foreign tourist quota. Correspondingly, an Indian resident abroad, with passport to prove it, is regarded as a foreign tourist.

To quote the SR timetable, 'the Indrail Pass ticket will also be issued for:

1) a foreign tourist demanding an Indrail Pass for his Indian wife; and
2) a foreign tourist preferring to take a guide instead of depending on local assistance.'

The pass is not transferable and the traveller should be prepared to show passport as proof of identity.

What it costs

Prices of passes have risen occasionally since the scheme was introduced, with the 1982 prices being increased by at least 15 per cent in January 1988, the date on which the prices quoted below came into effect.

Period of Validity	AC 1st Class		AC Sleeper 1st Class AC Chair		2nd Class	
Days	Adult/Child		Adult/Child		Adult/Child	
1	–	–	25	13	10	5
7	190	95	95	50	45	25
15	230	115	115	60	55	30
21	280	140	140	70	65	35
30	350	175	175	90	75	40
60	520	260	260	130	115	60
90	690	345	345	175	150	75

(Costs in US dollars)

A child is between the ages of five and 12 years. Children below five can travel free on the Indrail Pass of their parents.

One day pass

The one day pass was introduced to help people who want to make only a short journey, perhaps to Agra and back from Delhi, or overnight from one city to another and would like to have their ticket and berth reserved before they arrive in India. The one day (24 hours) pass for AC Sleeper is valid for travel in the AC Chair Car of Rajdhani Express trains but not in the sleeper coach. Unlike the other passes, it is not on sale in India.

Pass refund

The regular passes have to be used within one year of date of issue. The cost can be refunded, less 15 per cent of the face value, if it is returned to the office of issue unused at least seven days before the commencement of its validity. There is a deduction of 20 per cent after that period, and also of any cancellation charges for abandoned reservations. There is no refund possible after commencement of the pass's validity; if it is lost or stolen; or if the journey is undertaken in a lower class of accommodation.

The pass holder with a pass purchased outside India who decides while in India not to use it, should present it to a Station Master to have it cancelled and to obtain a dated cancellation certificate. The cancelled pass and the certificate should be kept to claim a refund eventually from the overseas office that sold the pass.

An Indrail Pass can be revalidated to commence on a different date by the overseas office of issue on payment of US$5. Cancellation of confirmed reservations and substitution of new ones incurs a penalty of US$10 outside India, or Rs 10 per change (up to a maximum of Rs 50) if changes are made in India.

Extension of the validity period of the pass can be made in India by the nearest Area Officer or gazetted Station Superintendent of it becomes necessary due to circumstances beyond the control of the pass holder, such as train delay.

Pass value

Is buying an Indrail Pass worth it? The answer is a big YES, but you have to take more than the cost per kilometre into consideration. On a straight comparison of costs (distance travelled on single journey tickets versus distance travelled on a Pass) there is little financial advantage, unless you spend all your time in India on trains just to clock up excess kilometres. It is being able to avoid the boring rules and surcharges that give it real value.

There is no financial advantage in buying a 2nd Class pass. Anyone who is prepared to travel at length in 2nd Class is likely to be young (in mind if not in age) and not impressed by the convenience and prestige that make an Indrail Pass worth having. The financial savings come with the 1st Class pass with its entree to superior accommodation in 1st or AC coaches. Its value is not only in kilometres travelled but also in the (free) nights spent on board in comfortable berths. The pass pays for itself in a few nights from the savings made on hotel accommodation alone.

The most expensive pass of all, the blue AC Class (ie: 1st Class Air

Conditioned Sleeper) Indrail Pass, brings a greater saving on buying single journey tickets since those tickets are themselves much more expensive. There is also the bonus of privileged accommodation in the luxury of 1st AC Class. Unfortunately, only a few trains (listed in Chapter 12) have 1st AC Class, so only buy that pass if most of your journeys will be on trains that do.

The ordinary 1st Class long period passes represent the best bargain financially. With a pass for 21 or more days you don't have to travel day and night to get full value from it. You can linger in different places and still be able to travel more kilometres than if you'd spent the same amount of money on single journey tickets.

With an Indrail Pass you will have freedom of the Indian Railways network. It is important, though, to remember that because of the demand for space on Indian trains, it is not always possible to jump on a train at random and expect to find a berth. You *have* to make a reservation, usually a few days in advance, if you want to be sure of travelling on a particular train, no matter what class of rail pass you have.

A fixed itinerary is what many rail travellers are keen to avoid, but the Indrail Pass helps the impulsive traveller too since, with it, you can turn up at a station three hours before a train's departure and try to get a reservation. Or you can simply find the conductor when the train comes in and try to arrange everything with him. The authorities hate these last minute arrangements, and so will you if there is no berth available, but you stand more chance with an Indrail Pass than without it.

RESERVATIONS

It was raining when I arrived in Secunderabad. My train from New Delhi had been delayed and I had missed my connection so the itinerary, painstakingly prepared for me by the staff of the ITB, was now useless. The SS sent me out of his station into the dark, wet night and I carried my two cases past the bus stand to the reservations office 600 metres away around a corner.

After a day of travelling, I felt dreadful; I was soaked to the skin and fed up. The prospect of queuing for a reservation made me feel worse, but I had to leave for Madras the next day. The reservations office was like a council hall with rows of seats in which people were waiting. There were no queues. I asked at the enquiry desk what I should do. The clerk told me to fill in a requisition slip.

The slip was headed 'Requisition for Reservation/Cancellation/Return/Onward Journey' and contained spaces for 'Station from . . . to . . . Date of Journey . . . Train number' and for the names of up to six passengers with age and sex columns. The name of the applicant, address and signature with date were also needed.

I returned the slip to the clerk and was given a number and told to sit and wait. I sank into a chair gratefully and composed myself for a long wait. Looking around I saw numbers flashing above the different ticket counters; to my amazement my own number was being displayed. The clerk at the counter took my Indrail Pass, scribbled 'R' on it and some numbers, and gave it back.

My reservation had been made and it was not the exacting process I feared. I was in a strange city, without friends and at my lowest ebb, expecting the worst. Yet the system worked perfectly, and I can only guess it was because I had an Indrail Pass.

Making a reservation

If you don't have an Indrail Pass you must buy a journey-cum-reservation ticket. In the Advance Reservation Centre fill in a requisition slip with details of when you want to travel, by what train and in what class, adding your name, age, sex and address. This has to be handed in at the appropriate reservations counter. When the reservation is confirmed, the journey-cum-reservation ticket issued by a man-operated reservation counter is endorsed on the reverse with the reservation details. It is only valid for the particular train and day for which it is endorsed. For a 1st Class booking it will have the letter 'R' written on it and the actual allotment of seat/berth will be done on the day of travel; you will see your allotted number on the lists posted in the station lobby and on the platform of your departing train. In the case of a reservation in 2nd Class, the seat/berth number will be quoted, such as S3-45 which means seat 45 in Coach S3. If the reservation office does not have a quota for the journey you will have to buy a ticket and wait at least three days for messages to be sent and replies received to confirm the reservation. If it can't be confirmed, the ticket cost can be refunded, as detailed under 'Lost Tickets and Refunds'. When the advance booking is done at a computerized reservations centre, a single coupon instead of a cardboard ticket is issued by the computer. If you have an Indrail Pass this serves as your ticket and after you have filled in a requisition chit, the reservation details will be entered on it. If computer reservation coupons are available, they will be issued to you as well, as confirmation.

Computer coupons

The computer-generated ticket/reservation coupon is approximately 15×9 cm in size, white and blue in colour and contains several numbers. The most important is the PNR (Passenger Name Record) number as this identifies the passenger. The passenger's name does not appear on the ticket although it will appear on the reservation chart pasted on the side of the train and on the station notice board showing berth allocations.

The coupon contains details of the class of travel (in English and

Hindi), the train number and date. The boarding and destination stations will be indicated together with the distance between them in kilometres. It will state whether the ticket is for an adult or child and the sex and age of the passenger are also shown (to prevent fraudulent use) as well as the seat/berth number. Additional information, such as where the train comes from and the journey routing will appear at the bottom of the ticket.

Types of reservation
There are two kinds of reservation: (1) Confirmed and (2) RAC. Confirmed passengers are allocated berths/seats at the time of booking and the details are endorsed on the tickets. RAC (Reservation Against Cancellation) provides a limited number of passengers, only at the train's originating station, with seats on the train in all classes. A berth is promised if one becomes vacant due to a cancellation or no-show.

RAC passengers are entitled to board the train at its originating station and to occupy the seats assigned to them. If an RAC passenger is actually provided with a berth, the sleeper surcharge and the difference in reservation fee is collected by the TTE.

If all berths and the RAC quota have been filled, the name of passengers with journey tickets are entered on the Waiting List. Wait List passengers are accommodated in the order in which their names appear on the list, subject to space being available, within the ten minutes before the departure of the train. Sometimes, extra carriages are added to a train, so it is worth having your name on the waiting list.

If you purchase a journey ticket and are assigned to the RAC quota or Wait List and then decide not to travel, you can claim a refund on your ticket. No cancellation charges will be levied unless a confirmed reservation was actually provided before you cancelled. A clerkage charge of Rs 2.00 will be deducted though.

Return reservations
Return journey reservations can be made at the originating station by filling in the requisition slip and purchasing a return journey (card or blank paper) ticket which will cost twice the single journey. A telegram is sent, at no charge to the passenger, to request accommodation from the return journey station. Some return journey quotas have been set aside on popular mail/express trains and berths can be allocated from the originating station.

Space
Stations have Advanced Booking counters, sometimes in a separate building adjacent to the station, where reservations are made. Many of these buildings are agreeable places in which to wait, and have coffee counters and magazine stalls. The availability of space on the train will be indicated by coloured discs or lights so you can see if there are

berths available on the train you want. The colour indicates the following:

Green:	Space available
Yellow:	RAC space available
Pink:	Wait List available
Red:	No space, fully booked.

If the train of your choice is shown as fully booked, don't despair. As a foreigner you have access to seats issued under different quotas (see below) and should apply at the separate counter for foreign tourists or to the CRS.

If you leave making your reservation until the day of departure, requests at the reservation counters are usually accepted up to three hours before the scheduled departure of a train. After that you must try the ticket collector (TC) or Conductor at the train's originating station during the hour before the train's departure.

Reservation charges

The fees payable to make reservations, and for which reservation tickets are issued, are:

AC Class	Rs 12
AC Sleeper	6
1st Class	6
AC Chair Car	5
2nd Class Sleeper	5
2nd Class Sitting	2
2nd Class RAC	2
2nd Class Sleeper	
– surcharge up to	
500 km journey	10
– surcharge over	
500 km journey	15

The fees and surcharges are the same for adult or child. No fees are payable by Indrail Pass holders.

Refunds

For single journey tickets, minimum cancellation charges are:

AC Class	RS 15
AC Sleeper	10
1st Class	10
AC Chair Car	10
2nd Class	5

The original reservation fee is not refunded; the journey cost will be refunded less deductions according to when cancellation is made.

Cancellation charges are not levied if an alternative reservation is made.

Cancellation charges of 50 per cent are levied on refunds when the cancellation is within two days before, or three hours after, the departure of the train. Refunds can also be sought on partially used tickets or due to the failure of a train's air conditioning equipment (if the ticket is for AC accommodation).

NB Foreigners who have reservations from the tourist quota should always cancel them if they cannot travel, as this releases the berths for other tourists who may be on the waiting list.

Lost reservation
It could be useful to record the number and date of your ticket in a safe place in case it is needed for future reference, as well as the number of the train, berth allocation (if any) and date of travel. However, if you lose a reserved berth ticket and there is a record of your name as being its purchaser, you can still travel on the same reservation. A payment of 25 per cent of the original fare paid will be levied for this duplicate ticket.

Special requirements
Reservations can be made only up to 60 days in advance of departure for all classes and on all trains except for some special expresses on

which the advance reservation period is reduced to 15 days or even less. This restriction does not apply to Indrail Pass holders.

An individual can book only up to four berths in the case of a party or a maximum of six berths for a family on the same train travelling to the same destination. It is sometimes possible to request a particular berth or seat: for instance, an outside lower berth or a berth in the ladies compartment, subject to availability. Reservations are not transferable.

For reservations from an intermediate station, the passenger must apply at least 72 hours before the departure of the train from its starting station. Reservations are not accepted by telephone. They are done in order of receipt of requisition slips.

Boarding the train

To make sure your reserved berth isn't given to someone on the RAC or Waiting lists, be at the station at least 30 minutes before the train is due to leave. This will give you time to find the platform, the train and your berth.

If you are boarding the train at an intermediate stop, arrive there with enough time to find out from the passenger lists which is your carriage and where it will be when the train pulls in. Some trains have 21 carriages so you will need to position yourself properly for boarding as there won't be time to run the whole length of the train searching for your carriage before it leaves.

Passenger lists are posted in prominent places in a station before a train's departure, and on the side of carriages themselves. The lists show the passengers' names, sex and ages with numbers of allotted berths and carriage number. Each carriage has its number painted on its side and also an indication of where numbered berths are to be found.

Reserved sleeping accommodation is provided between 2100 and 0600. During the day (0600 to 2100) overnight passengers must make room for seating passengers in the compartment, up to the number it is marked to carry.

The quota system

Many foreigners wonder why accommodation can be found for them on trains which are shown as fully booked. They suspect some inefficiency or corruption. In fact it is due to the miracle of the quota system.

Railway officials turn coy when you ask them about the various quotas and how the system works. Basically, it is a 'free sale' arrangement which enables a reservation clerk at a station to allot berths on a particular train without reference to the headquarters controlling the sale of berths on that train. This is done by headquarters assigning the station a specific number of berths, more than which cannot be sold by that station.

Lists of berths available at various stations appear in all the zonal timetables. For example, from the South Central Railway timetable, we discover that Aurangabad has a quota on Train 552, the Ajanta Express from Manmad to Kacheguda, to sell up to 10 AC Sleeper berths, up to 91 2nd Class 3 tier berths, up to four 2nd Class 2 tier berths and up to nine seats in the 2nd Class 2 tier carriage.

Foreign tourist quota

Trains which are popular with foreign travellers have a foreign tourist quota set aside for reserving at tourist-frequented stations. Any foreign traveller can request a berth from that quota, where it exists. If there isn't one, the foreigner must try to get a berth out of the general quota which is open to all passengers.

What happens if the general quota is sold out, as is often the case? That is when the system gets interesting and the officials get coy.

There are over a dozen different quotas formulated over the years to cover the needs of special passengers. As well as the General, Return Journey and Foreign Tourist quotas, there are the Parliamentarian, Defence, VIP, Outstation, Railway Employees and Emergency quotas.

Berths from all quotas which haven't been taken up by the time the train departs are released to the conductor to allocate according to priority on the RAC and Waiting lists. Where there is no foreign tourist quota, the SS or the CRS can apply (to the area manager) to have the foreign tourist accommodated on the Emergency quota. Preference is given to Indrail Pass holders over purchasers of single journey tickets.

A Reservations Guide is published in some daily newspapers showing the earliest date on which berths are available on trains from major stations. Trains are listed with class of accommodation alongside and the dates from which there are vacancies. Some trains, such as weekly expresses, are very popular and are likely to be fully booked from the day reservations open.

Reservation assistance in India

The following staff will help make reservations:

1. **Bombay (Central Railway)**
    *(a) Tourist Guide, Central Railway, Bombay Victoria Terminus Railway Station, Bombay.
    OR
    (b) Assistant Commercial Officer (Reservation) Central Railway Headquarters Office, Bombay Victoria Terminus Railway Station, Bombay.

2. **Bombay (Western Railway)**
   *(a) Tourist Guide, Western Railway, Upper Class Reservation Office, Church Gate, Bombay.
   OR
   (b) Deputy Chief Commercial Superintendent (Rates) Western Railway Headquarters Office, Church Gate Railway Station, Bombay.

3. **Calcutta (Eastern Railway)**
   *(a) Tourist Guide, Eastern Railway, Reservation Office, Fairlie Place, Calcutta.

4. **Calcutta (South Eastern Railway)**
   *(a) Tourist Guide, South Eastern Railway, Reservation Office, Fairlie Place, Calcutta.
   OR
   (b) Deputy Chief Commercial Superintendent (Rates), South Eastern Railway Headquarters Office, Koilaghat, Calcutta.

5. **Delhi (Northern Railway)**
   *(a) Supervisor, International Tourist Bureau, New Delhi Railway Station, New Delhi.
   OR
   (b) Assistant Commercial Officer (Reservation), Northern Railway Headquarters Office, Baroda House, New Delhi.
   OR
   (c) Deputy Chief Commercial Superintendent (General), Northern Railway Headquarters Office, Baroda House, New Delhi.

6. **Gorakhpur (North-Eastern Railway)**
   (a) Senior Commercial Officer (General), North Eastern Railway Headquarters Office, Gorakhpur.

7. **Guwahati (Northeast Frontier Railway)**
   (a) Senior Commercial Officer (General), Northeast Frontier Railway, Headquarters Office, Maligaon.

8. **Madras (Southern Railway)**
   *(a) Assistant Commercial Officer (Reservation), Southern Railway, Madras Railway Station, Madras.

9. **Secunderabad (South Central Railway)**
   (a) Assistant Commercial Officer (Reservation), South Central Railway, Headquarters Office, Secunderabad.

* These are the main reservations offices for foreign tourists.

Computerization
The recent introduction of a computerized reservation system has dramatically improved the booking process. Reservations are now

done by computer in Delhi, Madras, Calcutta and Bombay for trains originating from those areas. There is also a computer link between Delhi and Calcutta. As yet there is no target date for linking all computers so that instant confirmation of a reservation from, say, Bombay to Jammu Tawi, can be supplied by a computer in Madras.

At present, even stations with computers have to make reservations from stations outside their area by telex or telegram just like stations with a manual booking system. During 1989 at least six more stations were being computerized. Eventually computerized reservations will be possible in at least 70 per cent of the rail network.

In anticipation of this, new reservation centres are being built at many stations, and the whole reservations process is being streamlined. Since computers require careful maintenance in a dust-free, air-conditioned atmosphere, passengers are benefiting too with climate controlled, clean and comfortable areas in which to sit and await their turn. With less harassing conditions in which to work, the booking clerks have become customer-friendly too.

The computerized reservations system switches off automatically at the stipulated closing time, usually 2000 hours. So it's no good hoping to complete a complicated itinerary by starting just before 2000 hours since the operator, however helpful, can do nothing about it when the computer has closed down.

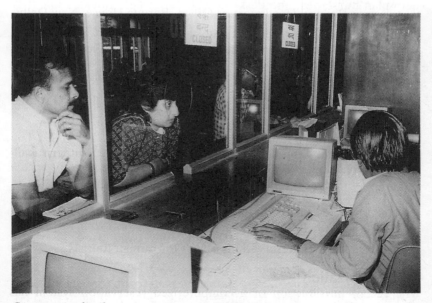

Computerized railway reservation terminal in Calcutta.

The International Tourist Bureau

The International Tourist Bureau (the ITB) is the flagship of Indian Railways' bureaux for dealing with foreign tourists. It is located on the first floor of New Delhi station, opposite the restaurant, and was opened in 1987 to cater for foreign travellers who no longer have to go to Baroda House to make reservations.

The ITB, sometimes known as Central Space Control, is the nerve centre of the Indrail Pass scheme which is coordinated by the Northern Railway. When a pass is sold by an overseas GSA (or by an agent in India) the GSA telexes the name, nationality and passport number of the purchaser, with the Indrail Pass number, class, itinerary and reservations required. A file is opened for the passenger at the ITB.

Apprehensive foreigners just arrived in Delhi who visit the ITB with their foreign-bought Indrail Passes are delighted to discover not only are their reservations confirmed as promised, but their full itineraries have been carefully recorded. This is possible because each GSA has an experienced reservations officer at the ITB who looks after the GSA's clients. When the telex containing the reservation request is received it is processed swiftly and confirmed by telex within seven days. Even if your Indrail Pass itinerary doesn't take you to Delhi, the details are recorded here.

The ITB is a brightly lit, cheerful office, open from 1000 to 1700 every day except Sunday. The staff take a break of 30 minutes for lunch from 1330 but tourists can wait in the pleasant conditions of the office during that period. There is a Tourist Guide on duty who will help plan itineraries, and desks at which travellers can sit while they discuss their requirements with reservation clerks and their computers. The Indrail Pass can be bought here and reservations on the pass as well as single journey bookings from the foreign tourist quota can also be made here.

Any resemblance to an efficient airline reservation office seems entirely deliberate. The ITB handles between 250 and 300 bookings a day. Over 100,000 foreign tourist reservations were made through the Bureau in 1988.

Only the foreign tourist quota on trains departing from the Delhi stations is controlled here. However, through telex, telegram and telephone, the ITB is linked with reservation offices throughout India and can confirm even complicated itineraries anywhere in India in about five days. It helps, of course, if they have your itinerary in advance from the GSA so you can pick up the computer reservation coupons, have your Indrail Pass endorsed, and be on your way.

In July 1988 a policy was introduced of accepting payment only in sterling pounds or US dollars for all bookings made by the ITB. The logic behind this is that since foreigners' reservations are made from the foreign tourist quota, they should be paid for in foreign currency. So don't change all your travellers cheques before going to the ITB.

Actually, buying a rail ticket from the ITB is a painless way of changing money. Pay by travellers cheque or foreign currency and the change is given in Indian rupees calculated at the day's bank rate. It saves a separate visit to the bank.

If you are unlucky enough to have changed all your foreign currency into rupees (as happened to one frustrated Californian trying to buy a ticket to Jammu Tawi when I was there), you will have to go to the main reservations counter and use your rupees to buy from the general quota. Or change the rupees back into US dollars if you are desperate to get a foreign quota berth. (The Californian did that since it was the only way to get a berth to Jammu Tawi in the summer season.)

The policy of accepting only pounds or dollars for reservations sold from the foreign tourist quota is spreading throughout India, so be prepared. However, not all stations which have foreign tourist quota allocations are able to accept foreign currency.

SS: The Sensible Solution
If nothing works out right, what to do? The office of the Station Superintendent (SS) is a haven for the troubled traveller. He is the man to resolve whatever travel problems you have. Travellers who barge into his office in high dudgeon are urged to sit down in one of the many chairs in front of his desk. A glass of water is offered immediately, followed by tea if the agony looks like being prolonged.

Station superintendents are usually men of great charm and personality who use tact and wisdom to soothe the irate traveller. Any foreign tourist who is bothered by an aspect of rail travel should go straight to the SS first. Shuttling around from one junior official to another will only compound your dissatisfaction. Save your temper and from the outset seek out the SS: he's the Sensible Solution.

Every station has a Station Master (SM) who deals with the operation of trains, while the SS is responsible for overall supervision. Smaller stations will only have an SM.

Chapter 4

Class Distinction

'You must,' said my publisher, 'travel 3rd Class. That's all that many rail travellers can afford and they'll want to read about it.'

The good news is that there is no '3rd Class'. 1st Class is being phased out too. A Divisional Railway Manager told me this is being done as part of a scheme to create a classless railway. It's not true, I discovered, but it sounded right.

There are, in fact, six classes defined by ticket cost, with variations in style and comfort depending on the age and status of the train and whether it's day or night travel. In rising order of expense, the classes are:

1. 2nd Class Ordinary (Passenger train seating)
2. 2nd Class (Mail/Express 3 tier sleeper)
3. Air Conditioned Chair Car
4. 1st Class (Non air conditioned sleeper)
5. Air Conditioned Sleeper (2 tier)
6. Air Conditioned 1st Class (sleeper)

In India, any class that's not 2nd Class is referred to as Upper Class. If the list seems complicated, it's going to seem worse as you read on.

Train type

Trains are either express/mail or passenger. Main line express/mail trains will include 2nd Class accommodation and one or more of the other classes on the list, unless they are 'Janata expresses' when they have only 2nd Class (non AC) carriages. Passenger trains are slower, often steam hauled, stop at every station and village halt and will generally have ancient 2nd Class carriages with wooden seats but usually with 1st Class accommodation even if its only two compartments in a combined 2nd and 1st Class coach. Incidentally, what I call a carriage or coach is also called a bogie in India.

For fast travelling, you need an express or mail train, preferably a superfast one since there are few expresses that manage to go very far – or fast – without stopping at a station. Broad gauge trains are capable of greater speed than metre gauge ones and, indeed, many metre gauge lines are being converted to broad gauge for more convenient travel.

CLASS STRUCTURE

Sometimes it is difficult to tell from the timetables just what the accommodation consists of. The daily Delhi/Howrah mail is shown as having: 'One AC 2 Tier, one AC I, two I and five II 3 tier sleeper car and three II.' The Tinsukia Mail from Guwahati to Delhi has 'one air conditioned II Class 2 tier sleeper coach' while a sister train runs from Dharmanagar to Guwahati with 'one II Class 3 tier cum 2 tier sleeping coach and one II Class coach.'

In those examples 'II Class' means 2nd Class. 'Air conditioned II Class 2 tier' is AC Sleeper. Some timetables call it AC II 2 Tier. Really you can only consider it as 2nd Class because it is the second most expensive way of travelling by train.

(1) 2nd Class Ordinary

The reference to 'II Class coach' means a 2nd Class carriage without sleeping accommodation, often called the general (ie: non reserved) coach. Passenger trains are composed of similar carriages; in other words the old style 3rd Class accommodation.

These carriages usually have a side aisle giving access to the open sided compartments of two wooden benches facing each other, and seating four (or many more) people on each bench. The luggage racks, of wooden slats, hang from the ceiling, giving extra space for passengers to sit or sleep (although signs say they are only for luggage). The luggage racks block out the light and add to the gloom of the compartment, as do the horizontal iron bars across the windows. Each compartment has two fans. On trains with a vestibule running its length, the linking door from the general carriage to the rest of the train is kept locked to prevent passengers slipping into the reserved carriages.

(2) 2nd Class Sleeper (see plan)

Long distance expresses and mail trains have 'II 3 Tier Sleeper Coaches' which means 2nd Class carriages with sleeping berths in three tiers: lower, middle and upper. There are 72 berths; the day time seating capacity is supposed to be 75 but usually expands beyond that.

The windows are always open in hot weather and closed tightly as soon as it begins to rain, hence the carriage gets stuffy. The windows have bars across them, like a mobile jail, although both doors at both ends of the carriage are usually left open so anyone can jump in, or out, as the train stops. There are three fans to each compartment (no AC) and they can be airy in the cooler months. In hot weather, nothing tempers the heat, and the dust billowing in through the open windows adds to the swelter.

The carriage is divided into nine open sided compartments. Each one has bench type seating for three people facing another bench for

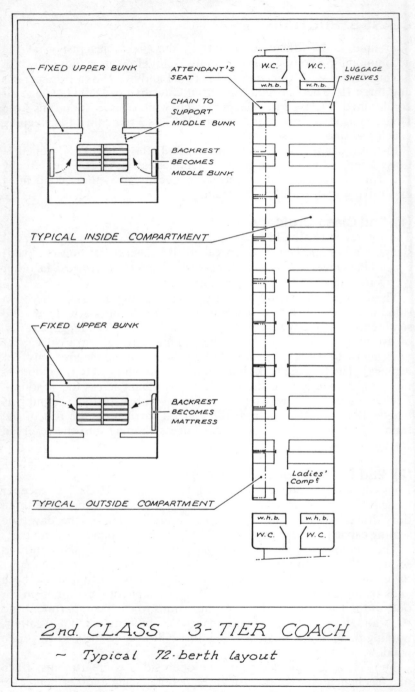

FIXED UPPER BUNK

ATTENDANT'S SEAT

CHAIN TO SUPPORT MIDDLE BUNK

BACKREST BECOMES MIDDLE BUNK

W.C.   W.C.

w.h.b.   w.h.b.

LUGGAGE SHELVES

TYPICAL INSIDE COMPARTMENT

FIXED UPPER BUNK

BACKREST BECOMES MATTRESS

Ladies' Compt

TYPICAL OUTSIDE COMPARTMENT

w.h.b.   w.h.b.

W.C.   W.C.

2nd. CLASS   3–TIER COACH

~ Typical 72·berth layout

three people. On the other side of the aisle is one single seat opposite another. The seats and benches have been converted from the old wooden ones and have been firmly padded and upholstered in rexine.

The padded back of the lower bench is raised to become the mattress of the middle berth, supported there by chains hanging down from the upper bunk. This upper bunk is a fixed, padded ledge suspended by permanent supports from the ceiling. The bunks formed in this manner have a width of 55 cm and a length of 184 cm.

Across the aisle are the 'outside' berths, converted out of the two single seats facing each other. The cushioned backs of these seats drop forward flat across the seats themselves to touch in the middle and form the lower bunk. The upper berth is fixed. These berths measure 55 cm in width with a length of 166 cm.

Thus, '3 tier' refers to what are known as the inside berths, while the outside berths (those parallel to the outside of the carriage wall) are two tier. This makes eight berths per compartment, all open to the aisle that splits them. Sometimes passengers hang clothes and towels as curtains but with so many people in a small space, there's not much privacy.

Each compartment has nightlights and clothes hooks. Access to the upper bunks is by scrambling up the metal hoops by the aisle; these also serve as handholds for people passing through the coach.

There are two toilets at each end of the carriage, but no shower. There are also mirrors and wash basins in the lobby by the entrance doors. At one end of the carriage there is a seat for the attendant and shelves for luggage. On a long trip the inside of the carriage gets dirty when people throw their rubbish on the floor instead of out of the open windows or in the bin at the end of the carriage.

Because the top bunk is fixed, it is frequently used for passengers' luggage. A family or friends travelling together might keep the middle bunk in place too during the day which adds to their lack of headroom and comfort.

The choice of where to sleep usually depends on the luck of the draw at the reservations centre. The lower bunk, being used as a seat, is only available for sleeping when the other passengers have retired to their own bunks. Similarly, the middle bunk can only be used when the seated passengers have finished sitting since it is their back rest. The upper bunk is available all the time, but requires agility to climb in and out and it's close to the fans and the lights. This is where an eye mask helps for sleeping.

Women travelling alone can request accommodation in the ladies' compartment which is a separate cabin, with a sliding door, at the end of some 2nd Class 3 tier carriages. It sleeps six. While men are not allowed in, they often spend time there during the day. Boys, up to the age of 12 if accompanying a lady, are permitted. On expresses with a

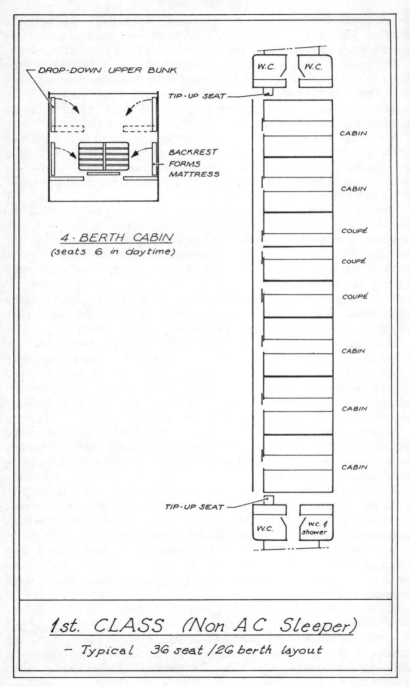

4 · BERTH CABIN
(seats 6 in daytime)

1st. CLASS (Non A C Sleeper)
— Typical 36 seat /26 berth layout

train superintendent on board, the ladies' cabin closest to the 1st Class is reserved for him as his quarters.

There are some odd combinations in 2nd Class such as 'II class 3 tier cum 2 tier sleeping coach'. This is a composite coach with both three and two tier sleeping berths but in separate compartments. The word 'tier' is frequently pronounced 'tire'.

(3) Chair Car Class

Chair car class has many variations and is usually encountered on day time journeys. Only some cars are air conditioned (the AC Chair Car class) with a separate fare structure, while others are non AC at 1st or 2nd Class fares.

AC Chair Cars seat from 56 to 73 passengers in a 2 × 3 layout. Some operate on overnight routes and a list of trains with AC Chair Car accommodation appears in Chapter 12. As well as the AC unit there are plenty of fans; the windows are sealed and the glass is tinted a sunset bronze. These carriages are a bit claustrophobic. The seats have tables which fold down from the chair back in front and a magazine pocket; they recline slightly. Be careful in locating your seat since when you think you've found, say, seat 45, because it says so above the fold-down table, you are actually in seat 40 because that's the number on the back of the seat your're sitting in. Western and Indian style toilets are available.

The 1st Class non AC version has 60 reclining seats in a 2 × 2 layout, with the aisle passing between the two pairs. There are fans and the windows open. Curiously, a seat in such a carriage can cost up to 60 per cent more than one in the newer AC chair cars.

Seats in the 1st Class, non AC coaches have a width between armrests of 44 cm and a cushion width of 50 cm. The armrest dividing the seats is broad and fixed. Leg space (pitch) from the front of one seat to the back of the one in front is 55 cm. There is a footrest, a pocket for papers in the seat back, and an ashtray at the side. All seats are forward facing except for a pair either side of the aisle at the end of the coach which face the others.

Seats in non AC 2nd Class are likely to be of wood in bench sections of 3 × 3, facing each other. There could be a total of 108 seats, plus two jump seats by the centre doors. Seats can be cramped when more than three people squeeze onto them and leg room is limited when there are passengers on the facing seat. There are Indian style toilets at both ends of this kind of coach.

(4) 1st Class (Non AC Sleeper) (see plan)

Forget the glamour and luxury associated with 1st Class travel; on Indian trains those comforts are now only to be found in the air conditioned coaches. No wonder 1st Class is being phased out. It would be hard to know what to call it when it ranks third in expense after AC 1st and AC Sleeper Class.

No new 1st Class carriages are being built; they are being replaced by AC Sleeper coaches since 46 people can be accommodated a night in an AC 2 tier coach compared with 26 in the same amount of carriage space in 1st Class. As a result 1st Class coaches are being allowed to deteriorate. They are often shabby with hard, bench type seats covered in a drab, patched, grey rexine. Passengers who don't like travelling in air conditioned isolation, or in the cramped conditions of 2nd Class, have only these neglected carriages to ride in. It's a shame.

Unless it's a Chair Car, all 1st Class coaches have sleeper accommodation. A typical 1st Class carriage is split into five compartments with four berths in each, and three two-berth 'coupé' cabins. There are four fans in the four berth cabins and two in the coupés. The glass windows open upwards and there are metal screens which can be lowered at night while the window remains open to let in air. There are bars across the windows, as in 2nd Class.

There are window screens that can be raised on the aisle side of the cabin too, and a sliding door which can be double-locked by bolts from the inside to keep out intruders. There is a metal loop fitted on the aisle side of the door (at its base) that enables the door to be secured with a passenger's own padlock. Some doors have a name card holder on them, a relic of the style of the old days.

The upper berths in these cabins can be raised during the day and bolted flat against the compartment wall. Many passengers keep them lowered though which obscures what little light there is, reduces the space available and becomes an obstacle when getting up from the seat below. (Mind your head.)

There are two foot rests that flip down from the cabin wall to help the passenger get into the upper bunk. A reading light and a pocket for personal items are fixed to the wall just above the bunk, and there is a shelf over the window.

The main disadvantage of being assigned an upper berth, apart from the process of getting in and out, is that it is close to the fans, fine in hot weather but they are noisy, and to the ceiling lights. Although these aren't very bright they can be annoying if the passenger in the lower bunk doesn't switch them off. There is a blue night light over the door.

The lower berth is formed by unbolting the cushioned back rest and letting it drop forward to make a wider mattress than the seat of the bench. At the aisle side it has a ledge for personal belongings and a holder for glasses or bottles, to which suitcases can be chained. There are also coat hooks, ashtrays, a pocket attached to the wall above the bunk and a reading light. There is a small table between the two lower berths, under the window.

The lower berth is easier to use but the occupant may feel obliged to wake early if the person in the upper bunk wants to sit on it, or to go to sleep late if the upper berth occupant stays up.

During the day the bench seats can accommodate three sitting passengers, which raises the total complement in the carriage to 39. The upper berth is 64 cm wide and 188 cm long, with the lower berth being 57 cm wide and 192 cm long.

The advantage of 1st Class travel, despite its recent deteriorations, is its spacious privacy. The cabins have enough room for four people to spend nights together in security and for six to travel companionably in the day. The coupés, while being perfect for a couple or loner who gets one for sole occupancy, are a bit depressing with only the cabin wall to face. 1st Class is as hot and dusty as 2nd Class, as the windows are always open, but it's not so dirty or noisy.

There are two toilets at each end of the carriage. At least one of these is western style. A marvel is that one of them will have a shower, such a boon on a long, hot journey. At one end of the coach is the attendant's seat, positioned so he has full view of the aisle. There is shelf space there too for meal service.

Many older carriages are still in use which is bad news for 2nd Class travellers since the seats are the old style wooden slats. But 1st Class passengers benefit from older coaches which have larger compartments than those built in the 1960s. They have wooden fittings, such as latches to keep the windows open, and a lime green interior instead of a grim grey. Toilets, too, are bigger with only one at each end but one is western style, and the other has a shower.

(5) AC Sleeper (2 tier) Class (see plan)

This kind of accommodation is also known as 'AC II class 2 tier' and shares with II class (2nd Class) a dormitory style accommodation. Its air conditioning, cleanliness, facilities, fixtures and fittings have made it superior to 1st Class (and more expensive). It has become the most popular with Indian upper class travellers.

The coaches have 46 seats/berths. Entrance is by doors at either end into a lobby which is cooled by a ceiling fan. At one end there are two toilets, a wash basin, the control panel for the AC unit in a glass fronted cabinet, shelves for storing meal containers and flasks, and a jerry can of drinking water and a seat for the attendant. A shelf drops down to serve as the AC unit technician's bunk. At the other end of the carriage there are two more toilets, a wash basin, more electrical controls and a cupboard for the storage of bed linen, which also serves as the attendant's cabin.

Self-closing doors lead into the air conditioned dormitory part of the carriage which has an aisle running its length. On the outside of the aisle are single seats, facing each other in seven pairs. Bunks hang down above them from the ceiling, although they can be raised and bolted back to the cabin wall.

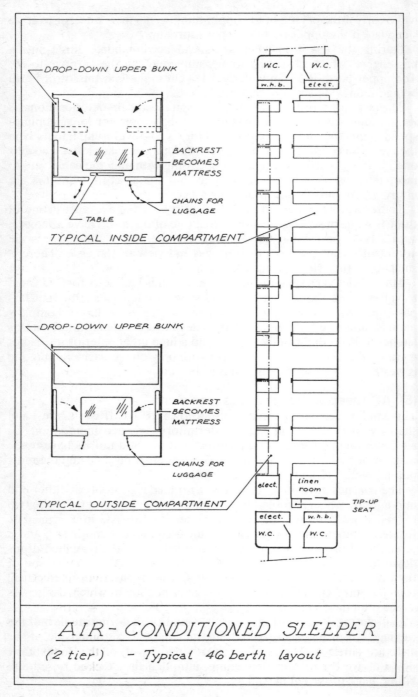

DROP-DOWN UPPER BUNK

BACKREST
BECOMES
MATTRESS

CHAINS FOR
LUGGAGE

TABLE

TYPICAL INSIDE COMPARTMENT

DROP-DOWN UPPER BUNK

BACKREST
BECOMES
MATTRESS

CHAINS FOR
LUGGAGE

TYPICAL OUTSIDE COMPARTMENT

W.C.

w.h.b.

W.C.

elect.

elect.

linen
room

TIP-UP
SEAT

elect.

w.h.b.

W.C.

W.C.

AIR - CONDITIONED SLEEPER

(2 tier) - Typical 46 berth layout

Each pair of seats converts, with the lowering forward of the chair back, into a lower bunk. At one end of the carriage there is only one lower bunk and no upper, making a total of 15 'outside' berths. One of the seats used to make this sole lower berth is actually an extra one. The worst berths are numbers 5 and 6 which are by the door and number 46 by the other door and under an ever-humming AC unit.

At the other side of the aisle are the 'inside berths' grouped in compartments of four each (two upper, two lower) with a curtain that can be pulled across to close the open space to the aisle. The upper bunks can be raised and bolted back flush to the wall to give greater space and light, but most passengers prefer to keep them down for day-time sleeping.

The lower berths are formed by letting down the cushioned back rest. The seats/berths are covered in a blue-grey rexine and are comfortable even on long journeys. A prominent sign says: 'Please pull up the backrest-cum-bed during 6 am to 9 pm to avoid inconvenience to sitting passengers.' Few people bother.

There is a shelf serving as a table, and two glass holders, below the windows. The windows have curtains; they are sealed and double-glazed and tinted, sometimes yellow, adding to the gloom within the carriage.

There is a strip light with push-buttons to switch it on or off by the window, and another strip light above the aisle, controlled by the passenger in the lower outside berth. Reading lights above each bunk are switched on automatically when the covering shade is raised. There is a fan above the aisle for each compartment, with a switch under the mirror on the inside wall.

Carriages have seven four-berth compartments with one having only three berths; two lower and one upper. Berths have different measurements. The outside lower one, converted out of two single seats, is 186 cm long and 53 cm wide. The berth above is 184 cm in length and 54 cm wide. Inside, the upper berth measures 184 cm long and 61 cm wide while the lower berth is shorter, at 173 cm long but wider at 65 cm.

Of the coach's four toilets, one is western style and another for ladies only. The 'Ladies' has side as well as full-face mirrors. Newer models of these carriages have fans in the toilets too, but there are no showers.

Carriages built in 1988 have several improvements over the original models. The end side seat, number 5, has a partition wall by it that protects its occupants from the ceaseless opening and shutting of the access door. Curtains have been added to the side bunks giving privacy and since each one is curtained off individually, the bunks adjoining the aisle are actually more private than those in the four berth compartments. Chains to which luggage can be padlocked have been fixed under the seats too.

These AC coaches have two attendants (one is the technician who looks after the AC unit) so they are usually well-maintained. Some passengers like the AC unit set at maximum, perhaps feeling that if they are not cool, they are not getting their money's worth. The usual temperature is around 72°C.

Attendants have different views on keeping the carriages clean. I've been in one carriage where the attendant was scrupulous in his job, crawling around on his hands and knees with a dustpan and brush and a damp cloth, and in another where rubbish was allowed to accumulate until passengers complained. There is a rubbish bin in the lobby at the end of the carriage, under the wash basin. The toilets are generally kept clean. Each AC carriage is issued an Opinions Book in which the attendant will try to get two entries every trip, preferably complimentary ones.

I've noticed in this class of coach that Indian passengers tend to spend the day lolling in their bunks in apparent boredom, whereas they seem livelier and more friendly in the 1st and 2nd Class carriages. I was curious to see several fellow passengers were very old men, with companions of equally advanced years. They turned out to be Freedom Fighters, pensioners who have been given an annual pass by the Government of India to ride free in 1st or AC Sleeper Class with a spouse or companion.

There are no separate compartments for ladies in AC class although women can request to be accommodated with other women. An appeal on board to whoever is in charge of berth allocation will usually be successful in achieving any necessary change. In theory, a woman travelling alone in this class is safer with 45 other passengers and two attendants than she would be alone in a 1st Class coupé.

Smoking is prohibited in the AC part of the coach: smokers congregate in the lobbies at either end.

The main appeal of this type of accommodation is the air conditioning. With the windows permanently closed, the dust and noise are kept out as well as the heat. However, you also miss much of the scenery since you can't see through the tinted windows clearly.

There is no spare space in the compartments and I personally find them claustrophobic and a bit dismal. However, if you can't stand the heat, this is an ideal way to travel. But if you want the windows open so you can see, feel, and smell, the India you are passing through, then a non AC coach is better.

(6) AC 1st Class (Sleeper)

Since it costs about double the price of a berth in AC 2 tier Sleeper Class (and about eight times the price of one in 2nd Class), you expect something splendid in AC 1st Class. I wasn't disappointed. The difference was apparent the moment I set foot in the carriage, with attendants eager to help and inordinately proud of their jobs serving in the best accommodation available to passengers on Indian railways.

The division of cabins and berths in this class differs according to the carriage and route. Where demand is small, berths are limited to ten; two cabins of four berths each, and one coupé.

The floor of each cabin is carpeted and the upholstery is a soothing brown. The upper bunks are bolted flush to the cabin wall during day time, with the lower berth serving as a comfortable rexine-covered seat for two. The seat converts into a berth at night by lowering the cushioned backrest down over it to serve as a mattress.

This mattress has been ingeniously designed with flaps down the length of its sides forming an envelope into which the bedding can be tucked. (This refinement, incidentally, is also to be found in the new generation of AC 2 tier coaches.) Freshly laundered bedding – and a hand towel – is included in the ticket price and the bed will be made up by the attendant.

Each passenger is given a packet containing soap and a plastic strip which I assumed was a toilet seat cover. There are at least two toilets, one of which is western with toilet paper provided or available on request. There is a shower and a fan in the toilet as well.

Each cabin has a sliding door, which can be locked from the inside, with a curtain to hide it. The windows, also with curtains, are sealed shut because of the air conditioning which is kept at an unobtrusive level; there are fans as well. Cabins have a drop-down table; some coupés have a miniature washbasin. There are ashtrays and a rubbish bin, a pocket for papers, and holders for glasses which are provided. Cold water is available.

A narrow, shallow closet contains a ladder to be removed for reaching the upper bunk, and some coat hooks, but no coat hangers. There is a range of buttons for putting on or switching off the strip lighting and night lights, or for summoning the attendant.

The only disagreeable feature of this cosy accommodation is a sign which says: 'Drinking of alcoholic drinks prohibited' which tends to spur all but the devout to disobedience.

AC 1st Class is only available on some 60 trains, not all of them daily, and only on major routes (see Chapter 12). Despite the cost, it is popular. Fellow passengers are likely to be government officials or top executives on expense accounts. For the less adventurous tourist, this is the best way to travel by train, especially if using an Indrail Pass which makes this top class a low cost bargain.

Double decker carriages

A novel feature in some trains operating to/from Bombay are the double decker carriages introduced in 1978 for 2nd Class travel. The Panchavati Express running daily between Manmad and Bombay VT, a five hour journey, has some of these.

By deft design, 144 to 148 people are accommodated in two decks of a single coach. The lower deck to which passengers descend by a few steps after entering by a door at the end of the carriage, holds 69 people. They sit on bench type seats, some of which are upholstered, with space for four on each. There are single seaters at the other side of the aisle.

The upper deck has seating in a 2 × 3 layout as well as singles, like thrones, and pairs, at the top of a tiny flight of stairs. When these carriages are empty, the clever use of space is impressive. When they are full, they are chaotic, hot and stuffy despite the fans. There are two toilets at both ends of the carriage.

Metre gauge accommodation

There are many combinations of berths and seats on MG trains which, like the Pink City Express, have had carriages custom-built for them. You will come across 2nd Class two tier sleeper coaches (non AC) with 16 upper berths and 64 seats and even three tier sleeper coaches with 48 berths and 64 seats. The MG Vaigai Express is all 2nd Class, but chair cars only. In AC class the layout differs from that of BG trains. For instance, the Pandyan Express (see Chapter 11) has 1st Class AC cabins in a carriage which also has 2nd Class AC (two tier) berths in cabins, instead of in the usual BG dormitory layout.

Metre gauge trains are renowned for their leisurely pace. There is a story about a travelling ticket examiner on an MG passenger train who asked an old man with a beard for his ticket. The old man gave it to him.

'This is a child's ticket', said the TTE in surprise. 'You can't travel on that'.

'Believe me', the old man replied, 'when I started on this train journey, I *was* a child'.

Rolling stock

Many trains on Indian Railways are very long, sometimes longer than the platform, and consist of at least 20 carriages. A major express will be made up of one AC 1st Class carriage (sometimes combined with AC Chair accommodation) and an AC sleeper (2 tier) carriage next to it. This will be joined to the pantry car with a 1st Class carriage the other side. The remaining carriages will all be 2nd Class 3 tier sleepers with two unreserved passenger coaches, one at the front and one at the rear making up the rest of the train.

Individual carriages on long distance mail and express trains are manned by railway staff. They will close and lock the doors five minutes before a train is due to depart, leaving one door open on the platform side of each coach so they can check late-comers. Doors open inwards.

The worst long distance trains are those without a corridor. It's difficult to know in advance whether a train will be vestibuled or not. Even when they do have a linking corridor, the attendants seem to delight in locking the doors so people can't walk up and down.

Why should you need a vestibule? Precisely so you can walk the length of the train to stretch your legs and to meet new faces in different carriages. And if the train stops in the middle of nowhere for 20 minutes you can get out and walk its length and not worry about hurrying back to your compartment when the train moves off, since you can board it anywhere and walk back along the corridor at your leisure.

When getting off a train, do remember to face the engine so if the train moves suddenly, you'll be able to recover your balance. Of course, never get off a train when it is moving, and always make sure the tracks are clear if you are clambering down on to them.

Train numbers

Trains share numbers, for example there are more than six express/ mail trains with the number 1. Trains are numbered from 1 to 198, with a few trains numbered in the 300s, 400s and 500s and there are some in the 800s. Trains numbered in the 900s are usually fast expresses that do not run daily, although some do. Most trains also have names, sometimes based on their route, e.g. 51/52 Howrah/Bangalore Expresses, or on local place names, e.g. 29/30 Malabar Expresses (on the Trivandrum/Mangalore route). Railway staff refer to a train as being an UP or DOWN one, a familiarization too complicated for the casual rail traveller to fathom.

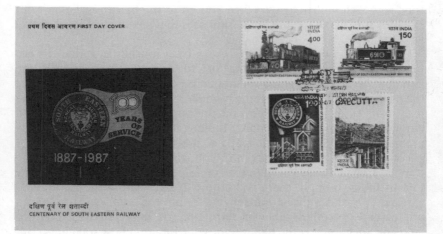

Chapter 5

On the Move

There's an air of excitement on the platform as the train's departure time draws close. You've found your name on the passenger list, together with the names of those in the compartment with you so you already know your fellow passengers' names, ages, sex and destination. People are pushing past you to get on as you show your coupon to the conductor and he tells you to board.

Your fellow passengers are settling in, staking out their claims to territory with too much luggage. A bell clangs but there is no slamming of carriage doors, no blowing of whistles and no shout of 'All aboard!' as in the States. The train simply draws out of the station while people stroll alongside and, with studied nonchalance, clamber on one after the other through the still-open doors.

You claim your own seat, pleased to be on the move. Since you have a long journey ahead in the company of strangers, what happens next will govern your enjoyment of the trip. You can start up a conversation and make friends, allies, quickly, or be anti-social and lonely for the whole of the journey. Of course, it depends on your personality but if you are travelling alone you'll need an ally, someone you feel you can trust to watch your luggage when you go to the bathroom. You can't isolate yourself completely on a train so if that's your style, train travel isn't for you.

I get a thrill out of the start of every train journey in India. It's not just the excitement of moving on to a new place, there's the anticipation of what's going to happen on the journey; the pleasure at the new acquaintances I'm going to make; the dissolving of city skyline into lush, rural landscape beyond the windows; and the heightened emotions of everyone on board. Indians love to travel by train; they are used to it and prepare properly so it becomes a picnic on wheels. I get a charge out of being part of it; you will too.

With Indian Railways, like everything else, you get what you pay for. In India, though, there is a bonus. If you choose the unreserved carriage on the slowest passenger train, you can be sure of an unpleasant overnight ride. In retrospect, it may provide you with amusing anecdotes at the expense of your Indian fellow travellers. But you're not seeing any more of the 'real India' than if you reserved a berth in affordable 1st Class on a superfast express with meals served

A typical Indian scene: Bari, near Agra. (Hugh Ballantyne)

The Doon Express from Dehra Dun (Delhi) to Howrah leaving Lucknow station. (Hugh Ballantyne)

Passengers waiting to board a train. Note bedroll in the foreground.
(Anthony J. Lambert)

Char Wallah at Santragachi, near Calcutta. (Hugh Ballantyne)

at your seat and fellow passengers who are lively, intelligent company. That's the bonus.

Part of the excitement of train travel is meeting new people who will pass on tips. However, some will regale you with their horror stories, seldom realizing that the fault could be theirs, or that of their guide books.

According to an article in an Indian journal, 'Travel guides dish out advice: when in India, think cheap, dress cheap, travel cheap, eat cheap and count on local hospitality and kindness to strangers to get you through.' The article urges foreign rail travellers to 'try to balance their experiences of cheap travel, and do themselves a favour, by travelling in a more comfortable class.'

For a foreigner, India is cheap but that doesn't mean you have to choose the cheapest and miss the best. Do the opposite. If you can't afford 1st Class in your home country, give it a try in India. You'll meet a cross section of the 100 million Indians who travel in upper class from time to time. Never stayed in a 5 star hotel? Now's the chance, since some of the world's best are in India at a third of the price you'd pay elsewhere.

Signals
The thrill begins with seven sharp rings struck on the warning bell (or sonorous piece of pipe) hanging outside the station master's office. That means Only Five Minutes Before the Train Leaves. At Bombay Central, though, seven bells indicates Ten Minutes to Wait. Two strokes on the bell means Departure Time.

The guard will wave a green flag, or a green light at night, and the journey begins.

When the train is passing through a station you will see a railway man on the platform holding out a green flag horizontally (at night he waves a green light). This signal tells the driver and guard that the train is 'proceeding in a safe and proper mannner.' If the watcher notices anything unusual about the train, he will hold out a red flag so the driver or guard know to stop it immediately.

If you need to stop the train in an emergency there is a communication cord. It is activated by pulling down a handle very much like the end of an old fashioned toilet chain and seems to be a relic of the Raj. It is placed close to where a standing passenger is likely to grab if the train jolted and he lost his balance. Be careful, especially in the toilet where it is tempting to pull the cord to flush the loo. There is a penalty of Rs 250 and/or imprisonment for up to three years for improper use.

Passenger rules
Compartments contain many notices advising passengers how to behave, such as 'Switch off lights and fans when you don't need them,'

and 'Discourage beggars,' and 'Smoke only if other passengers don't object.'

There is a rule about alcohol on trains. The Western Railway timetable says 'No passengers should consume alcoholic drinks in II AC Sleeper, II Class and AC Chair Car Coaches or be in a state of intoxication in any railway carriage.' The inference is that in 1st Class carriages, drinking is OK. But I've seen signs in 1st Class that state alcohol is prohibited there too. In practice, if it is done discreetly and without causing offence to other passengers, alcohol is consumed and even sold to passengers by trackside vendors, especially on the line to Goa.

Central Railway has a rule saying 'Case of transistor radios in an air conditioned chair car is not allowed except with an earphone'.

Train staff

Some expresses are under the command of a Train Superintendent (TS) who travels from the originating station to its destination. He is the train's manager and is usually a smartly dressed gentleman of great experience who will take a keen interest in foreign travellers requiring help. His office is likely to be a requisitioned Ladies Only cabin in the 2nd Class carriage near the pantry car.

A conductor travels in the 1st Class coach and joins the train only for the few hours it is in his railway zone, not for the entire journey. At wayside stations he helps joining passengers in all classes with their accommodation. He carries a reservation list as well as a complaints book.

He ensures that passengers are evenly distributed and prevents over-crowding. He has been instructed to 'exercise tact and firmness in dealing with passengers occupying more than their fair share of space in I and II class compartments either for themselves or for their luggage.'

A conductor's duties also include checking on the train's cleanliness, waking passengers who have to leave the train during a night halt, and taking orders from upperclass passengers for meals where these have to be ordered in advance. Conductors usually wear black jackets with a white shirt and a tie, and often with white trousers too. They are supposed to have a name badge.

Corridor Coach Attendants are less smart although they do have a khaki uniform of shirt and trousers, and name badge. They act as support for the conductor in 1st Class and have a passenger list and can help with berth location and check tickets if the conductor or TTE aren't available. They are supposed to 'keep a good lookout on the corridor of the coach from the attendant's seat, particularly during night time' and to see that everything is in order. Whereas the conductor will have a seat in a compartment, the attendant uses the tip up seat in the corridor of the 1st Class coach.

There will be several travelling ticket examiners (TTEs) on a train in 2nd Class who join at different stations for a few hours. As well as the obvious duties of checking passengers' tickets and assigning vacant berths, they also take orders for meals, see the carriage is kept clean, and 'look after generally the comfort and convenience of passengers'. They are supposed to see that upper berths are folded up and locked during the day.

TTEs usually wear uniforms of dark jacket and tie, and will sit in the coach they are in charge of. Travelling ticket inspectors in plain clothes will also be encountered occasionally. Since they are looking for fare dodgers, they are unlikely to be as affable as the TTEs or conductor.

The *Indian Bradshaw* contains hints for travellers, one of which says: 'Civility on the part of railway travellers to the railway staff who have frequently unpleasant duties to perform will, as a rule, command civility in return. Discourteous conduct on the part of railway servants should be reported to the authorities'.

Other train people you will meet are the pantry car staff. Bearers will come through the corridors with meals, snacks and drinks for sale. They are usually dressed in a drab grey uniform and tend to look scruffy. Since they have to live on the train in cramped conditions while it travels to its destination and back, this is not surprising.

The pantry car is under the control of a catering supervisor who has a white uniform but he sometimes wears his own clothes because of the difficulty in keeping the uniform clean.

The effectiveness of train staff differs by railway zones. Some trains do not seem to have enough TTEs to cope. In the north especially, 1st Class can become just as crowded as 2nd Class with ticketless interlopers and bogus free-pass holders. There are no restrictions on the beggars, pedlars and shoe-shine boys who invade the train and push their way through a carriage seeking money.

Loo lore

Perhaps what most puts potential passengers off train travel in India are tales about the toilets. I've got good news: they are not as bad as the anecdotes of travel writers and horror stories of tourists pretend them to be.

There are usually four toilets to each coach, a far better ratio of loo per passenger than on a jumbo jet. Some coaches have Ladies Only toilets, and there is no graffiti. At least one of the toilets in the upperclass coaches, and many in 2nd Class, will be western style. This means a flushable commode. Indian style is an aluminium trough with foot stands and a hole over which one squats.

For hygienic reasons, the Indian style lavatory is preferable to the western one. Often the western one won't have a seat and when it does you'll hardly want to put your bottom on it. At least the Indian version does not demand bodily contact. You will have to learn how to hang on while the train, as well as you, are in motion. There are strategically placed bars and handles for that purpose.

I am not advocating that, as a westerner, you abandon your personal toilet training and do it all Indian style. Carry your own toilet paper. (Contrary to popular belief, this can be bought in India, for about Rs 5 for a small roll.) There is a tap at knee level for personal hygiene and a lever to flush the trough.

If you are not sure how to use an Indian toilet, glance out of the train window as it goes through a town in the early morning and you will see people squatting with their backs to the tracks in the recommended position.

You need your own soap for handwashing and the basin will have cold water from a self-closing tap. There is a hand towel provided in every bed roll but this is small. If you are going to take a shower, you will need your own, larger towel. There are no showers in 2nd or AC Classes so if the train has a vestibule you'll have to use the one in 1st Class.

In the toilet, be careful where you hang your clothes since the hooks are so positioned that water from the shower will soak whatever is hung on them. Take a plastic bag and bundle your clothes and valuables in it so they can be hung safely from the handle that flushes the latrine. The water isn't heated and comes from a rose set into the ceiling.

Keeping clean

You'll be amazed at how dirty you get on a train, especially if you travel in a carriage where the windows are open. You can wash, and shower, in the toilets, but doing your laundry is not practical because of the drying process. That has to be done during overnight stops. Clothes dry quickly in India. Laundry is cheap and you can usually find someone at the railway retiring rooms who will arrange to have your clothes washed, pressed and returned before you move on.

When a train stops for a long period, you could even have a shower on the platform. Station waiting rooms have showers attached to them and there are also separate shower cubicles on many platforms, for which no charge is made. Take with you your own soap, and towel, and valuables in a plastic bag to place where you can keep your eye on them.

The cleanliness of the carriages themselves is fairly good although it depends on the attitude of passengers. The AC Sleeper Class coaches are usually the cleanest while 1st Class is somewhat shabby with compartment walls that are in need of a good scrub since repainting seems unlikely.

Freelance cleaners will hop on board some trains and make desultory sweeps with a broom of twigs and then pass around for tips. On the Tinsukia Mail from Patna to Malda Town there was a railway cleaner who swept out the carriage twice and then produced a book for passengers' comments, instead of asking for a tip. Since most people when confronted like that are unlikely to put down anything critical the cleaner was pretty safe. However, someone had the courage to write 'foul'.

SLEEPING

Many foreign travellers sleep in their clothes, seeing this as the best way of keeping all their possessions intact as well as avoiding the confusion and embarrassment of undressing in a crowded compartment.

Indians sleep with their briefcases under their heads, using them as a pillow. They might change into a cotton pyjama-style suit on the train, or wear a lungi. On one occasion when I shared a compartment with an Indian lady (and two men, all strangers to each other) I noticed she dived under her blanket every night still swaddled in her sari.

In the 2nd Class 3 tier coaches, you have little option but to sleep in your clothes with your valuables close to your skin. This is where your own blanket will come in useful. One regular rail traveller from England told me that he buys a new blanket every time he arrives in India. He uses it as a seat cover during the day since he wears shorts and the rexine gets uncomfortable, and to cover himself at night. He takes the blanket back to England after each trip as a colourful souvenir.

Air pillows can be bought at major stations with a choice of attractive woven pillow cases. Without air they do not take up much luggage space and they can be blown up very easily. They are useful as cushions for padding hard seats during day time travel as well as being better than a briefcase for resting one's head on at night.

Bed rolls

Travel bags, more popularly known as Bed Rolls, can be hired for overnight journeys in AC 2 tier sleeper class and in 1st Class if there are any spare. They are also available on some trains in 2nd Class 3 tier coaches. In AC 1st Class and on the Rajdhani Expresses they are provided free.

Bed rolls have to be ordered in advance, when making the reservation is the best time, and they cost Rs 5. For this you get a large canvas bag containing two bedsheets, one blanket, one pillow with pillow case, and one hand towel. The linen is crisply laundered and the blanket clean.

From October to March bed rolls hired from Northern Railway have an extra blanket, and cost Rs 6. The charge is per night and you have to pay double if you keep the bed roll for a second night. Get a receipt listing the contents which will be checked by the attendant when he

---

एक बिस्तर नं........................प्राप्त हुआ, जिसमें
निम्नलिखित वस्तुएं हैं :—

Received One Bedding Set No.................
Consisting of

1. दो चादर/Two Bed Sheets.

2. एक तकीये का गिलाफ़/One Pillow cover

3. एक कंबल/One Blanket

4. एक गद्देदार तकिया/One Foam Pillow

5. एक तौलिया/One Towel

6. केनवस/रेक्जीन बैग में पैक किया हुआ ।
    मैं बीच के कोई स्टेशन पर यात्रा विराम नहीं करूंगा ।
                              (कुल सात वस्तुएँ)

    Packed in Convas/Rexine bag.
                         (Total Seven Articles.)

        I do not intend to break Journey at any
    Station en route.

दिनांक/Date   यात्री के हस्ताक्षर पत सहित ।
                    Signature of Passenger with Address.

---

collects the bed roll the next day. There is no deposit payable but there
is a charge for anything missing.

If you forget to order one when you make your reservation, apply at
the station at least three hours before the train's departure. Some
zonal timetables show where bed rolls are available and there are
about 100 trains which provide this facility.

These are some of the trains which carry bed rolls for use by
passengers in 2nd Class 3 tier sleepers:

7/8	Ahmadabad Janata Express
17/18	Saurashtra Janata Express
19/20	Konark Express
23/24	Firozpur Janata Express
45/46	Girnar Express

101/102   Minar Express
123/124   Andhra Pradesh Express
929/930   Cochin/Hyderabad Express
931/932   Ahmadabad/Hyderabad Express.

Berth control

If you have a lower berth in either 1st Class or AC Sleeper Class, you will have to fold down the back rest over the bench seat to form the bunk's mattress. By laying your trousers and flat valuables on the seat before lowering the backrest mattress on top of it, you can keep them safe during the night, and your trousers get pressed too.

In full compartments you will have to develop an economy of movement in making up your bunk without disturbing other passengers. The upper bunk is the most difficult. In hot weather, the blanket can be used to sleep on. However, the temperature of the AC coaches is usually so cold you'll need the blanket on top of you instead of underneath.

Is it possible to get a good night's sleep on a train? When you think of the jolting, the constant stopping and starting of the train, the sudden shrieks of engines passing in the night, the insistent shouting of platform vendors when the train halts, the disturbance caused by passengers getting in and out during the night, and the worry about the safety of your belongings, it seems unlikely. Ear plugs will help. Since there are less people, in AC Sleeper or 1st Class you stand a better chance of sleeping in them than in 2nd Class. This is another argument in favour of not travelling the cheapest way but going for the best value.

Incredibly, after a day sitting on a train doing nothing very much, you will still feel tired at night. After a couple of night's practice, you'll be able to fall asleep easily, shutting out the noise and ceasing to worry about your belongings. I got so accustomed to sleeping on moving trains that occasional nights in a retiring room bed were sleepless ones because it was stationary.

SECURITY

The possible theft of belongings is a worry to foreign travellers but it need not occur if you take sensible precautions. Luggage in compartments should be padlocked to a fixed fitting so it can't be removed if you leave it for a few minutes. On platforms, never leave bags unattended. Carry valuables, whether money or documents, on your person, and sleep with them too.

If you're in a compartment with a door to the corridor, lock it on the inside at night. The four external carriage doors can be fastened and double locked from the inside to prevent unauthorized entry. The doors linking carriages on vestibuled trains are also locked at night.

Don't leave anything of value by open windows. Busy stations have gangs of urchins who cluster around trains as soon as they arrive. Many of them carry long sticks with hooks on the end with which they fish out discarded plastic cups from under the train. They could also catch your purse or bag if you're careless.

You will see notices on stations warning people not to accept food or drink from strangers. There are stories of passengers being given drugged food or drink and then robbed. It is hard to refuse an invitation to share a picnic lunch with a friendly Indian fellow traveller without causing offence. But if you are suspicious then plead an upset stomach.

Fellow travellers are just as likely to be thieves as urchins are, especially in the 3 tier carriages where you are sharing sleeping accommodation with 71 strangers. There is no need to become neurotic about losing things; if you do, your attitude could attract the very calamity you are anxious to avoid. Good sense will save you from most awkward situations.

If you are robbed while on a train, contact the conductor or guard immediately you discover it. They have forms for theft reports so it is not necessary for a passenger to leave the train to lodge the report at a police station.

Some trains have police travelling on them, especially when they are going through areas notorious for *dacoity* or demonstrations. The responsibility of providing security is undertaken by two agencies, the Government Railway Police (GRP) and the Railway Protection Force (RPF). The GRP works under the various State Governments and looks after the security of passengers and their belongings. There are about 32,000 railway police and a further 64,000 in the RPF, which concentrates on the protection of railway property.

An Indian newspaper carried an article in late 1988 about ticket collectors with canes trying to drive away young beggars who have made the railway stations their homes. Periodically these urchins are rounded up and despatched by lorry to an unknown destination.

'But lo', said the newspaper, 'the brats make a stormy entry into the station like homing pigeons before even the lorry comes back'.

Kids are attracted to the station because of the new packaging used by railway caterers. The discarded silver foil, casseroles and plastic cups can fetch their finders as much as Rs 40 a day. Consequently passengers are urged to crush their cups before disposing of them to prevent them being used again.

MEALS ON WHEELS

The use of foil casseroles for different dishes instead of serving meals on the traditional tray-dish, *thali*, is spreading throughout the railways and enhances the hygienic serving of food. The method of preparation, too, has undergone changes in recent years. Only in occasional circumstances are entire meals prepared on a train, even when there is a pantry car.

Orders for meals are taken from passengers and a message is sent to the base kitchen scheduled to supply them. Meals are cooked in base kitchens on demand, and according to strict standards, under the supervision of a catering inspector. There are no deep-freezer facilities, so the ingredients are freshly supplied every morning.

Many kitchens have been modernized with machines to churn dough and other innovations to make them capable of cooking the thousands of meals required daily. Major base kitchens are equipped with mobile heated cabinets in which the foil dishes are kept hot for delivery to a train's pantry car. If there is no pantry car, the meals are brought to each individual carriage and distributed to those who ordered them.

A long haul express of 21 carriages would probably carry about 1,100 people. At least a third of them will want meals every meal time. Others make do with food brought from their own homes, which is what many Indians prefer. They will also buy from vendors on the platform.

There is a variety of snacks on offer at the major stations and omelettes can be cooked in seconds over a kerosene stove on a trolley outside the train window. The platform vendors are either railway catering department employees or they work for a licensee. They are subject to inspection and food handlers have a regular medical check up.

Platform vendors sell on commission. In trains with a catering staff many of them are paid on a commission basis too, which is why there are frequent offers of refreshments by bearers passing up and down the aisle of every carriage. On trains without a pantry car, or a vestibule, unlicensed hawkers will board the carriage to ride it to the next stop selling snacks, or tea from a huge kettle. Tea costs one rupee a cup although sometimes tourists are charged more. Pay with the right money or ask an Indian fellow traveller to buy it for you with your money.

Special meals

If you are keen on food, you could meet the catering supervisor of the train and discuss special requirements with him, and be agreeably surprised. After a surfeit of standard base kitchen fare, I fancied chicken curry on one long journey. It was prepared in the pantry car and was delicious. Then it occurred to me to ask how they had managed to store the chicken since there was no freezer.

'We didn't,' said the supervisor. 'When we stopped at a station this morning, I bought a live chicken and we killed it especially.'

Bearer serving casserole meals in a moving train.

A typical non-veg meal: chicken curry, rice and chapati.

Bearer service

Where meals are put on the train from base kitchens, they will be served late if the train is late at the scheduled pick up station. On some journeys, the train stops long enough for bearers from the station restaurant to bring meals to passengers' seats. A typical vegetarian lunch served in that manner, as a *thali* meal, would be helpings of four vegetable curries (such as cabbage, potato, ochra and dhal) chapati and rice with curd in a chrome dish. A spoon could be provided on request if you haven't got your own cutlery, or you can use your fingers like Indians do.

The bearers who serve on trains come in all shapes and sizes. One I encountered was especially proud of the hygienic packing of the food he served me, pointing out the advantages of the foil casseroles for foreigners with sensitive stomachs. Having laid out the dishes on a table made up of my briefcase across my knees, he dug deep in his pocket and produced a plastic spoon. With a flourish, he polished it on the collar of his grubby uniform jacket before handing it to me.

His concern to give good service was impressive but it did make me wonder what sort of training he received.

'On-the-job training.' I was told by a top railway official. 'The bearer may not be sophisticated but he does know how to serve on a moving train'.

A superfast express with a pantry car could have 20 bearers/vendors on board with two cooks, two kitchen helpers/cleaners, a supervisor and an inspector. Breakfast and snacks are cooked in the pantry over charcoal or gas stoves. If possible, pick a train with a pantry car (some are listed in Chapter 12) to get food at meal times.

Pantry car panorama

One train to avoid because it has a pantry car but no vestibule is the Gorakhpur/Cochin weekly express. The bearers have to wait for the train to stop, at a signal or station, and then run down the outside to serve. Consequently meals arrive less than fresh and the service is unreliable since it depends on the train stopping and on bearers who have to work under impossible conditions.

Some trains which have a railway-staffed pantry car can also have a contractor service. This explains why nondescript vendors appear on trains alongside railway uniformed bearers offering coffee, soft drinks and snacks.

The Trivandrum/Guwahati Express is an excellent train run by the Southern Railway. It is fully vestibuled with a pantry car and a team of railway bearers. Yet north of Howrah the railway bearers do not sell. Instead, vendors with paraffin stoves (supposedly strictly prohibited on trains) boil water (taken from the toilet tanks) in the corridor to make coffee and tea. *Thali* meals are sold by other vendors. (The trays are actually put on the train in the afternoon for serving to passengers four hours later.)

After Howrah, heading south, the Southern Railway pantry car team is allowed to operate again. There are obviously reasons for this practice but the worrying aspect are those stoves blazing away beside the toilets, and cooked food lying in unhygienic conditions for hours before being served.

On a train with a pantry car the day starts with morning tea brought to the compartment about 0630 hours, as long as you've ordered it the night before. If, like me, you find the tea too strong when a bag has stewed in a flask of hot water for a long time, request the flask of hot water and the tea bag to be served separately and make the tea to your own strength. Indians prefer tea strong and milky and very sweet.

Breakfast is served about 0800 to order. On the Jhelum Express to Pune I was even asked if I wanted my eggs single or double fried. They were served in a casserole with tomato ketchup in a small polythene envelope, buttered toast and chips. Two hours later, cups of tomato soup were on offer while women with sacks of oranges sold them, one by one, to passengers.

Tariff

The price of meals served on trains is not the same in all railway zones, although the difference is slight. The menus are similar, with a choice: either vegetarian or non-vegetarian. In the south there are the special breakfasts which are a popular part of South Indian cuisine, such as Iddli and Vadai and Masala Dosal.

Typical meals and prices

(Rates are inclusive of taxes)

Breakfast (Vegetarian)		Breakfast (Non-Vegetarian)	
2 potato chops	100gms	1 Omelette	2 eggs
Tomato ketchup	20gms	Tomato ketchup	20gms
2 Bread/Butter slices		2 Bread/Butter slices	
Potato rounders	25gms	Potato rounders	25gms
Price: Rs 6.00		Price: Rs 7.00	

Lunch/Dinner (Veg)		Lunch/Dinner (Non-Veg)	
Rice	200gms	Rice	200gms
Vegetables	100gms	Roti/Chapati/Paratha	100gms
Dal	175gms	Egg curry (2 eggs)	215gms
Roti/Chapati/Paratha	100gms	with 125gms gravy	
Curd	90gms	Salad	20gms
Salad	20gms		
Price: Rs 7.00		Price: Rs 9.00	

Special Meal (Veg)		Special Meal (Non-Veg)	
Mixed veg pullao	150gms	Rice	200gms
2 stuffed parathas/		2 Roomali roti/chapati	
2 Roomali roti	100gms	paratha	100gms
Dal/Rajmah	100gms	Chicken curry	225gms
Muter panner/		Salad	20gms
vegetable	150–165gms		
Malal kofta	75gms		
with 90gms gravy			
Pickle	5gms		
Price: Rs 7.00		Price: Rs 15.00	

Beverages
Tea in pot (285ml)	Rs 2.00
Tea in cup (150ml)	Rs 1.00
Filtered coffee in pot (285ml)	Rs 2.50
Coffee in cup (ready made)	Rs 1.25

Service times

Meals are normally served on trains and in refreshment rooms and restaurants on stations during the following times:

Morning Tea	0600 to 0800
Breakfast	0800 to 1000
Lunch	1200 to 1430
Afternoon Tea	1500 to 1730
Dinner	1800 to 2100

As well as the normal beverages available on board, fruit juices are sold in cartons, the most popular being mango which costs about Rs 4. Soft drinks, fizzy sweet ones, cost about Rs 3 a bottle.

Generally, train food is perfectly safe for foreign stomachs, so do not be nervous about eating it. The problem is lack of variety, especially on a long journey when curried eggs for every meal can become boring. Meals can be brightened by fruit and other regional delicacies sold at wayside stations. If you do suffer from problems caused by food (or drink) while on a train, at least you are close to a toilet and being taken ill on a train will result in speedy attention.

OTHER SERVICES AND FACILITIES

Medical aid

There is a first-aid box on every passenger-carrying train and guards have some training in first-aid. If you're in need of assistance, ask the coach attendant or TTE to summon help. While it is not obligatory on the part of the railways to provide medical aid to passengers, it is invariably rendered. A simple scheme has been introduced to help staff find out if there is a doctor on board. On the reservation requisition form doctors are asked to indicate if they could be of help in an emergency. An asterisk is then marked against the doctor's name on the passenger list so train staff can find who and where the doctor is whenever necessary.

In an emergency train staff can arrange for a doctor to meet the train at its next stop. The doctor will supply medication or arrange for the patient to leave the train. The Northeast Frontier Railway has published a list of the charges a doctor is entitled to recover from a passenger:

Consultation fee for the doctor	Rs 10.00
Dose of mixture and tablet	.50p
Dose of higher antibiotics	Rs 1.00
Sterile dressing of wound	Rs 1.00
Injection, including price of common drug	Rs 4.00

Station facilities

Most stations have upper class and ladies waiting rooms. These are usually kept clean and have a zealous attendant at the door who will only allow entry to authorized ticket, or Indrail Pass, holders. The rooms have fans and most have attached bathrooms, often with showers, and luggage racks to which you could padlock your suitcase. The waiting area for other passengers is sometimes a spacious hall or a room with an enormous table (used as a bed at night).

Facilities vary according to a station's status. Main stations have closed circuit TV (CCTV) with train announcements transmitted live in colour from a studio actually on the station. CCTV is very popular with waiting passengers, but adds to station noise when sets are at full volume. Another feature of big stations are the juice bars selling canned and bottled apple juice from Kashmir.

Some stations have wheelchairs available for disabled passengers, and also self-help luggage trolleys.

The Railway Board has defined the basic amenities which should be at every Regular and Flag station as: 'adequate seating arrangements; a drinking water supply, minimum of two hand-pumps at wayside station; sanitized latrine with water arrangements nearby for hand washing purposes; electric light; proper booking facilities; shady trees'.

At Halt Stations: 'rail level platform of suitable length; a small waiting shed which will serve as a booking office; electric lighting where trains stop at night; shady trees'.

The following facilities are being provided, where justified as a priority: 'waiting halls; pucka platform surface for whole or part length; platform covers for adequate length; raising of platform from rail level to medium level/high level; coolers where piped water is available'.

A second priority programme is for stations to have: 'retiring rooms as required; upper class waiting rooms; bathrooms as per yardstick; enquiry office; refreshment rooms'.

As well as these improvements, some stations in each railway zone have been designated as Model Stations, which means they are being rebuilt to cope with rail users demands in the 1990s. As well as improved passenger comforts, the booking facilities are being upgraded to match the sophistication of the computer age.

Luggage

Main stations have 'cloakrooms' which are not toilets but where passengers may leave luggage for up to a month. The charge starts at Rs 1 or more per 24 hours for the first two days, then rises in day-stages according to the total time of deposit. There are also safe deposit lockers at some stations. A typical locker, such as those at Bombay Central station, is 90 cm wide, 52 cm in height and 42 cm deep; big enough to take a small suitcase. An advance payment of Rs 3 or more has to be made and the cost begins at Rs 5 per 24 hours for the first two days, rising each subsequent day.

There are regulations about the weight of luggage that may be carried into a train's compartment, but since the 2nd Class free allowance is 35 kg and the 1st and AC Class is 50 kg (it's 20 and 30 kg in an aircraft) this won't affect many foreign tourists.

From Western Railway comes the following information: 'In the case of air-conditioned First Class passengers with tiffin baskets including small ice boxes, small handbags or attache cases (not suit cases), walking sticks and umbrellas, are allowed free and will not, therefore, be weighed. In the case of second class passengers walking sticks, umbrellas and such articles of food as may be required on the journey are allowed free and will not, therefore, be weighed'.

Excess luggage should be booked and an excess fee paid. The luggage of upper class passengers exceeding 100 × 60 × 25 cm should be carried in the brake van, not in the compartment. The maximum size allowed in AC Chair Car is 63 × 37 × 20 cm. On the Pink City Express between Jaipur and Delhi, passengers are prohibited from carrying heavy luggage in the compartments. Maximum permitted size is 62 × 37 × 20 cm.

Regular train travellers are emphatic that the least amount of luggage you carry, the better off you'll be. One told me, 'the lack of luggage helps you to conserve energy, then you won't feel a need to drink so much water'. Another believes that his small, tatty bag indicates that he has nothing worth stealing.

Porters

Luggage you can carry yourself means you won't need a 'coolie', as porters are called.

Porters are licensed by the station authority and pay a fee for the privilege of carrying people's luggage. They are supplied with a uniform red shirt and with a brass armband showing their licence number. A system was devised for the porter to give a token with his number on it to a passenger in exchange for the passenger's luggage. Then the passenger would have proof of who was the porter if the luggage and porter disappeared. Instead, the token disappeared.

If you do have a porter, keep an eye on him. He is adept at loading your luggage into a taxi you don't want. On the other hand, although a porter's uniform of red shirt and red scarf tied around his head, makes him look like a brigand, he can be useful in locating the right train, or even to guard your luggage. He'll want at least Rs 5 from you because you're a foreigner, but the normal carrying charge is from Rs 2 to Rs 4 depending on the station's rates.

Complaints

Complaints, or compliments, can be made easily and effectively while actually on board the train. 'Suggestion-cum-Complaint' books are carried by the guard/conductor of mail, express and passenger trains, and also in the dining or pantry cars.

A request for the complaint book can cause great consternation among the train staff because all entries are investigated and can result in disciplinary action. The complainant is required to record full name and address and ticket number as well as the train number and date. As a foreigner, ou may be asked to write down your comments if the train or catering staff think you are likely to be appreciative.

Complaint books are available at large stations in the station master's office, in the goods shed or in the parcel office. Refreshment rooms and restaurants also have books. Suggestion-cum-Complaint Boxes are available at major stations for passengers' letters.

Many stations have 'Public Grievance Booths' where passengers can let off steam or register formal complaints to a railway employee. Letters of complaint can also be sent direct to the DRM or General Manager of the zonal railway.

It is worth using the complaints machinery. Some foreigners keep their complaints to themselves, then malign the railway system when they return home. Only if they make their comments known to the railway management can there be any improvement. An Indian once urged me to complain because 'a complaint from a foreigner can improve the system for all of us.'

Complaints relating to bribery and corruption are investigated by a special vigilance squad run by each zonal railway. The complainant should be prepared to give evidence before the investigating officer

Passengers riding on the roof at Bamourgaon station near Gwalior. . .

. . .despite official discouragement. (Photos by Anthony J. Lambert)

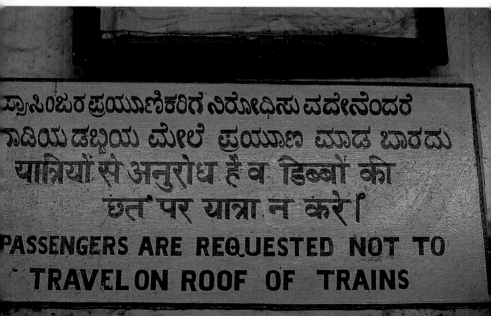

ಪ್ಯಾಸಿಂಜರ ಪ್ರಯಾಣಿಕರಿಗೆ ನಿರೋಧಿಸುವದೇನೆಂದರೆ
ಗಾಡಿಯ ಡಬ್ಬಿಯ ಮೇಲೆ ಪ್ರಯಾಣ ಮಾಡ ಬಾರದು

यात्रियों से अनुरोध है व डिब्बों की
छत पर यात्रा न करें।

PASSENGERS ARE REQUESTED NOT TO
TRAVEL ON ROOF OF TRAINS

An auto-rickshaw at Ajmer, decorated for the Divali religious festival. (Hugh Ballantyne)

Crossing the track. (Hugh Ballantyne)

and the original complaint should be sent by mail to the Chief Vigilance Officer at the HQ of the railway concerned.

Travellers' tips

Most foreigners you meet will be happy to share their tips. One told me that since local trains are slow, he actually prefers bus for short trips, only taking superfast trains on major trunk routes for long distance journeys. He travels 2nd Class, unreserved, during the day, not in the general coach but in a reserved carriage in which there are seats, and he pays the extra reservation fee, and surcharge, on the train (see Chapter 3 for how to do this). He travels during the day to see the scenery rather than at night. He was amazed by the number of rail routes in the eastern, Ganga, region where, he said, they probably only have a pair of trains a day.

An English couple told me: 'We travel by bus as well as train, but we don't like it. Not that it's crowded but it leaves you tired at the end of the day, and emotionally wrecked. The frenzy of driving, and the horror of watching near-misses the whole time, destroys whatever pleasure there could be'.

Another traveller said: 'To help avoid that feeling of lethargy that can be demoralizing on a long haul trip, I make a list from the timetable of all the scheduled stops and times of arrival and departure of the train I'm going to take.

'If the train leaves late, as often happens, I list my own idea of the ETA based on the amount of delay. In a third column I list the actual times of arrival and departure. It's amazing how some trains make up time despite inexplicable delays in the middle of nowhere'.

He added: 'I try to stick to a timetable of my own on a long journey, listening on my shortwave transistor radio to BBC World Service at 0730 and 1630 (Indian time) every day. A shower and a change of clothes works wonders for the self-esteem. The shower is usually empty during the hour before lunch or dinner since those passengers who use it at all are likely to do so in the early morning or late evening'.

Another tip: 'Conversing with fellow passengers really helps to pass the time, and relieves the isolation of being of no fixed abode. An eyemask (Gulf Air give them out free in economy class), is useful when you've had enough conversation and want to meditate or sleep without being disturbed. Indians usually respect such an extreme desire for privacy'.

Someone else told me: 'Earplugs are absolutely essential if you want an after lunch nap. It's not the noise of the train, which at least has a regular rhythm, that is disturbing, but the shrieks and caterwauling of the free-range children whose troublesome activities seem to be encouraged by their parents'.

Other tips I've gleaned from travellers met in India:

- A handkerchief placed on your seat will ensure that the seat won't be taken by another passenger when you go to the bathroom.

- The best seats, or berths, are those in the centre of the carriage where they are not over the wheels.

- Use timetables as a guide rather than as a guarantee of departure time or train accommodation. A check at the station in advance is vital since departure times can even be brought forward.

- If you have problems with officials at a station at night, head for the nearest hotel, check in, sleep, and wait for the next morning to resolve matters. Getting a good night's sleep is important if you are going to be quick witted enough to deal with Indian bureaucracy. Besides, in the morning, there should be different officials on duty who'll be more helpful.

- Try to adjust to the Indian tendency to make everything as complicated as possible. Remember there is no way to rush the system. You are the guest and don't have the right to dictate anything.

- Don't expect to get the right answer; you are told what people want you to hear. Nobody wants to be the one to tell you bad news.

The best advice I had was from a young Indian navy officer who wrote to me after our meeting on a train: 'Things may be difficult but you will encounter many people, many things, which will linger in your memory for long. Everything has a bad side – you must take them as a bad experience. I can assure you that definitely with time you will love this country'.

Chapter 6

Past Trains and Present Steam

To Madras goes the credit for the first plan to have a railway network in India when, in 1831, a parliamentary committee discussing the affairs of the East India Company, proposed the introduction of rail roads to improve the deplorable communications. Although the idea was considered again in 1836 nothing happened for 20 years.

Instead, Bombay did something about it in the 1840s with the result that the formal inauguration of the first railway line in India took place on April 16, 1853, when a train carried 400 passengers from Bombay to Thane. Actually, it had taken only 28 years after the start of the world's first commercial train service, between Stockton and Darlington in the UK, for India to have her own passenger trains.

Calcutta followed swiftly, inaugurating a 24 mile line from Howrah to Hooghly in August 1854. It would have happened sooner but the ship bringing the locomotives went to Australia instead. In South India, the first line opened in July 1856 for the Madras Railway Company: 63 miles of track between Veyasarpady and Walajah Road.

Meanwhile, in the north, a length of 119 miles of line was laid from Allahabad to Kanpur and opened in March 1859. Three years later, a line between Amritsar and Lahore opened for traffic.

Engineering feats
The achievements of the 19th century railway engineers are remarkable. The laying of a rail line from Bombay across the Bhore Ghats to Pune and the Thal Ghats to Bhusuval was the most difficult then undertaken anywhere in the world. Work began in 1860 with 40,000 men labouring for four years. The average daily consumption of gunpowder was 2½ tons. The two lines were opened in 1864, having been built without dynamite, pneumatic tools or any of the equipment used today.

More remarkable was the construction in 1874 of the 55 mile long metre gauge line at Godspeed from the left bank of the river Ganga to Darbhanga, forerunner of the present day North Eastern Railway. Major F.S. Stanton, Superintendent Engineer of the Rajputana Malwa Railway carried out the survey, acquired the land, moved material to the other side of the river, laid the track, commissioned the locomotives and opened the line for traffic, all in 65 days.

The government was anxious to attract private capital to develop the railways but private companies were cautious about the potential for their investments so a guarantee system was devised. After 1870, railway development became rapid.

For centuries, the growth of roads had radiated from the interior, from centres such as Delhi, Lahore, Allahabad and Agra, to the coast. With railways, the communications expansion was reversed with lines commencing at the major sea ports and penetrating inland. The line over the Bhore Ghats to Pune, for instance, was to serve as a connecting link with South India and the line over the Thal Ghats to Bhusaval went on to Delhi and Calcutta.

Rail fever

As well as tracks being laid throughout the country when rail fever took hold, stations were being constructed. The railway companies were the patrons of new architecture in the 19th century. Stations, big and small, were constructed in different styles: Classical, Gothic Arabic, Indo Arabic, Traditional and 19th century contemporary. The stations are still in use while the early locomotives have disappeared.

None of the three locomotives used on the first line from Bombay, they were called Sindh, Saheb and Sultan, exist now. Sindh did survive the two world wars and was kept on a pedestal at Matunga only to be sold for scrap. The first locomotive which hauled passenger trains on the East India Railway between Howrah and Raniganj is still preserved, however, at Jamalpur.

In the 1920s, the railways entered a new phase of development as the state began to take over the management of the various railway companies. A period of prosperity followed, including electrification which was introduced in 1925 by the Great Indian Peninsula Railway and in 1928 by the suburban section of the Bombay, Baroda and Central India Railway. The Madras suburban section was electrified in 1931.

The Second World War brought a setback to the railways when rolling stock and materials were shipped out for the war effort, and lines were dismantled and workshops used for ammunition manufacture. After Independence, the entire network of 42 separate railway systems came under State control. They were reorganized into six zones in 1951/52, which eventually became the nine zones in operation today.

Since the reorganization there has been a phenomenal growth in usage. In 1950/51, there were 1,284 million passenger journeys; in 1986/87 the figure was 3,580 million. The average distance travelled by a passenger in 1986/87 has been calculated as 71.6 km (compared with 51.8 km in 1950/51) while the average per upper class non suburban passenger was 528.4 km. The route kilometres of the railways now is

Many of India's narrow gauge railways were built by local maharajahs and only became part of the national network following independence. The 114 km Rupsa–Talband line in Orissa was once the Mayurbhanj State Railway, though the mahurajah did not provide locomotives or rolling stock; the line was worked by the Bengal Nagpur Railway. In 1966–7 the final 26 km between Bwagripoyi and Talband were closed. This ZE class 2–8–2, No 19, has been specially decorated with the peacock emblem of the maharajah. The locomotive was built in Germany in 1952. (Anthony J. Lambert.)

almost 62,000; almost twice the length of the national highways, with over ten million people travelling on the fleet of over 9,000 locomotives every day.

Rail museums

The history of Indian Railways can be traced in the excellent Rail Museum in Delhi (see page 124). A lesser-known museum exists at Mysore, and this is described on page 184.

STEAM IN INDIA – 1989
by Hugh Ballantyne

For convenience this brief guide to current steam working on India's vast railway system is divided into the nine railway zones. Trains from two or more different railways serve some places such as Agra with Northern, Central and Western trains, Varanasi with Northern and North Eastern, Lucknow with North Eastern and Northern and Pune with Central and South Central Railway.

India once had a bewildering variety of locomotive types but the variation has been simplified. On the broad gauge (BG) and metre gauge (MG) lines there are two operational and standardized classes to be seen and it is left to the narrow gauge (NG) lines to provide the variety.

The BG types are the WG class 2-8-2 and WP class 4-6-2. No less than 2,450 WG's were built between 1950 and 1970, with the first 100 being built in the UK by the North British Loco Co., and the others in India (at the Chittaranjan Loco Works in West Bengal) and in France, Germany, Austria, Italy, USA and Japan. Built for freight traffic, they are used on passenger trains as well. They are large, impressive and very functional machines and with an 18½ ton axle loading have the route availability to be found all over India where steam still remains in use. The WP class Pacific contains many standardized parts with the WG and was designed just after the Second World War as a passenger locomotive with the same axle loading as its WG goods counterpart. However, their appearance is quite different as the WP has a bullet nose smoke box door and semi-streamlined casing along the boiler, making it a very distinctive and attractive locomotive. A total of 755 were built between 1947 and 1967 with the original 16 coming from Baldwin Locomotive Works in the USA.

The MG railways have two standard types which at a quick glance look almost identical. These are the YG class 2-8-2 for goods and the YP class Pacific 4-6-2 passenger locomotive, so the same wheel arrangements are found on both BG and MG railways. 1,076 YG class were built between 1949 and 1972 and 871 YPs between 1952 and 1972. Until recently another standard post war class in use was the YL 2-6-2, an attractive and efficient all purpose engine for branch line use, and

For the independent traveller keen to explore some of India's remoter and less visited parts, the narrow gauge railways provide some interesting routes. Particularly recommended is a journey on the Satpura Express south from Jabalpur which passes through some delightful country in Madhya Pradesh. Another pleasing though shorter railway is the Parlakamidi Light Railway from Naupada to Gunupur, which follows the border between Andhra Pradesh and Orissa for much of its route. Motive power is provided by these little 0–6–4 tank engines built in Stoke-on-Trent in the 1920s, though work on upgrading the track to allow the use of diesels is under way. (Anthony J. Lambert.)

The "Family Tree" of the 9 Railway Zones

1853–1872	1873–1892	1893–1912	1913–1932	1933–1951	1958
Eastern Punjab E.I.R. (Lucknow Moradabad & Allahabad Div.	Rajpura Bhatinda Jodhpur: Bikaner state: B.B.C.I. (Delhi Rewari Fazilka section	Ludhiana Dhuri Jakhal Kalka Simla	Hosiarpur Doab Branch Jind Panipat Sirhind Rupar Kangra valley	Rupar Nangal Dam	Northern Railway
	Assam Bengal B.B.C.I: Kanpur/ Achnera sect. Bengal & N.W. Tirhut. Lucknow Bareilly Rohilkund. Kumayon Darjeeling Himalayan	Coochbehar State	Chaparmukh Silghat Katakhal–Lalabazar	Assam Bengal Assam	North Eastern Railway North East Frontier Railway
East Indian Eastern Bengal	Tarakeswar Dildarnagar Ghazipur State	South Bihar			Eastern Railway
	Bengal Nagpur	East Coast Northern Rupsa Talband Naupada Gunupur Purulia Ranchi branch Raipur Dhamtari Satpura	Central India Coalfields		South Eastern Railway

Madras Railway Southern Mahratta Rly. South Indian South Indian (MG)	Madras Railway Southern Mahratta Rly. Kolhapur State Pondicherry Branch French Mysore State	Kolar Gold Fields Shoranur Cochin Sangli State Nilagiri M&SMR. Travancore Peralam Karaikka	Bangalore–Chick Ballapur Light	Cochin Harbour Branch	Southern Railway South Central Railway
Great Indian Peninsula	Scindia State Bhopal Itarsi Nizam State	Bhopal Ujjain Bina–Goona Baran Nizam State Dholpur State Matheran Hill Scindia	Dhond Baramati Ellichpur Yeotmal Pachora Jamner Pulgaon Arvi		Central Railway
B.B. & C.I. Holkar State (MG)	Petlad Cambay B.B.C.I. Gaekwars Mehsana Bhavnagar Slate Gondal Porbandar State Junagadh State Gaekwars Baroda	Tapti Valley Nagda– Ujjain Ahmadabad Dholka Branch Ahmadabad Prantij Palanpur State Jetalsar Rajkot Jamnagar. Morvi. Drangadra State Jaipur State. Rajasthan Gujerat–Champaner Rajpidla State Morvi Tramways. Cutch	Boriavi Vadtal Jamnagar Dwarka Okham Andal Bodeli Chotaudaipur Gujerat–Godhra –Lunavada –Nandad –Kapadbhan Piplod–Devgod. Baria Shavnagar–Talja Manuja Tramways	Jodhpur–Marwar Phulad Section	Western Railway

264 were built between 1952 and 1956. It is possible a few will remain at work in odd places into 1989. Finally there is the WD class 2-8-2 which is the wartime American designed and built 'MacArthur' and were obtained from the USA Transportation Corps after the war, or later built new in 1948, and eventually totalling 304 engines in India. Some are still at work and one has been station pilot shunting stock at Agra Fort station for many years.

Of the four principal Indian cities only New Delhi and Calcutta see steam regularly and Bombay and Madras only occasionally.

Taking the railways clockwise from New Delhi:

Northern Railway   It is probably best to avoid the part of this railway to the north of Delhi in view of the political situation in the Punjab and concentrate on its eastern side. Good centres with steam sheds are Kanpur, Lucknow (highly recommended), Tundla (north of Agra), Bareilly, Moradabad and Varanasi. On MG, Delhi (shed in Sara Rohilla) and Jodhpur.

North Eastern Railway   This railway mainly operates on MG but there is some conversion to BG in hand. It is probably the best railway in India overall for concentrated steam activity. On BG Sonpur is the busiest shed with an allocation of 23 WP and 17 WG in 1988 plus its MG shed alongside. On the MG, Gorakhpur has about 36 MG steam hauled trains at its station every 24 hours, other good centres are Bareilly, Kasganj, Gonda, Varanasi, Lucknow (Charbagh), Samastipur and Darbhanga.

North East Frontier Railway   This operates mainly in a security area and is difficult to visit. The world famous Darjeeling–Himalaya Railway is a 2'0" (.610 m) gauge line in this region and if it is operating you are strongly recommended to travel on it. With its spirals and zig-zags, this amazing railway climbs to a summit of 2259 m at Ghum before descending by means of a double loop into Darjeeling, all steam worked with its beautiful B class 0-4-0STs. On the plains, connection is made at Siliguri with the MG, and at New Jalpaiguri with both MG and BG (see Chapter 11). Steam types to be seen at the latter are YG, YP and WD on MG and WG on the BG. Finally Katihar is also a good MG centre and with a new BG connection now opened sees WG class as well.

Eastern Railway   BG steam is still very active with plenty of WG and WP to be seen but mainly in deplorable condition. Best centres are Patna, Asansol, Andal, Sitarampur, Dhanbad, Burdwan (now known as Barddharman) and Mughal Sarai. On the NG the Burdwan–Katwa–Ahmadpur 2'6" (.762 m) gauge line has Bagnall of Stafford built 0-6-4T and 2-6-2Ts, although there are some railcar workings on the Burdwan–Katwa section.

South Eastern Railway   A BG railway with numerous NG but no MG at all. On BG still a lot of line work for both types with the best centres at Khurda Road, not far from the coastal resort of Puri, Waltair and Dongargarh (on the Nagpur–Durg main line). NG has six separate systems all 2'6" (.762 m) gauge. From east to west: Bankura–Rainagar uses CC class Pacifics dating from 1906. Ranchi–Lohardaga ZE class, a standard design NG type 2-8-2 dating from 1952 with a few BS class 2-8-2 from 1915 era on shunting duties. The Kotshila–Purulia railway also uses ZE class 2-8-2s as does the Rupsa to Bangraposi branch. The Naupada–Gunupur line further south has some attractive and beautifully maintained PL class 0-6-4T built by Kerr Stuart of Stoke-on-Trent 1924/28. The Raipur and the extensive NG lines around Gondia and Nagpur are all diesel operated.

Southern Railway   Broad gauge steam engines have been eliminated in the SR zone. However, there are about 160 MG routes which are served by steam-hauled trains. Some of the stations where you can catch a steam train are Tiruchchirappalli, Madurai, Rameswaram, Dindigul, Villuparam, Pondicherry, Thanjavur, Palghat and Mysore. There is also the popular steam loco ride on the rack and pinion line between Mettupalayam and Udagamandalam (Ooty). This MG line is operated by X class compound 0-8-2T built by Swiss Loco and Machine Works from 1920.

South Central Railway   Events are difficult to keep up with on this railway but on BG, check Rajamundry (south of Waltair on the main south east coast line), and a little activity at Secunderabad and at Daund. On MG, Hubli and the lines to the west have been extensively worked with steam haulage as have the branches off the main line going east towards Guntakal. There are no NG lines on this railway.

Central Railway   A very large BG network, nominal MG mileage but eight NG lines, six of 2'6" (.762 m) gauge and two of 2'0" (.610 m). Except in the Bombay area, steam does local work from nearly all the main centres and junctions on the BG. Sheds that have traditionally always had big allocations are Bhusaval, Jhansi, Jabalpur, Amla, Bina and Wardha. Some local work may still come to Agra Cantt, although the main line between Delhi and Jhansi is now electrified. On the NG the Daund–Bardmati uses standard ZE class 2-8-2 but is expected to go diesel soon. The Kurduvadi system known as the Barsi Light Railway is diesel. The Pachora–Jamner has ZE class 2-8-2, Murtajapur ZD class 2-8-2 and Arvi-Pulgaon some ZP class 4-6-2. At Gwalior there is a fascinating .610 m gauge system with lines going to Sheopur Kalan westwards and east to Bhind. It uses a variety of engine classes including three rare 4-6-4 of class ND. Between Gwalior and Agra at the junction of Dhaulpur another NG (.762 m gauge) line goes westwards to Sirmuttra and Tantpur through remote sparsely populated country using large 2-8-4Ts and some standard ZE 2-8-2s. The last two mentioned railways are within easy reach of Agra. Central Railway have three dozen routes served by broad gauge steam hauled passenger trains, the longest journey being the 392 km run from Bhusaval to Nagpur. Narrow gauge steam passenger trains operate on the following routes:

Pulgaon to Arvi	35 km
Pachora to Jamner	56 km
Murtajapur to Yavatmal	112 km
Murtajapur to Elichpur	76 km

Western Railway   A large and busy railway with important BG and MG main lines plus some NG branches. On the BG, Vadodara, Ratlam, Kota and Gangapur have busy sheds and one or two locos can usually be found if staying in Agra, at the small shed of Agra Idagh (which also has an MG shed on the opposite side of the running lines). The MG network is extensive and the two standard classes can readily be seen at such places as Ahmadabad (main shed is at Sabarmati), Mahesana, Rajkot, Ajmer, Jaipur Bandikui and, to the west Jetalsar and Bhavnagar. There are regular steam workings to Agra Fort but numerically not many locomotives to be seen. All the NG is .762 m gauge and the biggest system centred on Dabhoi, just south of Vadodara mainly uses a large fleet of ZB class 2-6-2s. To the north, at Nadiad, ZB work on Bhadran and WT class 0-6-4Ts, dating from 1925, to Kapadvanj. The Bilimora to Waghai line has W class 0-6-2T built from 1912 and the nearby Kosamba–Umarpada branch has four of the same type. The railway eastwards from Ankleswar uses ZB class 2-6-2s and WI class 0-6-2Ts for shunting and finally Champer Road to Pani Mines is using the standard class of ZB 2-6-2.

Permits

It is possible to visit locomotive depots but a permit has to be obtained first. Applications, stating the name of the sheds to be visited and when, should be sent to the Indian High Commission or Embassy in your home country. It will be forwarded to Delhi for official approval so allow at least three months for a reply. Often replies are delayed or permission refused for unexplained reasons. Applying before you go saves having to spend time coping with bureaucracy in India. Some of the smaller sheds can be visited on the spur of the moment without a permit, if you are lucky. Permits are also required for photography (see Chapter 2).

Chapter 7

Where to Stay

Retiring rooms

Guide books for the budget-conscious tourist and the travellers' grapevine concentrate on low-cost hotels and guest houses in most towns in India yet usually overlook the perfect place to stay within metres of the station platform: the railway retiring rooms.

At about Rs 50 for a double room with twin beds here is the best, cleanest and most secure accommodation you'll find at the price. It's also the most convenient since you don't have to traipse around town with your luggage looking for a place to stay.

Don't be put off by the term 'retiring room'. These are nothing less than comfortably furnished guests rooms, nearly all with attached bathrooms. The most luxurious are suites with sitting room, bathroom, pantry, TV, fridge and air-conditioned bedroom. Rooms are usually located off the main platform or on the first floor above the booking office.

Railway accommodation conforms to minimum standards that include adequate bedroom furniture and a rule that the bed linen be changed after every occupant. If you find the sheets are grubby when you arrive, ask for them to be changed. It will be done without rancour.

Towels are also supplied on demand. The bathrooms will have a shower (sometimes with hot water) and sometimes a western toilet, but no toilet paper. You will usually be given a padlock with a key to lock the door, or you can use your own. Many of the attendants are eagle-eyed women (wearing light blue saris) who won't let a miscreant near your door, so security is good.

The rooms in British-built stations are large and airy, with fans. Many of them open onto terraces that overlook the station forecourt. Limited room-service is usually available, such as bed tea and soft drinks; sometimes tea, soft drinks and a newspaper are included in the room rate.

There are twin-bedded rooms (known as 'doubles'), single bed rooms and dormitories. Dormitories will have their own shower and toilets attached, with a locker for each occupant to store his belongings in. If you are travelling alone and are wary about sharing a room, or dorm, with strangers, doubles can be let for single occupancy but you must pay the double rate.

Many rooms are air-conditioned with huge boxes containing alternators chugging away during the night to pump in cold air. I prefer a fan at night but I discovered that at some stations the AC rooms are much larger and, since they are regarded as prestige accommodation, they are cleaner and better serviced too.

I've only once found bed bugs under my mattress in a retiring room, in the same room where the attendant locked me in and wouldn't let me out, after waking me at 0300 hours to catch my train, until I'd given her a tip. I was pleased to notice on my second visit, after I'd complained to the DRM, that both bed bugs and attendant had gone.

Retiring rooms are charged per 24 hours. No matter what time of day or night you arrive, the room is yours for 24 hours from time of check in. Payment is made on arrival to the attendant in charge, or to the SS. Some stations increase the room rate by 25 or 50 per cent for the second 24 hours. Occupancy is only permitted to rail travellers with tickets, or to Indrail Pass holders.

Apart from the cost advantage, railway retiring rooms are ideal for those with pre-dawn departures. Their proximity to station facilities such as restaurants and, at New Delhi station, to the ITB, also adds to their appeal. A disadvantage can be the noise of the CCTV and of diesel engines hooting in the night, although waking up to the whistle of a steam engine shunting past the window could thrill the nostalgic.

A major snag is that, while foreign rail travellers may not know about railway retiring rooms, Indians certainly do. So they are very popular. At busy stations, you need to arrive early in the morning to secure one. Only one room per station can be reserved in advance, otherwise rooms are allocated on a first come first served basis.

To reserve a room write as far in advance as possible to the SS of the station, enclosing a rupee money order in favour of the SS for the cost of the room, giving details of date and time of arrival.

One of the best railway retiring room operations is at Varanasi where there are 70 beds, each with attractive patterned sheets. Most of them are in dormitories. A manager is in charge and he assured me the linen is changed after every occupant, even if a bed is vacated after only eight hours.

Railway hotels

In the New Delhi station compound a cross between a retiring room and an hotel has recently been opened. It is called Rail Yatri Niwas (New Delhi Railway Station, Gate No. 2, New Delhi 110002; tel: 3315445).

There are doubles and dormitories available, making a total of 224 beds. Only a dozen rooms have western style toilets and showers, and the dorms don't have attached bathrooms. There are fans but no AC.

Every floor has an attendant and there is a view of New Delhi station from the corridors on the upper floors.

Despite its rather intimidating atmosphere, the place is very popular. It is only open to rail passengers holding tickets for a journey of at least 150 km. There is room service from 0500 to 0800 and a cafeteria where coupons must be purchased for dishes on a price list in advance of ordering. Room rates are Rs 120 per day for a double room; Rs 30 to 35 for a dorm bed. There is a security deposit of Rs 50 payable at check in.

Two splendid old style hotels are operated by South Eastern Railway (SER). There is one at Ranchi, established in 1915, and another at Puri, built in 1925. Both are worth a visit for the pleasure of staying in them.

At Ranchi, the hotel is a sprawling bungalow type with 22 rooms and shuffling waiters wearing the livery of the former Bengal and Nagpur Railway. The waiters at the Puri hotel, which is in a garden setting near the beach, dress and serve in the same old world manner.

Double occupancy rooms begin at Rs 300. Reservations can be made through the Deputy Chief Commercial Superintendent (Catering), 14 Strand Road, Calcutta, 700001; tel: 232936, or direct with the hotel managers (address in accommodation list).

City hotels

When I want to stay away from railwayland in a town I've not visited before, the only option I consider viable is a good 5 star hotel. There are practical reasons for this. After several nights on a train, there is nothing better than to check into the best hotel and be pampered. You'll feel you deserve a comfortable hotel in which to sleep properly, have the laundry done, luxuriate in a hot bath, watch TV, indulge in a wide choice of good food, and drink a cold beer. (A 5 star hotel is about the only place where you'll get a drink on a 'dry' day.)

With rates from Rs 600 to Rs 1,600 ($40 to $106.66) a night, 5 star hotels are not for every traveller nor for every night, but the best are worth the extravagance, especially when set against the savings being made through travelling by rail.

For older train travellers who are suffering from lack of their usual comforts, a good 5 star hotel is the best antidote. Even one night tended by caring, alert staff who know their job can be a restorative and fortify for the journey ahead.

For younger rail travellers, some 5 star hotels are an experience not to be missed, as much as for the beauty and grandeur of their buildings as for the luxury of their service. It all costs far less than comparable hotels at home. Being able to pay with a credit card, including Visa and Access, is useful, too, since it preserves rupees for train expenses.

Sometimes an Indian 5 star hotel is not from the same constellation as international 5 star properties but those of the major chains like

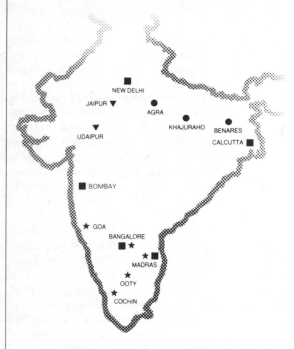

Oberoi, Taj and the Welcomgroup usually are. Oberoi Hotels have a pleasing mix of modern amenities and old world charm and tradition. (The modern New Delhi and Bombay Oberoi hotels actually have a team of butlers attending every room around the clock.) Oberoi was the first Indian hotel company to hire educated people for such run-of-the-mill jobs as waiters and bellboys, and to employ women in housekeeping and as receptionists and guest relations staff.

Welcomgroup run the remarkable Umaid Bhawan Palace Hotel which any visitor to Jodhpur should try to stay at for a taste of the Maharaja life style. They also operate the custom built colonial delight, the Windsor Manor Sheraton in Bangalore.

One of the most recognizable hotels in India belongs to another luxury hotel chain, the Taj group. Photos of the Lake Palace Hotel at Udaipur, as it seems to float on the blue waters of Lake Pichola are one of the enticements to visit India. It's not far from Udaipur railway station.

The luxury hotels and the ordinary retiring rooms (always the best bet for the low-budget passenger) where I've stayed are mentioned in detail under the destination headings. Low and medium budget hotels exist in every town and city and information on them can be found in the general guides to India (such as Lonely Planet's) and from state tourist offices.

Below is a list of some recommended Oberoi, Taj, Welcomgroup and other special hotels easily reached from railway stations. An asterisk (*) by an hotel indicates that I enjoyed staying there and think it's worth the train ride. The selection is followed by a list of railway retiring rooms. All rates are for 1989 so are likely to be higher in future years. Taxes, where applicable, are extra. (Rates in US dollars are calculated at US$1 = Rs 15 and are not necessarily the hotel's rate.)

A selection of recommended hotels

(Prices quoted are without meals, the minimum for a single and the maximum for a double, excluding suites. (CP) means breakfast is included; (AP) means full board.)

Establishment/Address	Telephone/Telex		Rates (Rs + US$)
Agra			
Taj View	64171	565202	825–1025
Taj Ganj, Fatehabad Road, Agra 282001. U.P.		TAJVIN	($55–$68)
Welcomgroup Mughal Sheraton Taj Ganj, Agra 282001. U.P.	64701	565210	1100–1800 ($73–$120)

Refinement, elegance, thoughtful
hospitality. The creation of a world touched
by a rare distinction. A name that
sets standards that others are
measured against.

Oberoi Hotels

BECAUSE YOU DESERVE THE BEST THE WORLD HAS TO OFFER

AUSTRALIA, EGYPT, INDIA, INDONESIA, IRAQ, NEPAL,
SAUDI ARABIA, SRI LANKA

Reservations through your travel agent or LRI worldwide.
Corporate Marketing Division:
Tel: 2525464 Tlx: 66303, 78163 OMDL IN Fax: 238347

Establishment/Address	Telephone/Telex		Rates (Rs + US$)

Aurangabad

| Welcomgroup Rama International R3 Chikalthana, Avrangabad 431210 | 82455 | 745212 | 600–900 ($40–$60) |

Bangalore

Taj Residency 14 Mahatma Gandhi Rd, Bangalore 560001	568888	8458367 TBLRIN	575–675 ($38–$45)
West End Hotel Race Course Road, Bangalore 560001	292281	845337 WENDIN	600–850 ($40–$56)
*Welcomgroup Windsor Manor Sheraton 25 Sankey Road, Bangalore 560052	79431	8458209	850–1500 (CP) ($56–$100)

Bhavanagar

| Welcomgroup Nilambag Palace Bhavanagar 364002 | 24340 | | 350–500 ($23–$33) |

Bhubaneswar

| *The Oberoi Nayapalli, Bhubaneswar 751013 | 56116 | 675348 HOBIN | 775–875 ($51–$58) |

Bombay

| *The Oberoi & Oberoi Towers Nariman Point, Bombay 400021 | 2025757 | 4153 OBBYIN | 1650–2000 ($110–$113) |
| Taj Mahal Hotel & Taj Mahal Intercontinental, Apollo Bunder, Bombay 400039 | 2023366 | 112442 TAJBIN | 1650–2100 ($110–$140) |

Calcutta

| The Oberoi Grand 15 Jawaharlal Nehru Marg, Calcutta 700013 | 292323 | 7248 OBCLIN | 1500–1650 ($100–$110) |

Cochin

| Malabar Hotel Willingdon Island, Cochin 682009 | 6811 | 8856661 MLBRIN | 600–700 ($40–$46) |

Establishment/Address	Telephone/Telex		Rates (Rs + US$)

Coimbatore
Hotel Sri Thevvar
153 Avanashi Rd,
Coimbatore 641018

| | 24135 | | 45–100 ($3–$6) |

Delhi
Holiday Inn
Connaught Plaza,
New Delhi 110001

| | 3320101 | 61186 HINDIN | 1450–1850 ($96–$123) |

Oberoi Maidens
7 Sham Nath Marg,
Delhi 110054

| | 2525464 | 66303 OMDLIN | 690–790 ($46–$52) |

*The Oberoi
Dr Zakir Hussain Marg,
New Delhi 110003

| | 363030 | 63222 OBDLIN | 1600–1750 ($106–$116) |

Taj Mahal
1 Mansingh Road,
New Delhi 110011

| | 3016162 | 314758 TAJDIN | 1500–1700 ($100–$113) |

Welcomgroup
Maurya Sheraton
Diplomatic Enclave,
New Delhi 110021

| | 3010101 | 61447 | 1450–2140 (CP) ($96–$142) |

Goa
Oberoi Bogmalo Beach
Bogmalo, Dabolim Airport,
Goa 403806

| | 2191 | 297 OBGAIN | 850–950 ($56–$63) |

Gwalior
Welcomgroup
Usha Kiran Palace
Lashkar,
Gwalior 474009

| | 23453 | | 400–700 ($26–$46) |

Hyderabad
*The Krishna Oberoi
Banjara Hills,
Hyderabad 500034

| | 222121 | 6931 OBHIN | 1050–1150 ($70–$76) |

Jaipur
*Rambagh Palace
Bhawani Singh Road,
Jaipur 302005

| | 75141 | 365254 RBAGIN | 900–1200 ($60–$80) |

Establishment/Address	Telephone/Telex		Rates (Rs + US$)
Jaisalmer			
*Hotel Jaisal Castle	62	Cable:	175–200
168 Fort, Jaisalmer,		JAISAL	($11–$13)
Rajasthan 345001			
Jhansi			
Jhansi Hotel	1360		
Shastri Marg,			
Jhansi, U.P.			
Jodhpur			
*Welcomgroup Umaid	22516	552202	775–1100
Bhawan Palace			($51–$73)
Jodhpur 342006			
Rajasthan			
Lonavla			
Fariyas Holiday Resort	2701	0113272	750–850
PO Box 8		ABAN	($50–$56)
Frichley Hill			
Lonavla 410401			
Madras			
Connemara Hotel	860123	418197	700–1000
Binny Road,		CHIN	($46–$66)
Madras 600002			
Taj Coromandel	474849	417194	900–1050
17 Nungambakkam High Road,		TAJMIN	($60–$70)
Madras 600034			
Trident	434747	4126055	850–950
1/24 G.S.T. Road,			($56–$63)
Madras 600027			
Welcomgroup Chola Sheraton	473347	417200	800–1400
10 Cathedral Road,			($53–$93)
Madras 600018			
Welcomgroup Park Sheraton	452525	416868	800–1050
132 TTK Road,			($53–$70)
Madras 600018			
Mangalore			
Welcomgroup Manjarun	31791	832316	300–700
Bunder Road,			($20–$46)
Mangalore 575001			

Establishment/Address	Telephone/Telex	Rates (Rs + US$)
Ooty (See Udagmandalam)		
Patna Welcomgroup Maurya-Patna South Gandhi Maidan, Patna 800001	22061 22352	610–1050 ($40–$70)
Puri SE Railway Hotel Chakratirtha Road, Puri	2063 Cable: SURF	235–525 (AP) ($15–$35)
Ranchi *SE Railway Hotel Station Road, Ranchi, Bihar	21945 Cable: RESTFUL	210–430 (AP) ($14–$28)
Shimla *Oberoi Clarkes The Mall, Shimla 171001	6091 206 OBCLIN	650–850 (AP) ($43–$56)
Tiruchchirappalli Rajali Hotel 3/14 McDonald's Road, Tiruchchirappalli, Tamil Nadu 620001	41301 455279	150–650 ($10–$43)
Udagmandalam (Ooty) *Fernhill Palace Udagmandalam 643004	3097 853246	150–450 ($10–$30) (More in season)
Udaipur *Lake Palace Pichola Lake, Udaipur 313001 Rajasthan	23241 33203 IPALIN	900–1500 ($60–$100)
Shivniwas Palace Udaipur, Rajasthan	28239 33226 IPALIN	600–1800 ($40–$120)
Vadodara (Baroda) Welcomgroup Vadodara R.C. Dutt Road, Vadodara Gujarat 390005	323232 175525	500–950 (CP) ($33–$63)

Establishment/Address	Telephone/Telex		Rates (Rs + US$)

Varanasi
Taj Ganges	42495	545219	700–800
Nadesar Palace Compound,		TAGAIN	
Varanasi, 221002, U.P.			

Railway retiring rooms

Prices in this list of stations with retiring rooms are for single or double rooms, and for a bed in a dormitory. Where there are two prices in one column, the higher one is for AC accommodation. Some stations have only one room available and where prices are low, the facilities could be quite basic. Many rooms have attached toilet and shower. Prices are approximate as they are subject to change.

(Rupees)

Station	Single Room	Double Room	Dormitory Bed
Abohar		35	
Abu Road		22	
Adia		26	
Adoni		35	
Agra Cantt		50/100	12
Agra Fort		44	12
Ahmadabad	50/100	100/150	30
Ajmer		35/60	5
Akola		50	12
Aligarh Jn		35	
Alipurduar Jn		15	
Allahbad		70/200	
Allahbad City		20	
Alwar		17	
Ambala Cantt			20
Amethi			10
Amlai		22	
Amritsar		65/90	
Anand	20	40	
Anantapur		30	
Annavaram		25	
Ara			9
Arakkonam		20	
Araku			7
Aravanakadu			15
Asand		36	
Aurangabad	25	35	12
Ayodhya		20	

(Rupees)

Station	Single Room	Double Room	Dormitory Bed
Badarpur Jn		15	
Badaun		24	
Badnera		20	
Bagaha		10	
Bagalkot		25	
Baheri		24	
Bahraich		50	
Baidyanathdam		35	9
Balasore		32	9
Ballia		20	
Balotra			20
Balrampur		30	
Balugaon			12
Banda		24	
Bangalore City		50/75	15
Bankura			13
Barajamda			11
Barauni		25	
Barddhaman		35	
Barmer			10
Bareilly		50	
Barpeta Road		15	
Basti		50	
Bathinda			7
Begusarai		25	
Belgaum	20	30	
Bellampalli		20/50	
Bellary		30	
Berhampur Court		70/125	
Berhampur (Ganjam)		34	11
Bettiah		24	7.50
Betul		30	
Bhadohi		30	
Bhadrachaam Road		25/50	
Bhadrak			11
Bhagalpur		36/70	11
Bharatpur		30	12
Bharuch	25	40	
Bhatni		20	
Bhavnagar		50	
Bhilwara		20	
Bhiwanu			20
Bhopal	23	46/100	15
Bhubaneswar		50/114	12
Bhuj		18	

(Rupees)

Station	Single Room	Double Room	Dormitory Bed
Bhusaval		50/100	
Bishnupur			13
Bilaspur		3	
Bikaner			30
Bijapur		25	10
Bokoro Steel City			13
Bolpur		36	
Bombay Cent		85/225	
Bombay VT		100/160	30
Bongaigaon		15	
Burnpur			11
Buxar			11
Calicut	30	40	10
Cannanore	20	30	
Chakradharpur		46	11
Champa		38	
Chandigarh		50	
Changanacheri		30	
Chandrapur		24	
Chchapra Jn		20	7
Chengannur	20	30	
Chengalpattu	10		
Chitrakutdham-Karwi		20	8
Chidambaram		20	
Chittaranjam	20		9
Chittaurgarh	15	25/85	
Chittoor		30	
Coimbatore		80/250	20
Coonoor		50	
Cuddapah		30/90	
Cuttack		50/114	
Darbhanga		24	
Davangere	12	16	
Dauram Madhepura		20	
Dehra Dun		60	15
Dehri-on-Sone			9
Delhi		100	35
Deoria Sadar		20	
Dhanbad		60/100	20
Dharmanagar		15	
Dharmavaram		30	
Dharwad		30	
Diamond Harbour		36	

(Rupees)

Station	Single Room	Double Room	Dormitory Bed
Dimapur		20	12
Dibrugarh Town		15	
Durg		50	15
Durgapur		36	
Dwarka		7.50	3.50
Eluru	15	30	
Ernakulam Jn		60	15
Erode	15	30	
Faizabad		25	10
Fakiragram Jn		15	
Falna		12	
Farukhabad		24	
Fatehpur		25	
Firozabad		20	
Firozapur		35	
Forgbesganj		15	
Gadag		20	
Galagokarannath		30	
Gandhidam	18	30	8
Gandhigram		50	
Gaya		70/125	
Ghazipur City		20	
Godhra	20	40	
Gomoh		35	
Gonda		55	20
Gondal		70	
Gondia			11
Gooty		15	
Gorakhpur	50/80	75/150	20
Gudur	15	30	
Gulbarga		30/60	
Guna		40	12
Guntakal		30/45	12
Guntur	20	40/100	
Guwahati		35	20
Gwalior		46/90	14
Hajipur		20	
Haldwani		34	
Hanumangarh			15
Haralpur		16	
Hardoi		20	

(Rupees)

Station	Single Room	Double Room	Dormitory Bed
Haridwar		40	15
Harmuti		20	
Hassan		15	
Hazaribagh Road		35	
Hospet		20	
Howrah		60/200	20
Hubli	20	35	12
Indore	25	45/85	10
Itarsi		40	12
Izatnagar		24	
Jabalpur		50/90	15
Jaipur	40	65/155	20
Jaisalmer		60	20
Jajpur-Kionjhar Rd			11
Jalandhar City		65/90	
Jalgaon		50/100	12
Jamalpur		36	
Jammu Tawi	35	90	6
Jamnagar		42	18
Jasidih		35	
Jaynagar		10	
Jhanjharpur		10	
Jhansi		46	14
Jharsuguda		38	11
Jodhpur		60	25
Jolarpettai		14	
Junagadh	30	80	20
Kadur		15	
Kakinada Town		30	
Kalka		40	
Kamakhya		20	
Kannauj		15	
Kanniya Kumari	20	30	10
Kanpur Anwarganj		50	
Kanpur Central		70/200	25
Karaikkuda Jn		20	
Karimganj		15	
Kathgodam		34	15
Katihar		20	15
Katni		44	14
Katpadi		30	10
Kazipet	15	25	

(Rupees)

Station	Single Room	Double Room	Dormitory Bed
Khagaria		25	
Khalilabad		30	
Khandwa		40	
Kharagpur		36/114	9
Khurda Road		34	11
Kishanganj		15	
Kiul Jn		35	9
Kodaikanal Road		20	
Kolhapur	25	35	
Kota		44/80	12
Kotawara		20	
Kottayam	25	40	
Kumbakonam	10	20	
Kurnool Town		35	
Laheria Sarai		20	
Lakhimpur		50	
Lar Road		20	
Lovedale		30	
Lucknow (NR)		60/120	20
Lucknow Jn (NER)	80	75/150	20
Ludhiana	35	65/90	
Lumding Jn		20	15
Madgaon		50	12
Madhubani		10	
Madhupur		35	9
Madras Central		60/150	20
Madras Egmore	30	50	10
Madurai	25	40/70	7.50
Mahesana		18	
Maihar		42	
Makrana			10
Malda Town		36/70	11
Mangalore		50	15
Mankapur		50	
Manmad		40	
Mantralayam Road		25	10
Mariani Jn		15	
Mathura		30/70	9
Mathura Cantt.		34	
Mau Jn		20	
Meerut City			20
Mettupalaiyam		20	
Midnapur		38	

(Rupees)

Station	Single Room	Double Room	Dormitory Bed
Miraj		35	10
Mirzapur		35	
Moradabad		30	15
Morbi	7	12	
Motihari		24	
Mughal Sarai		70	20
Murshidabad			9
Muzaffapur		40/120	15
Mysore		50/75	15
Nagappattinam		20	5
Nagercoil		30	
Nagore		20/40	5
Nagpur		50	15
Nainpur			7
Najibadad			8
Nanded	25	30	12
Narkatiaganj		24	
Nasik Road		50	12
Naugarh		30	
Nautanwa		30	
New Alipurduar		15	
New Bongaigaon		15	
New Coochbehar		20	
New Delhi		100/300	25
New Jalpaiguri		20	12
Nidadavolu	15	30	
Nidubrolu		30	
Nirmali		10	
Nizamabad		35	
North Lakhimpur		15	
Ongole	15	30	
Palani		16	5
Palanpur		25	
Palasa		34	11
Palghat	20	30	
Palimarwar			20
Parbhani	20	35	
Parlivaijnath	10		
Pathankot	20	35/80	
Patna Jn		40/100	20
Patna Saheb		35	9
Pilibhit		34	

(Rupees)

Station	Single Room	Double Room	Dormitory Bed
Pipariya	18		10
Pondicherry		30	
Porbandar		52	
Pune		70	15
Puri		46	12
Purnea Jn		20	
Purulia			13
Quilon	20	30	10
Rae Bareli		25/50	8
Raichur		35/50	12
Raigarh		30	
Raipur		50	
Rajahmundry	20	40	
Rajgir		35	9
Rajkot		28	
Rajnandgaon		26	
Ramagundam		30/50	
Rameswaram	20	30	10
Rampur		20	
Rampurhat		35	
Ranchi		46	15
Renigunta	14	30	
Ratlam		35/85	10
Raxaul		24	7.50
Rayagada			7
Renigunta	14	30	
Rewari			15
Roorkee		20	
Rourkela	50	64/75	13
Sagarjambagaru		15	
Saharanpur			20
Saharsa Jn		24	10
Sakri		10	
Salem Jn		30	
Samastipur		24	10
Sanchi		16	
Sasaram	20		
Satna		44	14
Saugor		36	10
Sawai Madhopur		30	12
Sealdah		60/200	20

(Rupees)

Station	Single Room	Double Room	Dormitory Bed
Secunderabad	30	75/150	
Shahganj		15	
Shahjahanpur		30	
Shantipur		36	
Shimla	25	50/100	
Sidhawalia		20	
Silchar		15	
Siliguri Jn		20	
Simaluguri Jn		15	
Sitamarhi		24	
Sivakasi		15	
Siwan		20	
Sitapur		50	
Solapur		30/60	10
Sonagir		40	10
Sonpur		20	
Sriganga Nagar			16
Srikakulam Road			7
Srirangam		20	5
Supaul		20	
Surat		200(a/c)	30
Surendranagar		12	4
Suri		35	
Talcher			11
Tarakeswar		40	
Tatanagar		88/314	13
Tenali	15	30	
Tenkasi			6
Thanjavur		30	
Tilsipur		30	
Tinsukia Jn		20	
Tiruchchirappalli		40/100	7.50
Tirur		20	10
Tiruchendur		20	
Tirunelvelli	15	25	6
Tirupati		40/90	12
Tiruvarur		20	
Trichur		40	
Trivandrum Central	35	50	15
Tuticorin	6	10	
Udagamandalam		60	25
Udaipur City	20	35	12

| | (Rupees) | | |
Station	Single Room	Double Room	Dormitory Bed
Ujjain	20	35	
Vadodara		60	20
Valsad			10
Varanasi Jn		60/150	20
Vasco de Gama	30	50	15
Veraval		60	20
Vijayawada	30	50/130	15
Villupuram		20	
Vindhyachal		20	
Virudhunagar	20	35	
Visakhaptnam		100/188	11
Vizianagaram		30	
Warangal		30	
Wardha			15
Wellington			15

Hotel Oberoi Maidens, Delhi.

Coolies (porters) playing cards at Ranchi station. (Hugh Ballantyne)

Self-catering on Bandel station platform. (Hugh Ballantyne)

Washing under a water column at
Mahesana Junction station.
(Hugh Ballantyne)

Family scavenging for coal.
(Philip Ferguson)

Chapter 8

The Journey Begins

Since most visitors to India arrive by air at the airports of Delhi, Bombay, Calcutta or Madras, their rail journey is likely to begin from a station in one of those cities. This chapter looks at the facilities in those cities, and in two other cities with airports served by flights from abroad: Trivandrum and Tiruchchirappalli. Goa is covered in Chapter 10.

DELHI

For many readers of this book, their first experience of Indian railways will be at New Delhi or Delhi stations. That is unfortunate because both stations give a dreadful first impression with which to begin your journey. They are quite unlike Delhi itself which is pleasant and enjoyable.

Much of the negative reaction inspired by Delhi's two main stations is due to a traveller's own frame of mind. If you go to the station straight off the plane after a long-haul flight, you're bound to be appalled by the heat and squalor. Allow yourself a chance to adjust to the time change, jet lag and culture shock before attempting to buy a ticket. At least the ITB (see Chapter 3) relieves most of the hassle, but you'll need to be in top form for the station itself.

There is a desk operated by Northern Railway at Delhi's Indira Gandhi International airport where reservations can be made by arriving passengers. It is open from 0000 to 0800 hours, the period during which many long-haul flights arrive.

Delhi is the headquarters of Northern Railway (NR), the biggest zonal railway in the country. Its 10,977 route kilometres serve a population of nearly 200 million in Punjab, Haryana, Uttar Pradesh, Rajasthan, Himachal Pradesh, Jammu and Kashmir, and parts of Gujurat as well as Delhi and Chandigarh. Stretching 1168 km from Amritsar to Varanasi, NR also connects with the Pakistan rail network at Atari and Munnabao. NR runs 270 mail/express and 650 passenger trains daily, carrying about 1,200,000 people a day.

The NR zone abounds in pilgrim places: Amritsar, famous for the Golden Temple; Haridwar, the holiest Hindu centre; Allahabad, the site of the Triveni sangam, the confluence of the Ganga, Yamuna and

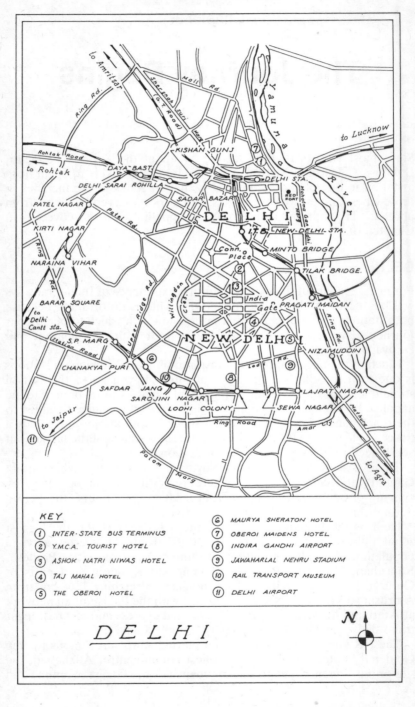

DELHI

the invisible Saraswati rivers; Varanasi, the oldest pilgrim centre. The
Himalayan resorts of Shimla and, via Jammu Tawi, of Kashmir, are
accessible by NR.

Trains from Delhi give access to colourful historical centres: Agra,
the capital of the Mughal empire, famous for the Taj Mahal; Fatehpur
Sikri with its magnificent monuments of Mughal glory; Lucknow, the
cradle of Muslim culture; Bikaner, a city renowned for Rajput chiv-
alry; Jodhpur, famous for its massive fort; and even the unique desert
outpost of Jaisalmer.

Since you'll have to pass through one of Delhi's stations to get to
those exotic places by train, it's as well to be prepared for a low-key
beginning.

New Delhi Station

It's not a major terminus in the grand style (like Bombay VT for
instance) but a depressing transit station with overstretched facilities.
The catering outlets are poor. At platform level, there is a snack
counter to serve a caged-off area which divides the station entrance. It
is staffed by people who make it obvious they have no interest in being
helpful. The restaurant upstairs, opposite the ITB, is like the canteen
of a small, rundown factory. The whole station has an unwelcoming
atmosphere and it's a relief to jump on a train and get out.

There are waiting rooms for upper and 2nd Class passengers, with a
separate one for ladies, and there are toilets with showers (towel and
soap, Rs 1.50). The general public have a waiting area with fans above
their seats. There are cloakrooms, a telegraph office, phone booths for
local and trunk calls and a post office.

There is a current reservations booking office for same day
departures as well as ticket counters for non reserved travel. On the
right as you enter the station building is an open lobby, beside the
caged-in snackbar area. Stairs from here (or a lift) lead to the first floor
where the ITB is located. It's a haven from the chaos below.

On the second and third floors are the retiring rooms. The point in
their favour is their proximity to the ITB. Rs 300 per night for the AC
room seems a lot, even if it does have an old fridge, a TV and free soft
drinks; it's just not very nice. There is a view from the terrace of the
small forecourt below, bright with colour from yellow-topped taxis and
red-shirted porters.

Reservations for the retiring rooms are made on the ground floor
where there is a desk in a lobby connecting the main platform with the
station entrance. A dorm bed costs Rs 20–25 and a non AC double
room is Rs 100. The 30 rooms are usually fully booked which shows my
own feelings about the station are not shared by everyone.

Actually, out of the station building and along the platforms, the
atmosphere does change. It becomes almost rural. At the end of
platform 1 there are plants in pots and hibiscus bushes in bloom. A

locked gate leads to railway offices and housing, and there are intriguing coaches parked in an adjoining siding. You might spot the royal blue Ultra Sonic Rail Testing Car URT100 Matix System here. At the other end of the platforms, there are nine in all, is a temple, serenity amidst the shunting trains.

Near platform 9 is the new base kitchen where 25 cooks prepare over 3,000 meals a day to put on trains. Also near the platform, across a compound, is the Rail Yatra Niwas, a hostelry for transit passengers opened in March 1988. It offers basic accommodation in non AC rooms and dorms, in a bureaucratic ambience rife with regulations (see Chapter 7).

Information on other places to stay can be gouged out of the staff at the Delhi Tourist office tucked away in a corner close by the lift to the retiring rooms. The staff are so fed-up with being asked the times of trains, their response to questions is almost automatically negative. But they have booklets to sell.

It is possible to walk from New Delhi station to Connaught Place, the hub of the city, and to the general reservation complex next to the station. Tourists, however, would fare better by using the facilities of the ITB for their ticket purchase and reservations.

Some of the major trains originating at this station are the Shatabdi and Taj Expresses starting early every morning for Agra, and the Rajdhani Expresses to Bombay or Howrah. To Madras there are daily departures by the 16 Grand Trunk and the 122 Tamil Nadu Expresses.

Other trains originating at New Delhi include the 922 North East and 510 Avadh-Assam Expresses to Guwahati, the 30 Lucknow Mail and the 120 Gomti Express to Lucknow, the 18 Prayag Raj Express to Allahabad, the 906 Karnataka Express to Bangalore, the 124 Andhra Pradesh Express to Secunderabad, the 126 Kerala Express to Mangalore/Trivandrum, the 47 Flying Mail to Amritsar, the 145 Shalimar Express to Jammu Tawi and the 195 Himalayan Queen to Kalka. There are dozens of other trains that transit New Delhi on the way north, or east to Howrah, and southwards.

Delhi Station

Delhi station (sometimes called Delhi Main) is to the north of New Delhi station and can be reached by train from there, either on suburban or main line services. It has a friendlier atmosphere than New Delhi but is bereft of more than essential amenities. Kiosks and snack counters are grouped along the length of the main platform where there is a charmless self-service restaurant.

There are 18 platforms, three of which are for metre gauge trains. There is a counter where reservations can be made for the retiring rooms. These are reached by a lift and many have old oak almirahs and seem pleasant enough. There are deluxe dormitories with beds at

Rs 35 and non AC double rooms at Rs 100 for 24 hours. There is a barber shop.

Reservations for departures from this station by foreign tourists can be made at the ITB. There is a computerized reservation booking office at the station for trains leaving from it. An occasional steam train can be seen puffing through the station which redeems its dismal atmosphere.

Metre gauge trains departing from Delhi include the 501 Pink City and 15 Chetak Expresses to Jaipur and Udaipur, the 143 Delhi to Ahmadabad Mail and Express, the 31 Aravali Ashram Express to Ahmadabad and the 93 Jodhpur Mail.

Some major trains on the broad gauge line are the 2 Kalka Mail to Howrah, the 12 Howrah Express, the 156 Tinsukia Mail to Guwahati, the 33 Jammu Mail to Jammu Tawi, the 137 Chchatisgarh Express from Bilaspur to Amritsar, the 38 Punjab Mail from Firozpur to Bombay VT, and the 84 Ganga Yamunu Express to Varanasi.

Do not get confused with your departure station since they are not close together. If you go to the wrong one, it will take at least 30 minutes by taxi to switch from one to the other.

Hazrat Nizamuddin Station

This is Delhi's third terminal, located in the south east of the city, close to the luxury hotel area. There are no retiring rooms here but a computer reservation office is close by. Nizamuddin is the main station on the ring railway commuter service system.

The 149/150 Mahakoshal Express terminates here when it arrives each morning at 1030 from Jabalpur, departing again at 1600. To Puri every day at 1250 via Agra, Tatanagar and Bhubaneswar goes the 77/78 Kalinga Utkal Express. It arrives at Nizamuddin at 1300.

Both the 175 Neelachal and 915 New Delhi/Puri Expresses originate and terminate at Nizamuddin station with a stop at New Delhi. The 3 Frontier Mail from Bombay to Amritsar and several other expresses also stop at this small station for a few minutes on their way to/from New Delhi.

Ring Railway

Delhi's ring railway gives a marvellous view of the backside of suburban city life, often literally as people use the line as a toilet. It was opened in 1982 and girdles the city, covering a distance of 35 km.

The trains make four circles clockwise and four anti-clockwise a day, from Hazrat Nizamuddin to 20 stations. There are two morning runs, and two evening ones. In the morning, one train provides a link from New Delhi (departing at 0740) to Delhi (arriving at 0753).

This is an EMU service, which means an Electrical Motor Unit is used to pull it. It is supposed to stop for only 30 seconds at stations so passengers have to move sharply. It is very popular with commuters; if you want to try it, the best time is at a weekend when it is not so busy. Tickets cost Rs 1.50.

The seats are wooden and there are lots of handles for standing passengers, as well as plenty of fans. The doors are kept open all the time and no smoking is allowed. One of its stations, Safdarjang, is near the Rail Museum.

Rail museum

The rail museum, set up in New Delhi in 1977, was the first of its kind in India. Engines and carriages, all refurbished and painted in their original colours, are exhibited on tracks of different gauges laid out in a 10 acre 'railway yard'. Six display galleries and a padlocked, glass walled building housing the museum's star exhibit (the Fairy Queen), a toy train and a restaurant, are included in the museum grounds.

For those fascinated by the sight of old locomotives, the museum is delightful. When I was there off-season (in July) it looked a bit neglected with bored attendants and overgrown gardens but nothing could detract from the majesty of the engines on view.

The Fairy Queen is unique as the oldest surviving locomotive in perfect working order anywhere in the world. It was actually purchased by the East Indian Railway barely two years after the inauguration (in 1853) of the first rail service in India. She was built by Kittson, Thompson and Hewitson of Leeds, UK, and looks eager to keep on running. Close to her is half an engine, a locomotive built in 1891 in Glasgow for the Nizam's Guaranteed State Railway, and sliced lengthways to show its workings.

On tracks among the grass, where you can wander at will, are more than two dozen vintage locos and a score of carriages, including an armoured train. Such trains, with 'Maxim Guns' were extensively used up to the 1920s by the British Army. The MG train in the museum was built in India prior to the First World War on wagon stock of the 1880s. Each carriage is provided with an armoured plate ½ inch thick, with felt lining 3 inches thick and another armoured plate of ¾ inch thick to protect the occupants against normal gun fire.

Other spectacular carriages are the white painted Vice Regal Dining Coach (1889) with its entrance platforms at both ends and the saloon coach of the special train of the Maharaja of Mysore. This coach could be run on broad gauge as well as metre gauge with a change of bogies without disturbing the royal family during their journey from Mysore to Madras. The other two carriages which made up the Maharaja's train are in the rail museum in Mysore (see Chapter 10).

The Prince of Wales saloon coach has its original fittings and furnishings. It was built for the visit to India of the Prince of Wales (later Edward VII) in 1876, and is provided with sunshades on both sides. A fourwheeler sheep van (built in 1929) is divided into four compartments with two tiers to accommodate 176 sheep. It also has sunshades.

The wooden Nilagiri passenger coach (built 1914) used on the rack and pinion railway up the steep gradients of the Nilagiris has canvas curtains as protection against the sun, wind and rain, its only difference from the wooden coaches in use today.

A new addition to the museum is an X-Class metre gauge loco of the types still used on the Nilagiri Mountain Railway. The Shimla Railcar (built 1931) fitted with a 4-cylinder petrol engine and painted in white and light blue, is a small version of the rail cars used on the Kalka/Shimla line.

Other delightful oddities include Ramgotty, with wooden brakes, built in France and converted from 4 ft gauge to 5 ft 6 in in 1896, and the steam monorail engine which ran on a single rail with an outrigger wheel running on the road alongside the track. Originally monorail trains were pulled by mules of the Patiala State Monorail Trainways on a 50 mile track.

A behemoth hulking over pygmy locos is the Garrat, built by Beyer, Peacock of Manchester in 1930 for the Bengal Nagpur Railway. This engine could easily haul 2,400 tons of trailing load on a 1 in 100 up gradient. Not all the engines are steam. Sir Roger Lumley built in 1930 for the Great Indian Peninsula Railway is electric powered. One of the first EMU coaches introduced on the Bombay suburban section of the Bombay, Baroda and Central India Railway (BBCI) in 1928 is also on display.

The galleries have a variety of mementoes and models of early as well as current Indian railway equipment. There is some of the Burmese teak furniture from the BBCI Railway; the Miraj station clock (1926), engine plates, special coach fittings and displays showing the development of signalling and telecommunications.

An astounding sight in the middle of the technology is the skull of an elephant whose firm refusal to budge from the track caused the derailment of the entire seven carriage Calcutta to Nagpur mail in September 1894.

Only a disappointing set of souvenirs (coasters, table mats, post cards and a bottle opener/ice breaker) were on sale during my visit, but there is a good, if out of date, guide to the museum available. The exhibits are well labelled with description, year built, builder and area of service.

Admission is Rs 2 for an adult, Rs 1 for a child, with a charge of Rs 5 for every camera taken in. On Tuesdays, entry is free for children below 12 years old. The museum is open from 0930 to 1730 but the ticket office closes at 1700 hours. It is closed on Monday and on Republic Day, Holi, Idn'l Fitr, Independence Day, Mahatma Gandhi's birthday, Dussehra and Diwali.

The most appropriate way to get to the rail museum is by train. It is five minutes walk from the ring railway station of Safdarjang, in the southwest of New Delhi. It is close to the Chanakyapuri Diplomatic Enclave, an easy ride by taxi or auto-rickshaw from the Welcomgroup Maurya Sheraton or Taj Palace hotels.

Rail Transport Museum, Shantipath, Chanakyapuri, New Delhi, 110021. Tel: 601816. Curator, Rail Transport Museum, Room 536D, Rail Bhavan, New Delhi, 11001. Tel: 383624.

Delhi Cantt

This station could almost be part of the museum. It has the period look of the 1930s, heightened by seeing the Palace on Wheels train which departs from here; the setting is perfect for its antiquated carriages. The station is off the road to the international airport on the western outskirts of the city, beyond the Dhaula Kuan roundabout.

The Jodhpur and Bikaner Mail trains stop here for a few minutes on their way to and from Delhi as do the 233 Shekhawati Express to Jaipur, the 15 Chetak Express to Udaipur City, the 31 Aravali Express to Ahmadabad, and some other MG trains.

There are several stations with the word Delhi in their name, but they are halts on the main or suburban passenger lines: Delhi Azadapur, Delhi Kishanganj, Delhi Safdarjang, Delhi Sara Rohilla and Delhi Shahdara Jn.

Delhi reservation offices

Indira Gandhi International Airport
ITB, New Delhi Station
IRCA Complex (adjacent to New Delhi station)
Delhi Junction
Hazrat Nizamuddin (near railway station)
Sarojini Nagar (near railway station)
Kirti Nagar (near railway station)
Delhi Shadara (near railway booking office)

Railway Enquiries:
Delhi/New Delhi/Nizamuddin stations. Tel: 3317575 or 3313535.
Reservations. Tel: 344877.

Where to stay

The nearest top hotel to New Delhi station is also the newest, the 500 room Holiday Inn Connaught Plaza (Tel: 110001) which opened in October 1988 and is about five minutes away. Rooms start at $96.

The Taj Mahal Hotel (1 Mansingh Road, ND. Tel: 3016162) is popular with New Delhi regulars. It has a lively bar off the lobby and a roof top restaurant, where Italian/Indian buffet lunches are served.

The rooms have twin beds and small bathrooms; there are 308 units including some magnificent suites. The practice of serving a tea bag in a plastic flask in my room for breakfast reminded me too much of railway retiring rooms, but a good feature is the illuminated 'Do Not Disturb' sign outside each room. Rooms from $100.

The Oberoi Maidens Hotel (7 Sham Nath Marg, Delhi. Tel: 2525464) is convenient for Delhi main station and is a firm favourite with British travellers, perhaps because of its colonial style as well as its superb value for money ($46–$52). It is one of the oldest hotels in India, and was the centre of Delhi's social life during the days of the British raj. It was *the* place to stay then, and there is a story about two young ladies who were guests there when their funds ran out. They telegraphed their father in England: 'Please Send Money Fast Or Can No Longer Stay Maidens.'

The Oberoi was India's first modern luxury hotel when it was opened in 1965. It is given warmth and soul by the butlers who attend guests in every room, an innovation that confused me at first as I wondered what a butler did. Mine organized my photocopying and shopping as well as polished my shoes. When I mentioned this book he gave me tips on which trains to try.

BOMBAY

For the rail traveller, Bombay is an exciting introduction to India: the city's stations have all the rail glamour you could want, as well as trains that go to most major destinations. The booking and information system works well, if you're patient, for it isn't that simple. There is the added attraction of Bombay itself – an exciting and bustling metropolis.

If you arrive by air, there is a railway enquiry desk and reservations centre at Bombay's international airport, open from 2300 to 0700, to coincide with flight arrivals. If your itinerary is complicated, though, wait until you get to the Foreign Tourist desk at Bombay VT station. As with New Delhi, I recommend a day to settle in before trying to sort out your onward rail travel.

Your first problem will be to find out whether your train leaves from Bombay VT or Bombay Central or even from Dadar, an important subsidiary station. The confusion is compounded by there being two railways in Bombay: Central and Western.

Central Railway (CR) does not operate trains from Central station but from Bombay Victoria Terminus, known as Bombay VT. Trains from Bombay Central station are operated by Western Railway (WR). It takes time to unscramble, especially if you try to make a reservation on a WR train which should be done at a third station, Churchgate, which is not a main line station but a suburban one.

Bombay VT

At first sight it seems unbelievable that the Victorian Gothic pile with its stained glass windows, cathedral arches and stone animals leaping from its walls like gargoyles, is a railway station. It is regarded as one of the finest station buildings in the world, from the architectural point of view. In May 1988 it was 100 years old.

Entry to the station is not actually through the portals of this glorious façade but around the back to the side of it. What you see when you stand and stare in amazement at the front of it is the administration building; for VT is the HQ of CR. The entrance gate is guarded by two massive stone animals, a lion and tiger, representing the United Kingdom and India.

Originally the Great Indian Peninsula Railway Company, CR has grown into one of the country's major railway systems. With 6,486 route kilometres, it traverses six states: Maharashtra, Madhya Pradesh, Uttar Pradesh, Haryana, Karnataka and Rajasthan. Within its jurisdiction are some famous tourists spots, including the Taj Mahal at Agra, Ajanta near Jalgaon and Khajuraho (which has no rail station) near Satna (which has).

The VT complex has reached saturation point having expanded as much as possible during its century of existence. As well as its suburban services, it handles 38 long distance trains which carry 75,000 passengers a day. Because there is no spare capacity for additional trains, a new terminal is planned at Kurla, north of Dadar, its other overflow station.

In the complex, a road separates the suburban station from the main line platforms. Anyone entering the concourse from the road is supposed to have either a platform or train ticket. Basic facilities and snack kiosks fringe the concourse and there is a place that inspires a glimmer of hope in the mind of anxious tourists: the office of the Foreign Tourist Guide. This is located opposite the platform entrances.

The glimmer becomes a glow of satisfaction when the tourists encounter a railway guide who really knows his lines, if he is the one I met in 1988. His office, shared with 'Public Grievances' staff, has been at the station since the 1970s. There are plans to shift it to the new computer reservations (CRS) building next door. This is necessary as the reservation ritual requires people who want to buy tickets from the foreign tourist quota to start at the guide's office. Then they must go to the CRS building and find another desk.

The guide's office is open 0900 to 1700 daily except Sundays with a lunch break from 1300 to 1330. (On Sundays, foreign tourist quota reservations are dealt with by the CRS supervisor.) The tourist guide puts a board saying 'Kindly Wait' on his desk when, as he frequently does, he leaves it to escort foreigners to the CRS building.

He alone deals with foreign tourist reservations and will stamp a

RACE COURSE to Dadar

Chowpatty Beach

BACK BAY

Malabar Point

GATEWAY OF INDIA

KEY

① BOMBAY CENTRAL RAILWAY STATION
② KAMALA NEHRU PARK
③ VICTORIA TERMINUS RLY. STN.
④ G.P.O.
⑤ CHURCHGATE RAILWAY STATION
⑥ OBEROI HOTEL
⑦ TOURIST OFFICE
⑧ AMERICAN EXPRESS & THOMAS COOK
⑨ AIR INDIA & INDIAN AIRLINES
⑩ TOWN HALL
⑪ TAJ MAHAL HOTEL
ⓣ TEMPLE

BOMBAY

0   1
km

N

passenger's requisition chit. This is the authority for the clerk on the
counter in the CRS building to issue the ticket/reservation from the
foreign tourist quota. The service is provided primarily for those who
wish to travel the next day but can handle reservations for periods up
to 360 days in advance for Indrail Pass holders, or up to 60 days in
advance for those who want a single journey ticket.

The CRS building is new (1987) and built to fit in with the Gothic
grandeur of the main building. It houses a computer reservations
system like the one in Delhi, with a telex room linking it with other
stations so instant confirmation of reservations on Central and Eastern
Railways can be given.

Counter number 2 is for foreign tourist quota transactions and all
tickets (as well as the Indrail Passes) have to be paid for in UK sterling
pounds or US dollars. Rupee change is given for travellers cheque
payments at the day's bank rate. The office is open 0800–1330;
1400–2000 daily except Sundays, when it's 0900–1330; 1400–1630. In
the station, there is a non-veg restaurant (open 0630–1400; 1430–2200)
on the second floor which serves the usual range of railway food. Its
attraction is the Victorian furniture: umbrella stands, dressers, and a
wooden and mottled glass screen concealing the kitchen. Modern
touches are the TV screens with train announcements and the careless
table settings. Also on the second floor is an attractive fast food
self-service snack bar (1100–1900 every day), and a veg restaurant at
the other end of the corridor.

The retiring rooms are located upstairs in the main station building,
with tall, polished wooden doors and huge brass bolts. The AC double
room costs Rs 160, non AC Rs 100 or Rs 135 (three beds) and there
are two dormitories with six beds in each at Rs 30 per bed. Waiting
rooms here are large and peaceful.

In the station concourse, strident CCTV has replaced the public
address system. There are electronic indicators, coach guidance
systems and train time indicators. It has all the amenities and ambience
of a major station with plenty of thrills, tearful farewells and the last
minute panic associated with train departures.

Services from this station go east and south and some northwards,
serving among others: Bangalore, Bhusaval, Chchapra, Cochin,
Delhi, Faizabad, Firozpur, Gorakhpur, Guwahati, Howrah, Hyder-
abad, Itarsi, Jabalpur, Jhansi, Kanniya Kumari (via Trivandrum),
Kolhapur, Lucknow, Madras, Mangalore, Miraj (for Goa), Nagpur,
Pune, Secunderabad, Sholapur and Varanasi.

The suburban services almost overwhelm VT station. The suburban
booking office is on the right of the main concourse; gaze up at the
ceiling and you'll feel you're in church. Every day 971 suburban trains
are operated from here, carrying 2.4 million passengers a day in
chaotic, crowded conditions which have become notorious. The trains
are fast and frequent and during offpeak hours are a pleasant way to
traverse the city; they have 1st Class and Ladies Only carriages.

Tickets can be bought (from Rs 1.50 depending on distance) at any counter in the booking hall. There are no waiting rooms on the eight platforms served by EMU trains and the free toilets are busy because the EMU trains don't have any. Electronic displays indicate train departures, platform and destination.

CR publish a small booklet twice a year containing details of all the suburban services from Bombay VT, heading northwards to Dadar and beyond.

Dadar Station

A small terminal was provided at Dadar in 1968 to cope with the increasing demand by passengers. It is the only Bombay station served by trains of both Central and Western Railways. It is used as a transfer station by passengers on Bombay VT bound trains who want to change to a train bound for Bombay Central or Churchgate, and vice versa.

WR's main line trains both outward and inward stop here and it is a main stop on WR's suburban service. Dadar is 8.85 km from Bombay VT, 4.48 km from Bombay Central, and 10.17 km from Churchgate.

Some main line trains which originate and terminate at Dadar are the 963 Chennai Superfast Express to Madras (it takes 24 hours), which departs at 1950 every day except Mondays and Saturdays; the 957 Dadar to Cochin/Mangalore Superfast Express on Mondays and Saturdays; and the daily 11 Dadar/Madras Express (which takes 26 hours).

The 961 Lashkar Superfast Express leaves on Mondays for Gwalior. To Amritsar there is a daily departure by the 57 Dadar/Amritsar Express which goes via New Delhi. At 0640 every morning, there is the 27 Dadar/Varanasi Express which stops at Bhusaval and Jabalpur on its way to Varanasi. The 39 Sewagram Express is a daily service from Dadar to Nagpur.

Churchgate Station

This station, under the control of Western Railway, was built in 1957 for suburban services. WR operate 819 suburban trains daily, carrying more than two million passengers. The station is in Bombay's central business area and is of interest to foreign tourists because of its proximity (across the road from its eastern exit) to WR's reservation office and a Government of India Tourist Office.

The tourist office is open from 0830–1800 Monday to Friday; 0830–1400, Saturday and holidays; closed on Sundays. It is staffed by charming ladies who hope you're not going to ask about train times since the rail office is next door. They will supply information or pamphlets on most places in India.

The counter dealing with foreign rail travellers is on the mezzanine floor of the CRS building. A Foreign Tourist Guide is here. Do not be put off by the sign in English above his desk which reads 'No Enquiry' as that is intended for Indian passengers only. The gentleman here is delighted to help foreigners and, in fact, without his authorization on the seat or berth requisition chit, you cannot get accommodation from the tourist quota. He writes down all the details, including starting point, so the tourist can find the right station as well as the right train.

His desk is open from 0930 to 1700 daily except on Sundays when the Chief Reservation Supervisor is available from 0900 to 1600. Payment for tickets is made at counter 28. The computers here are linked with those at Bombay VT and Bombay Central reservation centres. If you want to reserve a bedroll, you can do it at counter 16.

As the suburban terminal for WR, Churchgate station has 91 trains arriving during the three-hour peak period in the morning, with each EMU train discharging nearly 3,500 commuters.

The traffic is unidirectional which makes it a concentrated flow from north into Bombay in the morning and from south to north in the evening, like a human assembly line. Bombay's suburban services are the most intensively utilized in the country, carrying 70 to 75 per cent of India's commuter traffic.

There are 28 stations in the WR suburban network, extending 59.82 km from Churchgate to Virar. In 1988, electrified suburban services to Bombay completed 60 years. While WR is proud of its 95 per cent punctuality rate, delays are often caused when pedestrians use the tracks as a passage between built-up areas. In 1987, more than 500 people were run over or killed in the WR zone.

Tourists find the suburban system an excellent way to travel across the city, but not in rush hours. One family told me: 'It's clean, fast, safe, cheap and well sign-posted. The only problem is when you arrive at a station there are no signs to show which end of the platform has the exit you want. One is the main exit and the other leads to the back, but how do you know which one?' You don't.

Bombay Central Station

This station can be reached by the suburban line from Churchgate on one of the EMUs. A ticket costs Rs 1.50 or Rs 17 for 1st Class. The journey takes ten minutes. There is no direct suburban line link from Bombay VT to Bombay Central. So if you arrive at one station to leave from another, the best method is by taxi which is unlikely to take less than 30 minutes.

The entrance to Central station is surprisingly rural, a small building with a driveway. It gives way to a tiled lobby with local and long distance platforms and the usual station facilities including a pharmacy.

There are retiring rooms on the third floor (there's a lift) priced from Rs 85 for a non AC double room to Rs 225 for an AC one, called deluxe because of its veneered panelling. There is no dormitory. At platform level is a self-service vegetarian snack bar and a small composite restaurant (open 0800–1330, 1400–2000; Sundays 0900–1330, 1400–1630).

The reservation building is across an empty lobby which was used for reservations before computers. In September 1988 there was no counter dealing with foreign tourist reservations because in the past this was always done at Churchgate.

Since the three stations are now linked by computer, a foreign tourist could, in theory, make reservations at Bombay Central instead of having to go to Churchgate. But it seems that Churchgate controls Western Railway's foreign tourist quota.

For those wanting to go to Goa, there is an official tourist counter at Bombay Central station. There you discover that trains for Goa actually leave from Bombay VT station.

The Western Railway zone reaches up to Agra Fort and New Delhi, embracing Rajasthan (Jaipur and Ajmer) as well as the whole of Gujurat. It also has services branching eastwards across country to Jalgaon and Bhopal, destinations it shares with Central Railway.

The most important train from Bombay Central is the 151 Rajasthan Express which speeds for New Delhi on Mondays, Tuesdays, Thursdays, Fridays and Sundays, taking 16 hrs 45 mins for the journey. Other trains are the 19 Dehra Dun Express, the all 2nd Class 23 Firozpur Janata Express, the superfast 3 Frontier Mail, the 171 Jammu Tawi Mail (Mondays and Thursdays only) and the 25 Paschim Express to Amritsar. There are also several short haul expresses.

Enquiries
Central Railway: Tel: 2043535; Western Railway: Tel: 4937575/49333535.

Where to stay
The nostalgic head like homing pigeons for the Taj Majal Hotel with its Intercontinental Hotel appendage in Apollo Bunder (Tel: 2023366, rooms from $110). There is a new hotel, the Bombay Oberoi, which is also part of a pair as it is joined to the Oberoi Towers, a Rs 10 taxi ride from Bombay VT station (Nariman Point. Tel: 2025757, rooms, including butler, from $110). The management are proud of this hotel and it shows in everything, even down to the brightly polished buttons on the liftboys' spotless white uniforms. It's quite a wrench to get back on a train.

CALCUTTA

Calcutta is fun; a sophisticated city despite the teeming millions, but it is not the best city in which to begin a rail journey. If you do arrive at Dum Dum airport wanting to catch a train, there is a rail booking office there but your best bet would be to wait until you get to the Fairlie Place reservations office.

Calcutta is served by two main line stations, Howrah and Sealdah, and two railways: Eastern (ER) and South Eastern (SER). Both

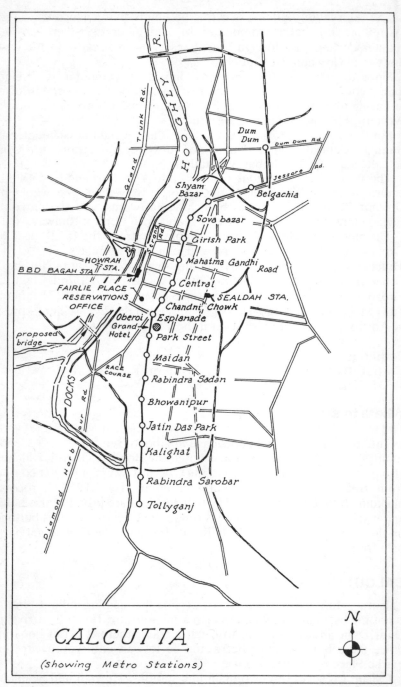

CALCUTTA

(Showing Metro Stations)

WP 4-6-2 between Daund and Manmad (east of Bombay), specially embellished for VIP passenger the Minister of Railways. (Anthony J. Lambert)

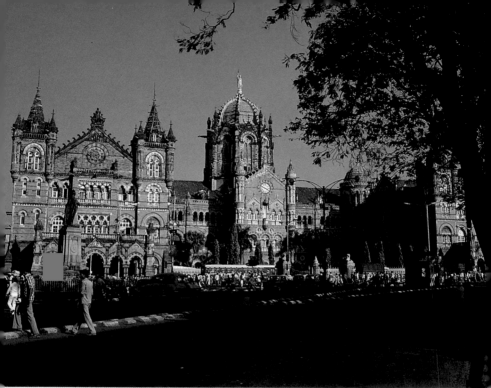

Victoria Terminus, Bombay. (Anthony J. Lambert)

Approaching Sealdah station, Calcutta. (Hugh Ballantyne)

railways have their headquarters in Calcutta although SER doesn't actually have a station to itself; it rents platforms at Howrah and Sealdah from Eastern Railway. There is also a circular railway run by ER and India's first underground railway, the Calcutta Metro.

The Eastern Railway network fans out westwards with Bangladesh to its east and the mouths of the Ganga to its south. It serves the states of West Bengal, Bihar, eastern Madhya Pradesh and part of Uttar Pradesh. It covers 4,281 route kilometres and 730 stations of which about 30 are on narrow gauge lines.

It handles 1,450,000 originating passengers daily who travel on 1,236 trains of which roughly two thirds are suburban trains. ER has approximately 1,118 locomotives, 3,000 passenger coaches, 1,000 EMU coaches and over 82,000 wagons.

It needs so many wagons as it is mainly a freight carrying railway, serving the major coalfields at Asansol, Jharia, Karanpura and Singrauli. Many of the tourist sites within the ER zone are religious, such as the footprint of Lord Vishnu at Gaya and the Buddhist temples at Buddha Gaya and Sarnath.

South Eastern Railway celebrated its centenary in 1987 as the direct descendent of the BNR. It serves stations in six states: West Bengal, Orissa, Andhra Pradesh, Bihar, Madhya Pradesh and Maharashtra. It deals with two lakhs of passengers a day at Howrah alone.

Despite having carried 192.08 million passengers in 1987–88, it is primarily a freight carrying railway serving an area rich in basic materials such as coal, iron and manganese ore, limestone and bauxite. The raw materials of seven major steel plants are carried by SER which also serves three major coalfields and two aluminium complexes.

With the coalfields in its area, it is not surprising that SER has lots of steam locos: in 1988 these amounted to approximately 341 BG and 56 NG engines. It also has 351 BG electric engines and 355 diesel, with 59 NG diesel. The railway has 2,760 BG and 472 NG passenger carriages with 51,700 BG and 1,803 NG wagons.

Another side of this industrial railway is seen in SER's afforestation programme. In five years from 1981 to 1986, 74.60 lakhs of saplings were planted by SER; with a survival rate of 80 per cent, that's a lot of trees. In its zone are the picturesque wilds of Saranda, the greens of Chhotanagpur and the foliaged heart of Madhya Pradesh.

Reservations

Eastern Railways is proud of its computerized reservation system (CRS) which enables 'an intending passenger to obtain a reservation for any train (ER or SER) in any class on any date within the advanced reservation period from any of the computerized reservation counters in Calcutta.'

There are six primary centres, New Koilaghat, Old Koilaghat,

Fairlie Place, Howrah, Sealdah and Rabindra Sadan with more than 100 reservation terminals. The second phase began with the opening of a satellite terminal at Dum Dum metro station in August 1988 which, with five other satellite stations (at Tollyganj Metro station, Bidhannagar Road, Bally, Ballygunge Jn and Majerhat station) will mean a passenger does not have to travel 'more than 2–3 km to get a reservation' according to ER.

Yet for the foreigner there is only one place where reservations can be obtained from the foreign tourist quota, that is Fairlie Place, which is not even near a mainline station. It is close to the BBD Bagh station which is on ER's circular railway but it is easier to get there from Howrah Station by ferry. The terminal for the Chandal Ghat Ferry is at the end of the road that splits Howrah station in two. The ferry operates at 15 min intervals from 0815 to 2000 daily, except Sundays. The fare is 50 paise for the ride across the river to the BBD Bhag ferry terminal. Once there, you walk across the railway line and Strand Road, then into the thoroughfare opposite, where the Fairlie Place building is on the right, at number 6.

There are two entrances, use the second one on the right. Inside the doorway, above a staircase on the right, is a sign saying 'Foreign Tourist Computerized Reservations'. This office is open 0930–1600 with a lunch break from 1300 to 1330. On Sundays the hours are 0900–1400.

The office is air-conditioned and box-like with chairs for waiting passengers, a counter with chairs in front of it and, when I visited in 1988, only one computer monitor. There is a railway guide to help plot itineraries and a very helpful staff although their ability to deal with lots of tourists is limited by having only one computer. In the season, there can be as many as 100 tourists a day trying to make bookings, so start early in the day.

Applications for reservations are made on the usual requisition slips and can be made here for all mainline trains leaving Calcutta, whether from Howrah or Sealdah, on Eastern or South Eastern railways.

Indrail Passes can also be purchased at Fairlie Place and, when possible, the staff try to accommodate passengers who want to begin travelling that very day. Reservations can be made for Darjeeling if the line is open, although a restricted area permit will be needed.

Howrah Station

The distinctive brick coloured station on the opposite bank of the river to the Fairlie Place office, was built in 1905. A few years ago there was an attempt to paint it lemon yellow but public protest kept it brick red. It handles 524 trains a day, for SER and ER as well as suburban services. A road (vehicles, except taxis, allowed for a toll of Rs 20) divides the station into north and south sections, and provides access to platforms 8 and 9.

The north side opens onto the non-ticket area running alongside the entrance to platform 1. It also links up with a subway entrance with shopping kiosks on both sides. The 2nd Class booking office is here and also lots of fresh fruit stalls. Upstairs is the computerized reservation office with an enquiry counter and the supervisor's office at the top. Foreign tourists can make reservations here only from the general quota. Hours of opening are 0900 to 2100 daily.

The north section also has a first-aid post with a doctor available for a few hours every day from 1000 and there is a medical hall (chemist) in the centre of the concourse. Bridging the road is a large mural over the platforms. The main entrance is flanked by ornamental wood panelling which used to front the old booking office. At this side of the station are three restaurants: a coffee corner serving non-veg meals (I had a very good western style lunch there) and, from 1400 to 2200 hours, Chinese meals. Adjoining this is a veg self-service restaurant, with waiters in attendance at meal times, and next door a non-veg restaurant with lurid green seats. Both are open 0600 to 2200.

On the first floor are non AC double rooms, two AC rooms and a dormitory with nine beds. Rates for the doubles include morning tea and a newspaper but the rooms, and beds, have seen better days. A grand staircase, close to the computerized train enquiries office, leads to the various classes of waiting rooms which are rather airless although there is a view of the river and the traffic-clogged Howrah Bridge from the terrace.

The West Bengal State Tourist Office on the station concourse is open from 0700 to 1300 hours. There is also a barber's shop on the south part of the station. Public announcements are made over the three dozen blaring CCTV sets.

Trains from Howrah are led by the 101 Rajdhani Express which departs at 1600 for the 18 hour run to New Delhi, but not on Wednesdays and Saturdays. The 7 Toofan Udyan Abha Express goes daily to New Delhi while the 81 AC Express goes on Tuesdays and Wednesdays and on to Amritsar on Saturdays; the 103 AC Express goes on Thursdays, and onto Amritsar on Sundays. Trains to Delhi are the daily 1 Kalka Mail, the 11 Delhi and the 39 Delhi Janata (2nd Class) Expresses.

To Bombay VT there is a daily departure by the 2 Bombay Mail and the 30 Bombay and the 60 Gitanjali Expresses. The journey takes over 30 hours. For Madras there are daily departures by the 141 Coromandel Express, the 3 Madras Mail as well as weekly departures by various through trains from Guwahati to Bangalore, Cochin or Trivandrum. Other expresses cover the east coast or cross India, either via Delhi or by-passing it.

Sealdah Station

The first thing to learn about this station is how to pronounce it. The locals say Sheldah. It deals mainly with suburban and local trains and is used by about a million passengers a day. The main station building, the north block, was built in the 1970s and has ten platforms. The computerized reservation counters on the first floor are open 0900–2100 and 0900–1400 on Sundays and holidays. In special cases, foreign tourists can make reservations here though there is no special counter, or even signs, for them. Better to head for Fairlie Place.

The retiring rooms are on the second floor. All four of them are non AC and rooms 2 and 3 are bright, with windows that open onto a view of the forecourt below. The dormitory is very basic, at Rs 20 per bed.

The first floor combined veg/non-veg restaurant has a cheerful 'caff' atmosphere and serves *thali* meals. The waiting rooms are spartan with stone benches. The SS here has two offices, one on the first floor and the other off the booking hall where he can be found during important train arrivals and departures.

Platform 8 is for VIP trains and has a VIP waiting room. There is a Passenger Guide on duty with his own desk and a 'May I Help You' booth open for important trains. There is a bookstall and a first-aid post as well as kiosks selling soft drinks. A novelty here is the cold water vendors who sell plastic sachets of water for 25 paise at the train side. A contractor operates the three 'Pay and Use' toilets where a pee costs 20 paise.

Departures from Sealdah include the 33 Sealdah/Varanasi Express every evening, and the morning departure 51 Jammu Tawi Express. The 43 Darjeeling Mail is a popular train which leaves every evening for New Jalpaiguri. The 53 Gour Express goes to Malda Town and the 303 Bhagirahi Express to Lalgoda.

Shalimar Station

Under construction and expected to open in the early 1990s, Shalimar station will be run by South Eastern Railways. The goods terminal there is being shifted to Sankrail. Completion is linked with that of the second Hooghly Bridge. It will handle main line and suburban trains.

Suburban services

The SER has had EMU suburban trains in operation since 1968 and runs 140 EMU local trains daily, carrying about 200,000 passengers. Services are Howrah to Kharagpur/Midnapore, Panskura/Haldia, Santragachi/Bargachia.

A circular railway system is run by ER operating a stretch of 10.5 km between Prinsep Ghat and Ultadanga Road stations with work under way on the final 3.5 km section to Dum Dum Jn. You can try this line from BBD Bagh station (the initials stand for Benoy Badal Dinesh) to Prinsep Ghat.

The Metro Railway

The idea for building an underground railway in Calcutta was conceived in 1949 but it was 20 years before the project was studied and a plan for a Mass Rapid Transit system prepared. The foundation stone was laid in 1972. That it was able to open at all amazed observers but in 1984 the first part was inaugurated. Now 10 km out of 16.43 km and 11 stations out of 17 are under commercial operation, from Tollyganj to Esplanade and Belgachia to Dum Dum.

When completed (in 1990?) it will carry more than 60,000 commuters per hour each way on trains following each other at intervals of two minutes. Every day about 1.7 million transit trippers are expected to use the Metro. From Dum Dum to Tollyganj will take 33 minutes. There are eight coaches per train, each one able to carry 218 passengers standing and 54 sitting.

A ride begins by buying a printed ticket, issued by a machine, from the ticket counter, at a cost of Rs 1 or Rs 1.50 depending on destination. Tickets can be bought in carnets of ten for the cost of nine. Entrance is through turnstiles where ticket checkers are on duty. The ticket must be kept to surrender at the exit turnstile.

The timetable says 'Do not squat, vend, eat, smoke or drink in Metro train or premises' and the cleanliness of the station owes much to the pride with which its users regard it. Potted plants grow undisturbed on platforms and the station walls are free of graffiti. Each station has a wide island platform with trains entering on either side. Murals adorn the entrances and walls of some stations and the customary CCTV plays full blast.

As soon as a train has pulled in, its doors open automatically. There is no time to dawdle as they snap shut within seconds, but only after a recorded announcement in Hindi, Bengali and English, and a bell, has warned that they are about to close.

The seats are metal benches running the length of the coaches, which have the familiar appearance of mainline carriages having been built at the same factory in Madras. They are fully vestibuled with no doors dividing them. Some of the carriages are very noisy because of the air-blowers which keep them cool. These drown out the recorded announcements, in three languages, made on the approach to each station, giving the station's name, and whether the platform is on the left or right.

Where to stay

There are several hotels of character in Calcutta, as befits the former capital of British India with its ornate Victorian architecture. The old tradition of gracious living is preserved at the Oberoi Grand which dates back to the 1870s. The style of the hotel is grand but not snooty. It is in Chowringhee which is practically equidistant from Howrah and Sealdah stations, in case you need an excuse to justify the enjoyable extravagance of staying there.

Rail data
ER Booking and Information, 6 Fairlie Place. Tel: 204025
ER Enquiries. Tel: 230138
SER Booking and Information, Esplanade Mansions (opposite Raj
  Bhavan). Tel: 289530
SER Enquiries. Tel: 239124.

MADRAS

Madras may not at first seem an obvious place from which to begin
your rail journey but it has a lot of advantages. The atmosphere is
right: hustling isn't brazen, people are polite and there seems to be a
feeling that rushing around isn't really worthwhile. Madras is a gentle
introduction to India.

There are now direct flights to Madras from Europe and there is a
rail booking-cum-reservation counter at Meenambakkam International airport. This is open 1000 to 1700 hours daily, and there is a
rail facility at the domestic air terminal too.

The major advantage of starting a rail journey in Madras is that it is
the HQ of the best railway in India: Southern Railway (SR). It's not
my view alone, ask Indians themselves. The trains are cleaner, the
service friendlier, the food better and the entire journey on an SR train
seems more enjoyable.

The reason is probably because SR is a passenger oriented railway.
SR's passenger earnings are almost 45 per cent of its total earnings
against an all Indian railway figure of 27 per cent. SR carries a million
passengers a day on 900 different passenger trains. (There are about
400 goods trains.)

The railway was founded in 1951 by the integration of the erstwhile
Madras and Southern Maharatta Railway, South Indian Railway and
Mysore State Railway. It traverses 6,729 route kilometres serving over
a thousand stations. It covers about 10 per cent of India's land area
with a passenger catchment of 14 per cent of the country's population.

It links the southern states of Tamil Nadu, Kerala, the major portion
of Karnataka, a small part of Andhra Pradesh and the Union Territory
of Pondicherry with the rest of India. It is an area of great variety for
the tourist with beaches, hill resorts, forests and animal parks,
monuments, temples and ancient traditions, with a welcoming people.

'It's the people that make Southern Railway better than the others,'
a passenger told me. 'Better staff and better passengers.' There are
better public relations, too, with 'May I Help You' booths located at
important stations to attend to passengers' problems.

A train conductor suggested that SR is better because the
competition from road transport is greater in the south than in the
north so, to keep business, Southern Railway must offer a better

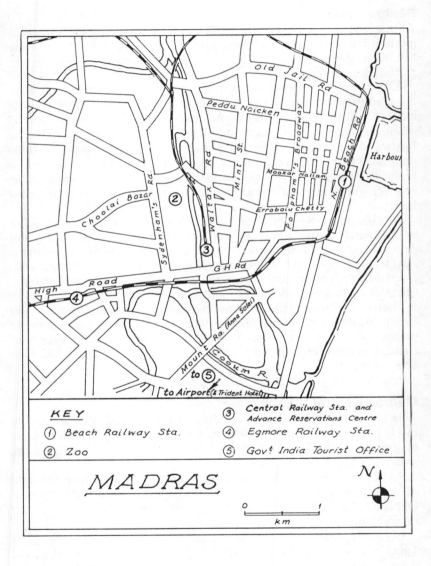

KEY

① Beach Railway Sta.

② Zoo

③ Central Railway Sta. and Advance Reservations Centre

④ Egmore Railway Sta.

⑤ Gov.t India Tourist Office

MADRAS

service. Another theory is that the nature of people in the south is placid so they do not misuse the railway.

Reservations

At one side of Madras Central station is a new building looking like a modern hotel; this is the advance reservations centre. It is part of the suburban station complex. There is an information booth on the ground floor and signs about which floor to go to.

The token system is in operation which cuts out queuing and there are comfortable chairs for waiting passengers. In addition, as another example of SR's concern for its passengers, there are snack counters on each floor and a magazine library where magazines can be borrowed for 50 paise. The office is open 0700–1300 and 1330–1930 daily, and 0700–1300 on Sundays. The best time to make reservations is early morning, 0700 to 1000. Bed rolls can be reserved from the same counter where reservations are made. There is a separate counter for ladies.

Foreign tourists should go to the first floor where there is an unfortunately named 'Foreign Tourist Cell' but the ambience is not prison-like. The tourist guide is in the same office as the reservations staff so the process of booking and getting confirmation is streamlined. Even if there is no foreign tourist quota on the train you want to go on, the staff make a special effort to find space.

There are three main stations in Madras: Central, Egmore and Beach, dealing with broad gauge, metre gauge and suburban services respectively. A rail minibus service (fare Rs 1) links Central with Egmore station, meeting important trains during the period 0500 to 2200.

Madras Central Station

This is a distinctive rust pink building with white trimmed arches but inside it is less romantic, overwhelmed by passengers and with a patina of grime. At night, when energy-saving yellow sodium lights are switched on, it looks Dickensian.

At this station the SS has his name in lights. His office is on the right of the entrance to the booking hall which leads from the forecourt. Opposite his office are counters for platform tickets and current reservations.

Before the barrier leading to the platform, on the right, there is a Tamil Nadu Tourist Office (open 0715–1900 every day). Twin flights of stairs lead up to the first floor where there are upper class waiting rooms and a restaurant (open 0600–1430 and 1530–2130). Both have wide balconies overlooking the station forecourt.

The waiting rooms (one is for ladies) have bathrooms with showers and toilets and mirrors. A table on the balcony of the restaurant is good for a meal with a view of the city; the staff will sometimes cook something special if you ask.

Activity on the passenger concourse can be watched from the landing in front of the restaurant. Down a passage to the left is a corridor leading to the retiring rooms. These are airless and depressing with king-size rats. Dormitory beds in a room with a breezy balcony next to the restaurant are Rs 20 each. A notice on the door says 'Securely closed between 2300 and 0400.'

Downstairs, the entrance to the concourse is on the left of the lobby with a large Higginbothams bookstall (open 0630–2130) just inside on the left. There is also an India Tourism Development Corp counter for tour bookings and a kiosk selling airpillows with hand woven pillow cases.

The veg refreshment room is a grubby, standing-only outlet with a self-service counter containing bins from which various snack items can be removed with tongs. Paper plates are charged extra; a public cup is chained to the water cooler. A medical shop is next door (open 0600–2200). There is also a cafeteria with various kinds of fried cakes and a coffee counter before the ticket barrier.

At the other side of the concourse, beyond the mass of people sprawled on the ground and in plastic chairs in the fan-cooled general waiting area, are more refreshment kiosks. A cloakroom, with a long queue for left luggage, has a notice saying 'Working Hours Around The Clock'. Self-help trolleys and wheelchairs are available outside the station master's office. A wall cabinet with its glass front broken contains mail addressed to passengers.

For passengers wanting to send letters, a post and telegram office is at the corner on the left of the station entrance near the suburban booking hall. It is open 0630–2045. The letter box, however, is on the other side of the station entrance, near the public telephone booths. In the lobby a diagram shows the location of ticket counters and a signboard gives the times of trains from Egmore station.

Outside is a taxi park with auto-rickshaws parked on the right and children asleep on the pavement. Taxi drivers have an agreeable approach and even the begging is restrained. One man asked me politely for the train fare home, saying he'd lost his ticket. I steered him towards the office of the SS, just in case he was genuine.

There are two crack trains a day taking about 34 hours to New Delhi, the 15 Grand Trunk and the 121 Tamil Nadu Expresses. To Bombay VT is a daily departure by the 10 Bombay Mail which takes just over 30 hours while to Dadar there is a daily morning departure by the Dadar Express, arriving 27 hours later. The daily 142 Coromandel Express takes 27 hours to reach Calcutta/Howrah and the 4 Howrah Mail also makes the trip daily but takes two nights to do it. Expresses pass through Madras from Trivandrum, Cochin and Bangalore on their way to Calcutta and/or Guwahati on different days of the week.

Nearly 30 express, mail and passenger trains a day leave Central station, with a further 20 trains providing a less than daily service.

Madras Egmore Station

If the minibus isn't available from Madras Central to Egmore station, a taxi costs about Rs 6 and an auto-rickshaw a couple of rupees less. Egmore station is exclusively metre gauge, serving the southern part of India. The station is a sedate, Victorian (1880s) style, brick red building with a covered courtyard entrance.

On the right of that is the current reservations counter, down a gallery. On the left, the special information counter is used only in emergencies. The SS is proud of his station winning the SR Best Kept Station shield in 1987/88. He is helpful to steam enthusiasts and I was treated to a test drive on a shunting steam engine.

The 1st Class waiting rooms and the retiring rooms are on the first floor. A unique feature of this station is cars being able to drive right onto the platforms. There are two suburban platforms as well.

One of the special trains that departs from Egmore nightly is the 117 Pandyan Express to Madurai with its 1st Class AC sleeper carriage and other comfortable accommodation (see Chapter 11). The fast day time all 2nd Class Vaigai Express also goes to Madurai. The 153 Cholan Express to Tiruchchirappalli is a popular day time train. The all 2nd Class 115 Pallayan Express also goes to Trichy, as does the overnight 177 Rock City Express.

Trains to Rameswaram from Egmore include the 113 Sethu Express overnight and the 101 Rameswaram Express. The 119 Nellai Express goes to Tirunelveli while the prettily named 103 Pearl City Express leaves for Tuticorin every night. The 105 Quilon Mail meanders through the south, taking 19 hours overnight to reach the west coast town of Quilon.

Madras Beach Station

This is the main suburban line station located behind Burma Market, a street of kiosks selling luxury imported (smuggled?) goods that runs parallel to the platforms. There are six platforms in the station, and a veg restaurant. It is the terminating station for MG trains. There is an EMU MG service to Tambaram/Chengalpattu and there are BG suburban services.

Rail data

Central station enquiries. Tel: 20048.

Where to stay

Madras has some very good budget hotels, especially around Egmore station. At the airport there is an orange courtesy coach which meets all flights to take passengers to the nearby Trident Hotel. A useful

Madras Egmore station.

feature of this garden hotel, opened in 1988, is its special 12 hour rate. This is not the same as a day rate since it applies for any 12 hours, even overnight such as 0200 to 1400. It works out at 40 per cent less than the rack rate of $63, double. Ideal if you just want to recover from a flight before taking an overnight train.

TRIVANDRUM

One of the pleasantest places to arrive to begin a rail journey is Trivandrum, capital of Kerala, in India's deep south. The airport is small and leisurely with none of the frenzy of India's major airports; it is only 6 km from Trivandrum central station and served by seasonal charter flights from Europe as well as by scheduled flights from Colombo, the Maldives and the Gulf States, and by domestic flights.

The station building is Victorian, extending the length of its main platform. 1st and AC Class tickets for current trains are sold from a counter on the left of the main entrance where timetables and platform tickets are also sold. The entrance lobby itself is small; steps lead from it upstairs to the SS's office and a porticoed gallery where the nine excellent retiring rooms are located. There is also a dormitory with eight beds.

The main ticket office is in a building adjoining the station. Downstairs are the counters selling 2nd Class tickets for same day trains. Up the stairs at the side is the long room where advance reservations are made at counters marked by destination. The office is open 0700–1930, lunch 1300 to 1330; only current reservations, enquiries and cancellations on Sundays.

Indrail Passes can be bought here. The Chief Reservation Supervisor (CRS) has his office at the head of the stairs and foreign tourists should go in and see him. 'They can stand in a queue at one of the counters if they like,' he told me, 'but we don't insist.' In fact, foreigners who do join a queue are quickly directed to his office.

Although Trivandrum is not computerized, foreigners who do not have reservations can register their names with the CRS who will try to secure berths for them. 'I hope,' the CRS said, 'we get the same special treatment in your country.'

Trivandrum Central has all the atmosphere of a major station with none of the hassles. There are three platforms, number 1 having the usual offices, restaurants and waiting rooms. The Deputy Station Superintendent's office is near the entrance and that's where to apply for a retiring room by filling in a requisition slip.

The lobby of kiosks includes a milk counter, a fruit stall, a nut vendor (cashews are locally grown), a bookstall and an apple-juice bar. A notice at the station entrance warns 'Beware of pickpockets, jewel snatchers and baggage lifters'.

Although it is so far south, Trivandrum Central is a gateway to all parts of India with daily direct trains for New Delhi (3054 km), the 125 Kerala Express; Bombay (2061 km), the 81 Kanniya Kumari Express; (Madras (907 km), the 20 Madras Mail; Mangalore (635 km), the 49 Parasuram and 29 Malabar Expresses; and Bangalore (851 km), the 25 Bangalore Express.

There are also trains daily to Shoranur (302 Venad Express), Ernakulam Jn (304 Vanchinad Express) and Cannanore (47 Cannanore Express) and Kanniya Kumari (express and passenger). Weekly, or bi-weekly, there are direct trains to Jammu Tawi (3642 km), the 907 Himsagar Express; to Guwahati (3625 km) by the 901 Guwahati Express and to Ahmadabad (2732 km) by the 904 Ahmadabad Express.

Popular destinations from Trivandrum are Quilon (65 km) which can be reached by northbound expresses or slower passenger trains, and Coimbatore (for Ooty) on the main line to Madras. To go to Cochin from Trivandrum, take a northbound train to Ernakulam Jn.

The beach resort of Kovalam is 16 km away. Its somewhat lack-lustre Kovalam Ashok Beach Resort is the foremost hotel in the area.

Trivandrum central enquiries. Tel: 62966/63066.

TIRUCHCHIRAPPALLI

Tiruchchirappalli, mercifully shortened by everyone to Trichy, has an international airport 15 minutes from the main station, Tiruchchirappalli Junction. The airport, served by international flights (from Colombo) is a frustrating experience due to the slow processing of passengers by immigration. Trichy Jn station, however, is well run and good for starting a journey, especially by metre gauge train through the south Indian countryside.

Trichy is a town of nearly 400,000 inhabitants, dozens of exotic temple towers and no less than six railway stations. It is situated on the banks of the Cauvery River and is a blend of history and tradition as well as a pilgrim centre and a thriving commercial city.

The main station serves broad and metre gauge. All the express trains are diesel hauled, while about 75 per cent of the passenger trains are pulled by steam locos. Built in 1935, the station has been selected for transformation into a model one.

To the left of the spacious forecourt a new building houses the reservations centre. Although not yet computerized, it has the atmosphere and facilities of an efficient system, with a bright waiting area, CCTV, fans, a refreshment stall, a pay toilet, and a suggestion box. My suggestion was that there should be a sign indicating which counter attends to foreign tourists. Counter number 3 deals with enquiries and foreign tourists should start there. Hours are 0700–1300, 1330–2000.

The station has a good Tamil Nadu tourist information office on the right of its entrance. Steps lead up to refurbished retiring rooms (12 doubles, one with AC) and dormitories which are being extended. Room service is available. The rooms are fronted by a wide verandah with a view over the station forecourt where local buses wait for major trains.

The platforms are linked by a tunnel and five of them are for MG trains. Platform facilities include veg and non-veg restaurants, a bookshop and book trolleys that meet all important trains. One of these is the fast 115 Pallavan Express running daily between Trichy and Madras Egmore. It is all 2nd Class chair car with a pantry car, and is painted an eye-catching silver grey and white.

Some MG trains also stop at Tiruchchirappalli Town, a new (1988) temple-like station at the end of a pot-holed village street. The reservation and booking counter there is open 0700–1130, 1430–1730, and there are pleasant waiting rooms with toilets and showers. The station handles mainly commuters although it is an ideal halt to see the nearby Rock Fort.

Srirangam Station (10 km from Trichy Jn) is another new building designed to fit in with its surroundings. It is popular with pilgrims who come to visit the Vaishnavite temple with its 21 towers built in the 13th century AD. The upstairs of the station has two twin bed retiring rooms with writing desks at only Rs 20 per room, and dorm beds at Rs 5. Trichy's other MG station is Golden Rock. Two other BG stations are Palakkarai and Trichy Fort.

Where to stay

Possibly the best value accommodation in Trichy is Room 8 at Trichy Jn station. This AC twin bedded room is as big as a hotel suite with wallpaper, wall to wall carpet, dressing table, settee and armchairs, lots of lights, fans and a dining-cum-work table. A dressing room leads to a large bathroom with western style toilet, and loo paper, and a hot water shower. There is even a private balcony with a view over the platform roof of the sunrise. All this for Rs 100.

The Rajali Hotel is a luxury hotel with low rates (single Rs 154– Rs 213 (AC); double Rs 213–Rs 330 (AC) per 24 hrs – any period of 24 hrs, not just from check-in to noon) only minutes walk from the station, or Rs 5 by auto-rickshaw. The Rajali Hotel has 78 bedrooms and suites and a renowned restaurant. There's a friendly atmosphere, especially in the Soaring High bar by the swimming pool (the only one in Trichy and open to non-residents). A teleprinter in the lobby chatters out the UNI news. Address: 3/14 McDonalds Rd, Trichy. Tel: 41301.

Chapter 9

Around India by Rail

DESTINATIONS

A list of the most popular destinations for foreign rail travellers, after the cities of Delhi (the top favourite). Bombay, Calcutta and Madras, has been compiled by studying the travel patterns of foreign tourists from bookings made at the ITB (see Chapter 2). Rail tourists tend to follow itineraries of their own devising, to the chagrin of the planners at ITB who have prepared itineraries which rail travellers ignore.

For many rail travellers, part of the fun is poring over timetables to draw up one's own itinerary. The *Trains At A Glance* timetable is the best for that (but watch for misprints, such as Table 67 frequently mentioned in the index which refers to Table 76). Zonal timetables are useful for local passenger trains.

Indian Railways has a directorate of rail tourist guides who are professional itinerary planners. The directorate can be contacted in advance if help is required. (Directorate of Tourism, Railway Board, Government of India, Rail Bhavan, New Delhi. 110001.) Another source of help would be the Chief Public Relations Officer (CPRO) of each zonal railway.

From their starting stations, the main trains which serve the most popular destinations are listed below. Intermediate stations are not shown but it is possible to catch a train wherever it stops, not only from its starting point. Most of the trains run daily, except where indicated.

To **Agra Cantt** from:
Ahmadabad: (to Agra Fort via Ajmer and Jaipur) 6 Agra Fort Fast Pass Exp.
Amritsar: (via New Delhi) 58 Dadar Exp. 138 Chchatisgarh Exp.
Bangalore: 905 Karnataka Exp.
Barmer: (to Agra Fort via Jodhpur & Jaipur) 8 Agra Exp.
Bilaspur: 137 Chchatisgarh Exp.
Bombay VT: 37 Punjab Mail.
Bombay/Dadar: 57 Amritsar Exp.
Calcutta/Howrah: (via Patna & Allahabad) 7 Toofan Exp.
Delhi/New: 2002 Shatabdi Exp. 80 Taj Exp. 126 Kerala Exp. 906 Karnataka Exp. 168 Malwa Exp. 16 Grand Trunk Exp.
Delhi/Nizamuddin: 150 Mahakosal Exp. 22 Hyderabad Exp. 78 Kalinga Utkal Exp.
Firozpur: (via New Delhi) 38 Punjab Mail.

Gorakhpur: (to Agra Fort via Lucknow) 63 Avadh Exp.
Gwalior: 79 Taj Exp.
Hyderabad/Secunderabad: 21 Hyderabad/Nizamuddin Exp.
Indore: 167 Malwa Exp.
Jabalpur: 149 Mahakosal Exp.
Jaipur: (to Agra Fort) 22 Agra Fort Exp.
Jammu Tawi: (via New Delhi) 178 Jhelum Exp. 132/908 Himsagar Exp.
   Weekly.
Jhansi: 2001 Shatabdi Exp.
Kanniya Kumari (via Trivandrum & Madras) 907 Himsagar Exp. Weekly.
Kathgodam: 12 Kaumaon Exp.
Lucknow (see Gorakhpur).
Madras Central: 131 Jammu Tawi Exp. Mo/Th/Su. 15 Grand Trunk Exp.
Patna: (see Calcutta).
Pune: 177 Jhelum Exp.
Puri: (via Bhubaneswar) 77 Kalinga Utkal Exp.
Ratlam: (to Agra Fort) 64 Avadh Exp.
Sriganganagar (via New Delhi) 8 Udyan Abha Toofan Exp.
Trivandrum: 125 Kerala Exp.

To **Aurangabad** from:
Kacheguda: (via Secunderabad) 551 Ajanta Exp.
Manmad: 552 Ajanta Exp. 96 Ellora Exp. 594 Nanded Exp.
Nanded: 593 Manmad Exp.
Nizamabad: 95 Ellora Exp.

To **Bangalore City** from:
Ahmadabad: 903 Trivandrum and 937 Cochin weekly Expresses.
Bombay VT: 129 Udyan Exp. 303 Mahalaxmi Exp. (via Miraj).
Calcutta/Howrah: 51 Bangalore Exp.
Cochin: 938 Ahmadabad Exp. Weekly.
Delhi/New: 906/928 Karnataka Expresses. Not daily.
Guwahati: 976 Bangalore Exp. Weekly.
Hyderabad: 85 Bangalore Exp.
Madras Central: 7 Bangalore Mail. 23 Bangalore Exp. 39 Brindavan Exp.
Miraj: 208 Kitur Exp. (MG) 204 Mahalaxmi Exp. (MG).
Mysore: 205 Exp. 209 Exp. 211 Nandi Exp. 215 Chamundi Exp. 221 Kaveri
   Exp.
Solapur: 241 Golgumbaj Exp.
Talaguppa: 284 Pass Mail.
Tiruchchirappalli: 31 Bangalore Exp.
Trivandrum: 25 Island Exp. 904 Ahmedabad Exp. Weekly.
Vasco da Gama: 202 Kitur Exp. (MG).

To **Bhubaneswar** from:
Bangalore: 975 Guwahati Exp. Weekly.
Calcutta/Howrah: 9 Sri Jagannath Exp. 45 East Coast Exp. 141 Coromandel
   Exp. 3 Madras Mail. 979 Tirupati Exp. 51 Bangalore Exp. Weekly. 952
   Cochin Exp. Not daily. 21 Dhauli Exp. 7 Puri Exp.

Cochin: (via Madras) 951 Howrah Exp. Not daily. 939 Guwahati Exp.
Weekly.
Delhi/Nizamuddin: (via Agra Cantt) 78 Kalinga Utkal Exp. (via Lucknow) 178
Neelachal Exp. Not daily. (via Gaya) 916 Puri Exp. Not daily.
Guwahati: (via Howrah) 976 Bangalore Exp. Weekly. 902 Trivandrum Exp.
Weekly. 940 Cochin Exp. Weekly.
Hyderabad: 46 East Coast Exp.
Madras Central: 142 Coromandel Exp. 4 Howrah Mail.
Puri: 77 Kalinga Utkal Exp. 8 Howrah Mail. 10 Sri Jagannath. Exp. 175
Neelachal Exp. Not daily. 915 New Delhi Exp. Not daily.
Secunderabad: 20 Konark Express.
Tirupati: 980 Howrah Exp.
Trivandrum: (via Madras) 901 Guwahati Exp. Weekly.

To **Gorakhpur** from:
Ahmadabad: 165 Sabarmati Exp.
Barauni: 153 Vaishali Exp. 505 Kanpur Exp.
Bombay VT: 115 Gorakhpur Exp.
Calcutta/Howrah: 19 Gorakhpur Exp. 947 Purvanchal Exp. Not daily.
Chchapra: 44 Gwalior Mail. 1 Gorakhpur Exp.
Cochin: 911 Gorakhpur Exp. Weekly.
Delhi/New: 974 Saheed Exp. Not daily. 154 Vaishali Exp. 510 Avadh Assam
Exp.
Guwahati: 509 Avadh Assam Exp.
Gwalior: 43 Chchapra Mail.
Hatia: 27 Maurya Exp.
Kanpur: 506 Barauni Exp.
Lucknow: 165A Sabarmati Exp. Not daily. 508 Gorakhpur Exp.
Muzzaffapur: 166A Sabarmati Exp. Not daily.
Ratlam: 64 Avadh Exp.
(From Gorakhpur there are daily passenger trains to Nautanwa or Naugarh for
Nepal.)

To **Jaipur** from:
Agra Fort: 5 Agra Fort Fast Pass Exp. 7 Barmer Exp. 21 Jaipur Exp.
Ahmadabad: 2 Delhi Mail, 4 Delhi Exp. 506 Ashram Exp. 6 Agra Fort Fast
Pass Exp.
Ajmer: 516 Exp.
Barmer: 8 Agra Exp.
Bikaner: 238 Exp.
Delhi: 3 Ahmedabad Exp. 501 Pink City Exp. 1 Ahmedabad Mail. 61
Mandore Exp. 33/233 Shekhawati Exp. 505 Ashram Exp. 15 Chetak Exp.
Jodhpur: 514 Marudhar Exp. 62 Mandore Exp.
Lucknow: 513 Marudhar Exp.
Sawai Madhopur: 237 Exp. 17 Exp.
Sriganganagar: 12 Exp.
Udaipur: 502/516 Pink City/Garib Nawaz Exp. 16 Chetak Exp.

To **Jaiselmer** from:
Jodhpur: 4 JPJ, 2 JPJ Pass.

To **Jalgaon** from:
Ahmadabad: 931 Hyderabad Exp. Weekly. 941 Navjivan Exp. Mo/Tu/Fr/Sa.
903 Trivandrum Exp. Weekly. 937 Cochin Exp. Weekly.
Amritsar: (via New Delhi) 58 Dadar Exp. 3 Bombay Mail.
Bombay VT: 37 Punjab Mail. 115 Gorakhpur Exp. 1 Calcutta Mail. 29
Howrah Exp. 170/913/945 Bombay/Bhagalpur/Muzaffapur/Guwahati Exp.
Bombay/Dadar: 39 Sewagram Exp. 57 Amritsar Exp. 27 Varanasi Exp.
Calcutta/Howrah: 2 Bombay Mail. 30 Bombay Exp.
Cochin: 938 Ahmadabad Exp. Weekly.
Firozpur: (via New Delhi) 38 Punjab Mail.
Gorakhpur: 116 Bombay Exp.
Guwahati: 946/169/914 Bhagalpur/Mauzaffarpur/Bombay Exp.
Hyderabad: 932 Ahmadabad Exp. Weekly.
Jammu Tawi: (via New Delhi) 178 Jhelum Exp.
Kolhapur: 83 Maharastra Exp.
Madras Central: 942 Navjivan Exp. Not daily.
Nagpur: 40 Sewagram Exp. 84 Maharastra Exp.
Pune: 177 Jhelum Exp.
Trivandrum: 904 Ahmadabad Exp. Weekly.

To **Jammu Tawi** from:
Bombay Central: (via New Delhi) 171 Jammu Tawi Exp. Mo/Th.
Calcutta/Howrah: (via Lucknow) 173 Himgiri Exp. Tu/Fr/Sa.
Calcutta/Sealdah: (via Lucknow) 51 Jammu Tawi Exp.
Delhi: 33 Jammu Tawi Mail.
Delhi/New: 145 Shalimar Exp.
Kanniya Kumari: (via Trivandrum, Madras & New Delhi: India's longest train
ride) 907 Himsagar Exp. Weekly.
Madras Central: (via New Delhi) 131 Jammu Tawi Exp. We/Sa/Su.
Pune: (via New Delhi) 177 Jhelum Exp.

To **Jhansi** from:
Ahmadabad: 165 Sabarmati Exp.
Amritsar: 58 Dadar Exp.
Bangalore City: 905 Karnataka Exp.
Bilaspur: 137 Chchatisgarh Exp.
Bombay VT: 37 Punjab Mail, 115 Gorakhpur Exp. 933 Lucknow Exp.
Bombay/Dadar: 57 Amritsar Exp. 961 Lashkar Exp.
Chchapra: 44 Gwalior Mail.
Cochin: 911 Gorakhpur Exp.
Delhi/New: 126 Kerala Exp. 906 Karnataka Exp. 124 AP Andhra Pradesh
Exp. 2002 Shatabdi Exp. 168 Malwa Exp. 16 Grand Trunk Exp. 122 Tamil
Nadu Exp.
Delhi/Nizamuddin: 150 Mahakosal Exp. 78 Kalinga Utkal Exp. 22 Hyderabad
Exp.
Firozpur: 38 Punjab Mail.
Gorakhpur: 912 Cochin Exp. Weekly. 116 Bombay Exp.
Gwalior: 43 Chchapra Mail. 107 Bundlkhand Exp. 962 Lashkar Exp. Weekly.
Hyderabad: 21 Nizamuddin Exp.
Indore: 167 Malwa Exp.
Jabalpur: 149 Mahakosal Exp.

Jammu Tawi: 178 Jhelum Exp. 132 Madras Exp. (via New Delhi). 908 Himsagar Exp. (via New Delhi) Weekly.
Kanniya Kumari: (via Trivandrum & Madras) 907 Himsagar Exp. Weekly.
Lucknow: 934 Bombay Exp.
Madras: 131 Jammu Tawi Exp. 15 Grand Trunk Exp. 121 Tamil Nadu Exp.
Pune: 177 Jhelum Exp.
Puri: 77 Kalinga Utkal Exp.
Secunderabad: 123 AP Exp.
Trivandrum: 125 Kerala Exp.
Varanasi: 166 Sabarmati Exp. 108 Bundelkhand Exp.

To **Jodhpur** from:
Agra Fort: 7 Agra/Barmer Exp.
Ahmadabad: 228/28 Marwar Ranakpur Exp. 508 Jodhpur Exp. Th/Sa. 265 Jodhpur Exp.
Barmer: 98 Barmer Exp. 8 Barmer/Agra Exp.
Bikaner: 27/227 Marwar Ranakpur Exp.
Delhi: 93 Jodhpur Mail, 61 Mandore Exp.
Jaiselmer: 3 JPJ, 1 JPJ Pass.
Lucknow: 513 Marudhar Exp.

To **Madurai** from:
Coimbatore: 715 Rameswaram Exp.
Madras/Egmore: 103 Pearl City Exp. 105 Quilon Mail. 117 Pandyan Exp. 119 Nellai Exp. 135 Vagai Exp.
Rameswaram: 716 Coimbatore Exp.
Quilon: 106 Madras Mail. 762 Trichy Exp.
Tiruchchirappalli: 761 Quilon Exp.
Tirunelveli: 120 Nellai Exp. 180 Villupuram Janata Exp.
Tirupati: 199 Madurai Exp.
Titicorin: 104 Pearl City Exp.
Villupuram: 179 Tirunelveli Janata Exp.

To **New Jalpaiguri** from:
Bangalore: 975 Guwahati Exp. Weekly.
Bombay: 945 Guwahati Exp. Weekly.
Calcutta/Howrah: 57 Kanchenjunga Exp. Not Sats. 59 Kamrup Exp.
Calcutta/Sealdah: 43 Darjeeling Mail.
Cochin: 939 Guwahati Exp. Weekly.
Darjeeling: 2D, 4D.
   (To Darjeeling from New Jalpaiguri: 3D, 1D) (service suspended).
Delhi: 156 Tinsukia Mail.
Delhi/New: 510 Avadh Ashram Exp. Not daily. 922 North East Exp.
Guwahati: 60 Kamrup Exp. 921 N.E. Exp. 155 Tinsukia Mail. 509 Avadh Assam Exp. Not daily. All weekly: 976 Bangalore, 902 Trivandrum, 940 Cochin, 946 Bombay Expresses.
Trivandrum: 901 Guwahati Exp. Weekly.

To **Puri** from:
Bhubaneswar: 7, 9, 78, 176, 916.
Calcutta/Howrah: 7 Puri Exp. 9 Sri Jagannath Exp.

Delhi/Nizamuddin: 78 Kalinga Utkal, 176 Neelachal Exp. Not daily. 916 Puri Exp. Not daily.

To **Quilon** from:
Ahmadabad: 903 Trivandrum Exp. Weekly.
Bangalore: 26 Trivandrum Exp.
Bombay VT: 81 Kanniya Kumari Exp.
Cannanore: 48 Cannanore Exp.
Delhi/New: 126 Kerala Exp.
Ernakulam: 303 Vanchinad Exp.
Guwahati: 902 Trivandrum Exp. Weekly.
Jammu Tawi: 908 Himsagar Exp. Weekly.
Kanniya Kumari: 907 Himsagar Exp. Weekly. 82 Bombay Exp.
Madras Central: 19 Trivandrum Mail.
Madras/Egmore: 105 Quilon Mail.
Mangalore: 125/126 Kerala Exp. 30 Malabar Exp. 50 Trivandrum Exp.
Shoranur: 301 Venad Exp.
Trichy: 761 Quilon Exp.
Trivandrum: 302 Venad Exp. 304 Vanchinad Exp. 29 Malabar Exp. 49 Mangalore Exp. 47 Cannanore Exp. 125 Kerala Exp. 20 Madras Mail. 25 Bangalore Exp. 904 Ahmadabad and 901 Guwahati Expresses, both weekly.

To **Rameswaram** from:
Coimbatore: 715 Rameswaram Exp.
Madras/Egmore: 101 Rameswaram Exp. 113 Sethu Exp.
(The ferry service from Rameswaram to Sri Lanka is suspended.)

To **Shimla (Simla)** from:
Bhiwani: (to Kalka) 409 Ekta Exp.
Howrah: (via Delhi to Kalka) 1 Kalka Mail.
Delhi/New: (to Kalka) 195 Himalayan Queen.
Kalka: 1KS, 257, 253.
(Other connections via Ambala to Kalka.)

To **Udagamandalam (Ooty)** from:
Coimbatore: (to Mettupalaiyam) 555.
Coonoor: 568, 566.
Madras Central: (to Mettupalaiyam) 5 Nilagiri Exp.
Mettupalaiyam: 562, 564.
(Trains from Trivandrum and Madras to Coimbatore.)

To **Varanasi** from:
Agra Cantt: (see Mathura).
Ahmadabad: 165 Sabarmati Exp.
Allahabad City: 82 Fast Exp. 6 Triveni Exp. 38 Varanasi Exp. 36 Varanasi Exp.
Amritsar: (via New Delhi) 82 AC Exp. Not daily. 6 Howrah Mail. 50 Howrah Exp.
Ballia: 31 Varanasi Exp.
Bhatni: 49 Varanasi Exp. 5 Triveni Exp. 81 Fast Exp.

Bombay VT: 193 Mahanagri Exp. 965 Varanasi Exp. Not daily.
Bombay/Dadar: 27 Varanasi Exp.
Calcutta/Howrah: 81 AC Exp. Not daily. 173 Himgiri Exp. (via Patna). 9
    Doon Exp. 5 Amritsar Mail, 49 Amritsar Exp.
Calcutta/Sealdah: (via Patna) 33 Varanasi Exp. 51 Jammu Tawi Exp.
Dehra Dun: (via Haridwar) 10 Doon Exp. 66 Varanasi Exp.
Delhi/New: 950 Varanasi Exp. Not daily. 158 Kashi Vishwanath Exp.
Delhi/Nizamuddin: (via Lucknow) 176 Neelachal Exp. Not daily.
Dhanbad: 407 Ludhiana Exp.
Durg: (via Allahabad) 159 Sarnath Exp.
Gorakhpur: 33/28 Varanasi Exp.
Gwalior: 107 Bundelkhand Exp.
Jammu Tawi: 174 Himgiri Exp. 52 Sealdah Exp.
Lucknow: 428 Varanasi Varuna Exp.
Madras: 139 Ganga Kaveri Exp. Not daily.
Mathura: (via Agra Cantt) 188/84/114 Ganga Yamuna Exp.
Puri: (via Gaya) 175 Neelachal Exp. (Not daily).

To **Vasco da Gama (Goa)** from:
Bangalore: 201 Mail/Pass MG.
Bombay VT: (change at Miraj to MG) 311 Sahyadhri Exp. 307 Koyana Exp.
    303 Mahalaxami Exp.
Miraj: 298 Mandovi Exp (MG). 206 Gomantak Exp. (MG).

ITINERARIES

New Delhi/Agra/New Delhi
If you only have time for one rail trip in India, it will probably be this: to Agra to see the Taj Mahal. There are two good trains from New Delhi which allow enough time to see the sights and return in the evening, but it means an early start.

Shatabdi Express	New Delhi: leave 0630 arrive 2215 ↑
	Agra Cantt: arrive 0825 leave 2010
Taj Express	New Delhi: leave 0705 arrive 2200 ↑
	Agra Cantt: arrive 0950 leave 1845

Delhi/Jaipur/Delhi
The Pink City Express is another popular train which allows a few hours for sight seeing on a day trip, in this case to Jaipur.

| Pink City Express | Delhi: leave 0600 arrive 2215 ↑ |
| | Jaipur: arrive 1105 leave 1610 |

Delhi/Jaipur/Agra/New Delhi
This itinerary, combining two popular places, is possible over two or

three days:

Delhi	501 Pink City Exp.	lv:	0600
Jaipur		ar:	1105
(Overnight in Jaipur)			
Jaipur	22 Agra Exp.	lv:	0610
Agra Fort		ar:	1100
Agra Cantt	2001 Shatabdi Exp.	lv:	2010
New Delhi		ar:	2215

Indian Railways has several set itineraries for Indrail Pass holders for which reserved train accommodation can be guaranteed as long as arrangements are made at least 90 days in advance. A selection of the itineraries is included here although I don't think the trains they recommend are very practical.

For instance, there are many timings like this:

> Day 3. Arr: Varanasi 0200
> Dep: Varanasi 2350.

That makes a long day without sleep. So I am not quoting the suggested trains, only the stations as a guide to the best sequence of travelling.

7 day tours

Buddhist tour: New Delhi / Gaya / Varanasi / Gorakhpur / Naugarh (for Lumbini in Nepal by road) / Lucknow / New Delhi.

Rajasthan tour: Delhi / Jodhpur / Jaiselmer / Udaipur / Jaipur / Agra / New Delhi.

Temple tour: New Delhi / Agra / Jhansi (for Khajuraho by road) / Varanasi / New Delhi.

To Goa: Delhi / Jaipur / Agra / Jalgaon / Bombay / Vasco da Gama.

City & Cave: New Delhi / Jalgaon (by road to) Aurangabad / Secunderabad (by road to) Hyderabad / Madras / Bombay.

City & Cave: Bombay (Dadar) / Madras / Bangalore / Lonavla / Bombay.

Temple & Hill: Calcutta (Howrah) / Varanasi (by bus to) Mughalsarai / New Jalpaiguri / Darjeeling / New Jalpaiguri / Calcutta (Sealdah).

Temple Tour: Calcutta (Howrah) / Nalanda / Rajgir / Gaya / Varanasi / Gorakhpur / Agra / New Delhi.

15 day tours

Temple & Beach: Bombay / Jalgaon (by road to) Aurangabad / Secunderabad / Madras (change at Khurda Road) Puri (for Konark). Varanasi / Agra / Jaipur / Delhi.

Desert & Caves: Dehli / Jaipur / Jodhpur / Jaiselmer / Udaipur / Khandwa / Jalgaon (by road to) Aurangabad / Secunderabad / Agra / New Delhi.

North to South: New Delhi / Madras / Madurai / Kanniya Kumari / Trivandrum / Cochin / Ooty (by road to) Mysore / Bangalore / Hyderabad / Bombay.

Religion & Wild Life: Delhi / Jaipur / Bharatpur / Agra / Jhansi / (for Khajuraho by road) / Varanasi / Haridwar / Dehra Dun / Delhi.

City Tour: New Delhi / Bombay / Madras / Bangalore / Bhubaneswar / Calcutta / Varanasi / Amritsar / Delhi.

South Tour: Madras / Bangalore / Mysore (by road to) Ooty / Cochin / Trivandrum / Kanniya Kumari / Madurai / Trichy / Thanjavur / Villupuram / Pondicherry / Villupuram / Madras.

21 day tours

Miscellany: New Delhi / Sawai Madhopur (wild life) / Jaipur / Agra / Varanasi / Calcutta / Puri / Madras / Bangalore / Vasco da Gama / Lonavla / Bombay.

New Delhi / Jammu Tawi (by road to Srinagar and back) / Varanasi / Gaya / Calcutta / Madras / Bangalore / Secunderabad / Agra / New Delhi.

Calcutta / Puri / Madras / Bangalore / Secunderabad / Bombay / Aurangabad (by road to) Jalgaon / Agra / New Delhi / Varanasi / Calcutta.

30 day tours

Madras / Puri / Calcutta / Darjeeling / Varanasi / Haridwar / Delhi / Agra / Jaipur / Udaipur / Chittaurgarh / Indore (by road to) Mhow / Jalgaon / Bombay / Miraj / Vasco da Gama / Miraj / Bangalore / Trichy / Madras.

Circular tours

The zonal railways have devised their own circular tours for which a circular journey ticket (CJT) can be purchased at the station of origin, with reservations made at the same time. These samples are useful for comparison of routes and costs:

Northern Railway
New Delhi / Bombay / Calcutta / New Delhi.
4,800 km. 1st Class: Rs 1328. 2nd Class: Rs 322. Valid 32 days.

New Delhi / Bombay / Vasco da Gama / Bangalore City / Mysore / Bangalore City / Ooty / Trivandrum / Kanniya Kumari / New Delhi.
7,550 km. 1st Class: Rs 1956. 2nd Class: Rs 454. Valid 51 days.

New Delhi / Puri / Calcutta / Darjeeling / New Delhi.
4,730 km. 1st Class: Rs 1486. 2nd Class: Rs 350. Valid 32 days.

South Central Railway
Secunderabad / Hyderabad / Pune / Lonavla / Bombay / Surat / Vadodara / Ahmadabad / Rajkot / Dwarka / Porbandar / Ahmadabad / Abu Road / Marwar / Ajmer / Jaipur / Delhi / Saharanpur / Haridwar / Rishikesh / Moradabad / Lucknow / Varanasi / Allahabad / Jabalpur / Itarsi / Nagpur / Secunderabad / Hyderabad.
6,825 km. 1st Class: Rs 1802. 2nd Class: Rs 422. Valid 47 days.

North Eastern Railway
Gorakhpur / Howrah / Puri / Madras / Rameswaram / Madurai / Kanniya Kumari / Trivandrum / Bangalore / Bombay / Porbandar / Dwarka / Ajmer / Jaipur / Mathura / Delhi / Haridwar / Gorakhpur.
9,652 km. 1st Class: Rs–2432. 2nd Class: Rs 560. Valid 64 days.

Western Railway
(This railway has 74 circular tour itineraries available.)
Bombay / Ahmedabad / Udaipur / Jaipur / Agra / Delhi / Jammu Tawi / Chandigarh / Shimla / Haridwar / Dehra Dun / Varanasi / Calcutta / Bhubaneswar / Puri / Vishakhapatnam / Madras / Trichy / Rameswaram / Madurai / Trivandrum / Cochin / Coimbatore / Ooty (by bus to) Mysore / Bangalore / Secunderabad / Aurangabad / Manmad / Bombay.
10,539 km. 1st Class: Rs 2752. 2nd Class: Rs 622. Valid 71 days.

Tour group itineraries

There are few travel agencies which specialize exclusively in organized tours by rail in India, although many tour operators do feature some rail travel in their package holidays to India.

All India Rail Tours are run by J.A. Butterfield, Burton Fleming, Driffield, Yorkshire YO24 0PQ. Tel: 0262 87230. (See Chapter 11, *Great Trips*)

The Romance of India by Rail Tours are run by International Railtours, 60 Cable Road, Whitehead, County Antrim, BT38 9PZ, Northern Ireland. Tel: 0232 231498.

The Palace on Wheels tour can be booked through major travel agencies or in India through Central Reservations, Rajasthan Tourism Development Corporation, Chandralok Building, 36 Janpath, New Delhi 110 001. Tel: 3321820; telex: 03163142. The itinerary is: Delhi Cantt / Jaipur / Chattaugarh / Udaipur / Jaiselmer / Jodhpur / Bharatpur / Agra / Delhi Cantt. 7 days. (See Chapter 11, *Great Trips*.) Prices, inclusive of meals and tours, start at Rs 1550 per person per day for the 88/89 season.

TRAVEL TIMES

The time it takes to travel by the fastest trains between Delhi, Bombay, Calcutta and Madras, and some popular destinations is listed here in hours and minutes. Where there is no time given, there is no direct service from that city, so a change of train will be necessary.

From:	DELHI	BOMBAY VT/CEN	CALCUTTA	MADRAS
To:				
Agra	1:55	23:40	29:20	32:40
Bhubaneswar	31:33		7:05	19:40
Bombay VT/Cen	17:00	–	32:15	30:30
Calcutta	17:40	32:10	–	27:05
Delhi	–	16:45	17:50	33:45
Jammu Tawi	10:10	29:55	37:25	60:25
Jhansi	4:30	18:50		27:35
Madras	33:15	30:30	26:20	–
Secunderabad	26:20	14:20	30:40	14:00
Trivandrum	52:45	44:35	48:00	16:40
Varanasi	13:00	27:00	14:40	38:30
Vasco da Gama		21:00*		

(*Includes wait of 30 minutes for change of train from BG to MG at Miraj.)

(A blank space indicates no direct service.)

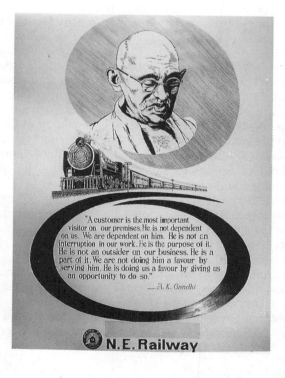

"A customer is the most important visitor on our premises. He is not dependent on us. We are dependent on him. He is not an interruption in our work. He is the purpose of it. He is not an outsider on our business. He is a part of it. We are not doing him a favour by serving him. He is doing us a favour by giving us an opportunity to do so."

—A. K. Gandhi

N.E. Railway

Chapter 10

Profiles of some Popular Rail Destinations

AGRA

Agra has seven stations (see plan) but only two of them, Agra Fort and Agra Cantt, are frequented by tourists. **Agra Fort** station was built in 1891 as a halt for colonials on picnic expeditions to the Red Fort and Taj Mahal. It is a Western Railway station with MG trains to Rajasthan and Gujarat. There are also BG trains to Lucknow, and it is a stop for the Toofan Express linking Delhi with Howrah. There is one BG platform and three MG ones, which actually have a separate entrance at the city side of the station.

Walls of the Red Fort tower over the station and the Taj Mahal is a Rs 10 auto-rickshaw ride away. There is a fine view of the Red Fort from the terrace in front of the six-bed dormitory (Rs 12 per bed) and the retiring rooms (Rs 44 a double room). The railway offices and waiting rooms are off platform 1 (BG) but the cloakroom is on platform 4 (MG). In the main lobby, the reservation office is on the left and the BG booking office on the right. First class reservations on all trains can be made at the counter by the enquiry office.

This enquiry office is a separate kiosk where foreign tourists can obtain help. A useful feature of Agra Fort station (which could be copied by other stations with lots of foreign passengers) is a sign which states: 'In case of difficulty, the Indrail Pass holders should approach CRS.' Although it doesn't explain what CRS means, it's nice to know foreigners are being thought of.

The auto-rickshaw drivers and their touts lurking to prey on tourists in the small forecourt are rapacious. Be firm, though, and they will soon lower their prices. The fare to Agra Cantt station drops from Rs 20 to Rs 10 after stern bargaining and it is an exotic ride through bazaars and pot-holed roads.

At **Agra Cantt** station, the taxis and rickshaws are organized by their own unions and have printed tariff cards which they show to passengers as they come off the train. Taxis and tour buses park on the right of the forecourt with auto rickshaws gathered around the circular gardens and cycle rickshaws and tongas on the left. The tour buses are

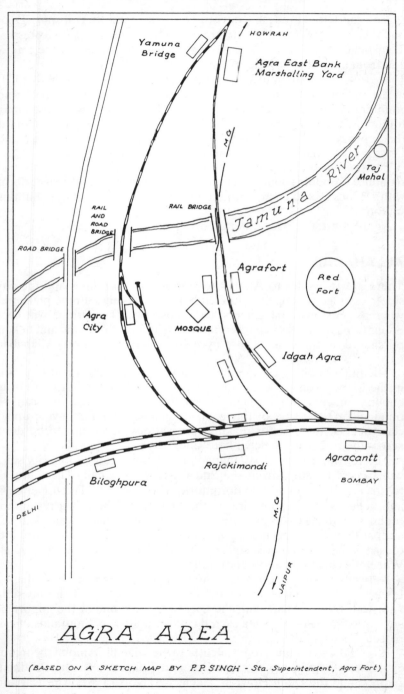

AGRA AREA

(BASED ON A SKETCH MAP BY P. P. SINGH - Sta. Superintendent, Agra Fort)

run by the Uttar Pradesh Tourism Dept and the UP Transport Dept and link with the arrival/departure of the Shatabdi and Taj Expresses. Tour tickets (taking in the major sights) are sold on board the trains, and from a booth on platform 1.

There is a very helpful Uttar Pradesh tourist bureau (0700 to 2000) in the station lobby and a range of ticket/reservation counters but no counter dedicated to foreign passengers. This is puzzling since so many foreigners use the station and the Indrail Pass can be bought there (at the upper class counter, but there's no sign saying so). There is a 2nd Class booking hall for local trains in an annexe to the station.

The present station was constructed in 1960 and has retiring rooms: six non AC double rooms and two AC (Rs 50/Rs 100) and a large dorm with 10 beds (Rs 15 each). Bottled mineral water can be bought at this station.

Agra Cantt: Tel. 65244. Agra Fort: Tel. 76161.

ALLAHABAD

There are two sides to Allahabad station: the civil lines and the city side. A bridge was opened in October 1988 linking all nine platforms whereas previously passengers had to use two. The bridge will be a boon for passengers since reservations are done on one side and tickets purchased on the other. Close by there is another station, Allahabad City, for MG trains.

The main booking counters for 2nd Class reservation and tickets is in the lobby. None of the counter signs are in English but there is an enquiry office (with its sign in English) where directions can be obtained. At the side of this complex is a counter for buying upper class tickets, but not for making reservations which has to be done across the bridge on the civil lines side.

The retiring rooms at Allahabad are on the second floor, city side, with access by steps from the 2nd Class waiting hall. There are 13 rooms (Rs 70/200) and two dormitories (beds Rs 20). The upper class and ladies waiting rooms are on the first floor. There is a restaurant (open 0730 to 2300) off platform 1 with ancient, grouchy waiters. It has a separate section specializing in 'South Indian dishes'. There are lots of snack bars and book stalls: Allahabad is the HQ of the A.H. Wheeler's chain of station bookstalls.

Notices on the platform say 'Alight here for Sangam Pilgrimage'. Located at the confluence of the Ganga, Yamuna and the invisible Saraswati rivers, Allahabad, the City of God, is one of the important ancient cities of India. As a sacred centre, it attracts thousands of rail passengers every day.

It is on the main line from Calcutta to New Delhi. Among the major expresses stopping are the Tinsukia and Kalka Mails, the Rajdhani Express and the Delhi/Howrah, Neelachal, North East, Amritsar and

A view of Agra Fort. (Photo by Anthony J. Lambert)

Toofan Expresses; Delhi is 627 km distant, Howrah 814 km. There are lots of trains from Allahabad to Satna where there is a road link to Karjuraho.

AMBALA CANTT

Ambala is a major transit station in the Northern Railway network where passengers from Shimla connect with Lucknow and Jammu Tawi trains. It can be a pleasant place to wait. Just outside the station are some open air restaurants with comfortable seating and brick ovens for cooking chapatis. There is also an English wine shop open all day selling Indian spirits and chilled beer. The NV restaurant at the station has some magnificent pieces of antique furniture, almirahs, dressers, a hat stand and screens, in daily use. There is no special counter for foreign tourists but there is a helpful reservations counter open 0930 to 1630 daily.

AURANGABAD

Aurangabad, a popular place to stay while exploring the caves at Ellora (30 km distant) and Ajanta (106 km) is on the metre gauge line from Kacheguda (Secunderabad) to Manmad. A daily overnight express leaves Kacheguda at 1745 and Secunderabad at 1825 to arrive at Aurangabad at 0605 the next morning. The return journey is by the same train (the 551/552 Ajanta Express) which leaves Aurangabad at 2230 and arrives at 1035 the next morning at Secunderabad.

Getting to Aurangabad from Bombay and New Delhi involves a change of train (from broad to metre gauge) at Manmad, a routing which has given Aurangabad the reputation of being difficult to reach. However, a good connection from Bombay is the 27 Varanasi Express which leaves Dadar station at 0640 daily and stops at Manmad at 1148. That gives time for lunch there which is fortunate because Manmad has a pleasant and clean restaurant with alert staff. Then you catch the 594 Nanded Express leaving at 1500 and arriving at Aurangabad 2 hours 45 minutes later. From New Delhi, the best connection is by the superfast 906 Karnataka Express which leaves ND at 2330 on Wednesdays, Fridays and Sundays bound for Bangalore. It stops at Manmad at 1755 in time for the 1945 departure of the 552 Ajanta Express.

At Aurangabad station there are two retiring rooms (one double, one single) and a dormitory with four beds (Rs 12 each).

Some travellers prefer to go to Jalgaon instead for access to the Ajanta Caves (59 km distant), since many trains stop at Jalgaon as it is on a broad gauge line linking it with Bombay and other main stations (see Chapter 9 for connections).

Aurangabad Station enquiries: Tel. 4815.

BANGALORE

Bangalore is expanding so fast as an industrial and business centre, its beauty as a garden city has been obscured. Infrastructure is struggling to keep up but the railways recognized the boom and, in 1981, made it a fully fledged division of Southern Railway. Bangalore is about to become the fourth major metropolis of India, overtaking the position held by Madras. In 1988 a new railway administration building was opened, next to the City station, and it has been crowned with the nose of a metre gauge steam engine as an authentic replica of the Indian Railways emblem.

At **Bangalore City** station, the high-ceilinged lobby has a booth for the Karnataka State Tourism Development Corporation (open 0630–2000 every day) promoting its tours. A city tour leaves from the station at 0730 and 1400 hours. The bus station is opposite the railway forecourt and tourist agencies line the road to the right. Also in the entrance-lobby is a police, information kiosk where a notice warns passengers about unauthorized 'ticket nippers'. The chemist (open 0600–2200) sells bottled mineral water and the bookshop (0900–1300, 1400–1700) has lots of locally produced guides about India.

Tickets for same-day departures can be bought in an annex to the lobby. For advance reservations go to the new building on the right of the station forecourt where there is a special Indrail Pass counter where foreign tourists can buy tickets and make reservations. It is open Mon–Sat 0700–1300, 1330–1930; Sun 0700–1300. The station has 12 platforms, six BG and six MG, with self-help trollies, wheel-chair assistance and 270 licensed porters.

There is a vegetarian restaurant off platform 1 with mechanized food mixers and fast-food boilers. A non-veg restaurant is on the upper floor, beside the gallery overlooking the booking lobby. Waiting rooms are also there. The retiring rooms are much in demand at Bangalore City and more are being added on the station's second floor. Double rooms all have twin beds, fans, settee and armchairs, a writing desk, dressing room and bathroom with hot water and towel at Rs 50 for the room. A dorm bed in a ward-like atmosphere costs Rs 15.

In keeping with its new image as the city of the future, Bangalore has an extensive system of direct rail links with the rest of India. There is a nightly departure by the superfast Karnataka Express to New Delhi, a journey of just over 40 hours. The Udyan Express takes 24 hours to Bombay while an MG mail passenger train gives a daily service to Vasco da Gama (Goa). To Madras, there are morning, afternoon and evening departures taking between six and seven hours for the 362 km journey. Details of all links are in Chapter 9.

Bangalore Cantonment station is more rural with light blue tiles lining the platform walls and an odd cluster of arches opposite platform 1. No trains originate here; it is a halt for those going to and from Bangalore City station. It has a bank to facilitate customers clearing freight from the goods yard that adjoins it. Bangalore is an inland port linked with Madras for imports and exports. In one shed in the yard I saw hundreds of drums of aspirin being loaded into a rail container for direct shipment to the UK.

Not far from both stations is the Welcomgroup's Windsor Manor Sheraton hotel (25 Sankey Road, Bangalore. Tel: 79431), an Indian architect's interpretation of an English stately home. Although constructed in 1983, it blends in perfectly with Bangalore's genuine historic buildings. The hotel is popular with local and foreign tourists and business visitors both to visit (the Royal Derby bar reeks of British nostalgia) and to stay (from Rs 850 a night).

Bangalore City station enquiries: Tel. 258465. Bangalore Cantt station: Tel. 74172.

BERHAMPUR

A small station with fantastic connections. You can get here any day from Howrah or Bhubanswar by superfast trains, and also from Madras (on the Coromandel Express or Howrah Mail) or from Hyderabad by the East Coast Express, and from Tirupati too. Once a week, expresses stop from Trivandrum, Guwahati and Cochin. It is described by its fans as a pleasant station with mountains on one side and sea in the distance on the other.

You go to Berhampur to get to Gopalpur On Sea, a beach resort on the Bay of Bengal. It is also the station closest to the huge (70 km by 15 km) freshwater Chilka Lake, which the railway runs beside. There are dorm beds at Rs 11 at the station and doubles at Rs 34. Buses and taxis go to Gopalpur On Sea, 18 km distant.

BHUBANESWAR

There are plans to make Bhubaneswar into a model railway station with a new building opposite the existing station to house a computer reservations facility and other offices. In the meantime, foreigners who want to make a reservation have to join the throng at the reservations counters (open from 0800 to 1700 every day but closed for lunch 1200 to 1230. The station built in 1965, is on the Calcutta–Madras main line with the railway tracks separating the new town from the old. Bhubaneswar is famed as the temple city of India and taxi drivers pester passengers with offers of city temple tours as soon as they arrive.

A staircase off the booking hall leads to the retiring rooms of which the best are the AC rooms at Rs 130 which includes tea and newspaper. I didn't fancy the dormitory (Rs 11.50 a bed) nor the gloomy waiting rooms. On the same floor are doors marked Veg and

*CS class 775 was one of the four smallest engines used on Indian Railways.
Photographed at Krishnanagar City Junction on the Shantipur to Nabadwhip Ghat
line in 1981, it was replaced by diesel in 1985. (Hugh Ballantyne)*

*Immaculate WP 7557 used for passenger trains at Agra Idgah shed, 1984.
(Hugh Ballantyne)*

Itinerant musicians by the Parlakamidi Light Railway, Andhra Pradesh.
(Anthony J. Lambert)

Non-Veg which open into the same restaurant. The 2nd Class waiting hall is downstairs at platform level. As well as the Wheelers bookstall there is a Sarvodaya stall with locally produced guide books among the religious tracts. I was astonished to find a telex bureau (open 1000–1700 except Suns and holidays) off the booking lobby.

Bhubaneswar's attractions are historical as it is part of ancient India although its proximity to the coast resort of Puri (reached by train) and to the Sun Temple at Konark (reached by bus) draws visitors. Puri is nearly two hours distant at a cost of Rs 6 and Rs 12 in 2nd Class and Rs 42 in 1st. There is an hotel (the Oberoi) at Bhubaneswar built in 1985 that has become an attraction in itself because it has been conceived along temple lines with an outer sanctum leading to another and on to the inner heart of the hotel, in this case a pool and garden surrounded by rooms. At this hotel, before serving my beer, the barman asked 'Are you German or English, sir?' When I said English he tilted the glass and poured the beer frothless and to perfection. The hotel is 4 km from the station, at Nayapalli. Tel: 56116. Rooms from Rs 775.

Bhubaneswar station enquiries: Tel. 52233.

CHANDIGARH

A modern looking station with very clean waiting rooms, on the line from Delhi to Kalka (for Shimla). There are two retiring rooms, both at the end of the office block on the sole platform. The reservation office says it's open 24 hours but is actually closed between 0130–0200, 0630–0900 and 1800–1830. Chandigarh is the capital of Punjab and Haryana States and the station is 8 km from the centre of the city planned by Le Corbusier. The 0600 hours departure of the 195 Himalayan Queen express from New Delhi gets to Chandigarh (244 km distant) at 1020 and the station is on the run of the 1 Howrah to Kalka mail which arrives at 0440 daily after leaving Delhi at 2245.

Chandigarh station enquiries: Tel. 22105.

CHITTAURGARH

Set in the plains of Rajasthan, Chittaurgarh station is on the MG line and served mostly by steam trains. It has a long tree-lined platform which doubles as 1 and 2 with retiring rooms, refreshment room and separate Ladies and Gents upper class waiting rooms beside it. The station is basic in appearance with a lobby that leads to a combined enquiry and reservation kiosk (open 1000–1700) with signs in English. A booking office for general tickets is on the left and a waiting hall on the right. The station is 6 km from the impressive fort ruin which is what visitors come to see.

A portion of the 501 Pink City Express takes nearly 12 hours for the

622 km day-time journey from Delhi, arriving at 1752 three times a week. Overnight there is the 1300 departure from Delhi by the 15 Chetak Express which gets in at 0502. The same trains link Chittaurgarh with Udaipur 117 km away. You can get here from Secunderabad (a distance of 1129 km) on the daily 1635 departure of the 582 fast MG passenger train to Ajmer which arrives at 1310 after two nights, or on the faster 1940 departure of the 70 Express to Jaipur, arriving at 0508, two nights later. From Jaipur, there is the 69 Express and two other trains a day come from Ajmer.

COCHIN

The real name for this station on India's south-western coast is Cochin Harbour Terminus and it is built on Willingdon Island in a natural harbour famous for its maritime history. Access to Cochin is also via Ernakulam Jn station (qv) where through trains from north and south halt for at least ten minutes.

From the rail point of view, Cochin is remarkable for the long distance trains which terminate here. At 0735 three times a week arrives the superfast 935 Netravati Express from Bombay VT, having taken nearly 36 hours for the 1852 km journey, and twice a week, the 957 Express comes from Dadar. Three expresses (from Gorakhpur, Bilaspur and Indore) arrive once a week on different days at 1535. Also once a week, the 940 from Guwahati arrives at the end of a 3362 km journey covered in 68 hours. The superfast 952 Howrah to Cochin Express operates three times a week. Weekly trains include the 937 from Ahmadabad via Bangalore and the 930 from Hyderabad. There is a daily express (No. 41) from Madras and another (No. 65) from Tiruchchirappalli.

There are no retiring rooms at the station, but budget accommodation is available. The Malabar Hotel, part of the Taj group, is on Willingdon Island. Tel. 6811. Rooms from Rs 600.

Cochin H.T. station enquiries: Tel. 6050.

COIMBATORE

This station, perhaps because it's new (1987), is one of the cleanest on Indian Railways. It isn't particularly pretty – they call Coimbatore the Manchester of South India because of its industry – but it is neat, tiled, bright and well-run. You can judge a station's efficiency by the number and appearance of the mobile vendors on its platforms. Coimbatore excels: they are many and they are smart, even the profit/loss accounts are displayed on the wall of its NV restaurant. You change trains here on the way to Mettupalaiyam for Ooty (see *Udagamandalam* in this chapter), unless you are coming from Madras on the 5 Nilagiri Express which stops in transit for 30 minutes. The station is served by a dozen major trains daily, and by a score more on a weekly or bi-weekly basis.

The spacious lobby has an expanse of granite floor tiles and natural light from its many windows. On the left on entering from the forecourt is the cloakroom and a Tourist Information Centre (0700–1900, except holidays: 1000–1730). A tunnel leads to each of the station's six platforms, numbers 5 and 6 being MG.

Unreserved tickets are sold at the counters to the right of the lobby. Reservations are made in a separate hall upstairs (open 0700–1330, 1400–2000; Sundays 0700–1330). There are no foreign tourist quota berths available but an enquiry to the CRS or SS (his office is on the ground floor) will bring instant and friendly help. On the first floor, on the other side of the gallery overlooking the lobby, are the retiring rooms where a non AC double costs Rs 100 and an AC apartment is Rs 250.

Coimbatore has no luxury hotels but the Hotel Sri Thevvar, 500 m from the station near the flyover (153 Avanashi Road, Coimbatore, Tamil Nadu 641018. Tel: 24135) has rates even less than the station retiring rooms. A single is Rs 45, a double Rs 65 and a double AC Rs 100, all with attached western style toilets and showers. There is day-time room service, a restaurant and a cellar bar (1100–2300) where drinks are sold at close to retail prices.

DEHRA DUN

This station is the rail gateway for the Mussoorie, 22 km distant by bus or taxi. Mussoorie is a picturesque hill resort commanding views of Himalayan snow ranges to the northeast and of the Doon Valley, and Haridwar to the south. There are retiring rooms at the station, with the usual rate of Rs 45 for a double room being increased to Rs 60 during the May to October peak season. The station is served by the daily 19 Dehra Dun Express direct from Bombay via Delhi, a 1701 km journey covered in 42 hours. From Delhi (320 km away) the trip takes 10 hours overnight by the 41 Mussoorie Express or nine hours during the day by the 19 Dehra Dun Express. The 9 Doon Express terminates in Dehra Dun at the end of its 36 hour (1524 km) run from Howrah via Lucknow. There is also an Express (number 65) from Varanasi. By train to Shimla or Jammu Tawi is via Laksar and Ambala Cantt.

ERNAKULAM JN

This is Cochin, although trains bound for Cochin terminate at the Harbour Station on Willingdon Island. If yours doesn't go there, alight here for the 8 km ride by bus or taxi, unless you are staying on the mainland. There are no special facilities for foreign tourists at Ernakulam Junction although the station does have three double retiring rooms (at Rs 60 each) and a new dormitory with beds at Rs 15 each. It is served by major trains with direct expresses from Bangalore, Bombay, Delhi, Madras, Mangalore and Trivandrum while other trains stop at Ernakulam Town station. A rail link from here to Alleppey is due to be opened in late 1989.

Ernakulam Jn enquiries: Tel. 353100. Ernakulam Town: Tel. 353920.

GAYA

This Eastern Railway station teems with begging children, shoe cleaners and vendors of *gram* which people spit into your face as they talk with mouths full. Yet this is the station from which to travel (15 km by bus or taxi) to the great pilgrim centre for Buddhists, Bodhgaya. Gaya itself is a centre for Hindu pilgrims. The station has four retiring rooms with two beds in each, at Rs 70 per room, and two with AC, at Rs 125. It is well served by main line trains and can be reached by direct expresses from Delhi (984 km in 18 hours, approximately), Howrah (458 km/8 hrs), Bombay (1715 km/30½ hrs), Jammu Tawi, via Lucknow and Varanasi on train number 52 (1509 km/36 hrs), Puri via Bhubaneswar (589 km/17–18 hrs), Patna (92 km/2 hrs) and Ranchi (337 km/8½ hrs).

GORAKHPUR

Gorakhpur is the HQ of the North Eastern Railway served by broad and metre gauge trains (see Chapter 9). Its attraction to foreigners is as a transit station to Nepal or for a visit to Kushinagar where Lord Buddha died. It is a spacious station with its upper class facilities centred around the main entrance, under a clock tower. In this lobby, there is a Foreign National Booking Counter with foreign currency exchange available for ticket purchase by foreigners. It is closed 2330–2400, 0730–0800 and 1530–1600. The reservation and enquiry offices are next to it. Train timetables are in Hindi although there is an illuminated sign in English giving current departures and platform numbers. A left luggage office (Rs 2 per piece) is on the right, with the sign in Hindi.

The lobby leads to the platforms where there is a book stall (open 0430–0130 daily) and a combined veg and non-veg restaurant (0630–2130) with an all-night refreshment stall outside it. Waiting and retiring rooms, some with AC, are upstairs. The one I stayed in actually had toilet paper to go with its western toilet. Rates are from Rs 50 for a single to Rs 150 for a deluxe double with TV, fridge and two cold drinks. There are 25 beds in three dormitories; plans are in hand to construct a 35 bedroom railway hotel at the station.

An Uttar Pradesh Tourist Bureau is on platform 1 where an

excellent set of leaflets is available, including one about Buddhist pilgrimages in the area. It is open 0600–2100 every day except state holidays and a lunch break 1300–1400. There are also police assistance, tourist help and grievance redressal booths on the platform. People in a hurry who have a complaint can collect a stamped lettergram to complete at their leisure and mail back to the station. Buses meet the main trains and from the nearby bus station buses leave on the hour for the 54 km ride to Kushinagar. Kushinagar can also be reached by bus (35 km) from Deoria Sadar station, 45 minutes by train from Gorakhpur.

There are several ways of reaching Nepal. Nautanwa (close to the border) is served by a daily MG passenger express which departs from Gorakhpur at 0615 and arrives at Nautanwa two hours later. The fare is Rs 53 1st Class and Rs 13 2nd Class. The train leaves Nautanwa at 0900 and arrives back at Gorakhpur at 1115. The closest station in India for Lumbini (Buddha's birthplace in Nepal) is Naugarh. This can be reached via the MG loop line from Gorakhpur to Gonda with the passenger train taking 85 minutes to Anandnaga which is a junction from where trains go to Naugarh (a further 52 minutes). Another way to Naugarh is by bus from Basti, a station on the main line from Delhi and Bombay which has the cleanest dormitory bathroom of any I've seen in India. The journey via Raxaul station involves too many changes to be practical. The final leg over the border is by bus or taxi.

Visas for Nepal are necessary and can be obtained at the border. You'll need a re-entry visa to return to India but this has to be applied for at the time you apply for the original visa to enter India (ask for a double or triple entry then). When you arrive at Gorakhpur from Nautanwa by train, you could be subjected to a casual customs search on the bridge from the MG platform to the station exit. If you are coming from Kathmandu or Pokhara in Nepal, beware of travel agents there who offer tickets on Indian Railways. A Chief Travelling Ticket Inspector (CTTI) on NE Railway told me he has discovered at least 20 cases of foreigners being overcharged. He proved it when we met a young German who had been charged Rs 200 more than the correct fare for his ticket to Cochin.

'The foreigner is an innocent, we must help him', the CTTI said. He advises foreigners travelling from Nepal to leave purchasing their Indian Railway tickets for onward journeys from Gorakhpur until they are actually in Gorakhpur. The Indrail Pass is sold there and single journey tickets are available. If reservations are difficult, the CRS or SS could be asked for help; it's better than being ripped off.

HARIDWAR

Situated at the foot of the Shivalik Hills and on the banks of the Ganga River where it enters the plains from the mountains, Haridwar is one of the holiest of Hindu religious places. It is on the line to Dehra Dun (qv) and is served by the same trains. The holy town of Rishikesh with its hanging bridge over the Ganga is 24 km and about an hour away by passenger train. There are several wild life sanctuaries within a few kilometres drive from Haridwar.

HYDERABAD

Look for Hyderabad – 'the City of Love' – in *Trains At A Glance* and it says 'Please see Secunderabad' but this station is the terminus (and starting point) for several important trains and is the one foreign visitors are likely to use when coming to see the city's best known landmark, the Charminar, four minarets, built in 1591 (5 km distant). The station has a large courtyard and six platforms and a reservation office in the main building. It is more relaxed than its twin, Secunderabad, and handles about half the number of passengers. There are no retiring rooms.

It is served daily by the 53 Madras and 59 Charminar Expresses from Madras (793 km/16½ hrs) and once a week by the 929 Cochin Express which also terminates here. It is the final destination for the daily 22 Express from H. Nizamuddin (Delhi) station, via Agra, 1675 km in 35 hours and for the weekly 931 Express from Ahmadabad via Vadodara, 1398 km in just over 26 hours. The 31 Bombay Express via Pune also terminates here, taking 18 hours for the overnight 730 km journey from Bombay VT. The 45 East Coast Express comes daily from Howrah via Bhubaneswar and Berhampur, and the 7 Godavari Express provides a daily link with Visakhapatnam. It is 10 km from Secunderabad station and trains generally stop at both.

There is only one five star hotel in Hyderabad, the Krishna Oberoi (Banjara Hills, Hyderabad. Tel: 222121) and it is so new that taxi and auto-rickshaw drivers don't know it, so you'll have to ask for 'Five star hotel' to get there. It is 7 km from Hyderabad station, 5 km from the airport. The hotel is an extravagant fantasy of white marble in a created garden setting; even the lifts have marble floors. There are 286 rooms (rates from Rs 1050) and a smart Indian restaurant with an electrically operated punkah.

JAIPUR

Jaipur station has been built (in 1956) in imitation of the flamboyant buildings which abound in this laid-back city of pink proscenium arches and turreted palaces. A new reservation complex is due to be opened opposite it; in the meantime foreigners have no special counter for bookings and must use the general counters (open 0630–1330, 1430–2130) which are labelled according to destination. Yet the Indrail Pass is supposed to be on sale here.

Retiring rooms (there are 36 of them, doubles costing Rs 65, dorm beds Rs 20) are on the first floor where there is also a restaurant (0600–1700). There is another restaurant at platform level open 0600–2300. As well as the usual facilities, waiting rooms, etc., the station has a post office (at the front) and a tourist office with well presented literature about Rajasthan including an elaborate map available free. It is open 0600–2000.

Jaipur, known as the Pink City and the Gateway, and Jewel, of Rajasthan, is one of the most popular destinations for foreigners and has been extensively covered in guide books and colour supplements. It is easy to reach from Delhi, by MG trains (see chapter 9), and is a convenient day trip. If you do want to stay, and fancy a night in a former Maharaja's palace, the Rambagh Palace (Bhawani Singh Rd, Jaipur. Tel: 75141), run by the Taj group, is Jaipur's finest hotel with superb lawns and palatial atmosphere where room rates start at Rs 900.

Jaipur Railway station, enquiries: Tel. 72121.

JAISELMER

After a day or night run through the desert from Jodhpur (the only way to get there by train) the sight of Jaiselmer station, small though it is, is welcome. Its sand-coloured buildings date from 1967 when the line to Jaiselmer was laid. A sign saying Retiring Rooms points vaguely into the desert and the rooms are to be found in a separate complex beyond the end of the platform. A bed costs Rs 20 and a 'Suit' Rs 60. There is a reservations office open 0800–1100 and 1400–1600 for the two trains (at 0900 and 2115) to Jodhpur. Trains leave Jodhpur for Jaiselmer at 2245 (arrives at 0800) and at 0820 (arrives at 1810). The trip of 295 km is dusty, hot (no AC) and slow (it's MG) but worth it. Take your own bottled water.

Jaiselmer is about 120 km from the Pakistan border, which is perhaps why there are signs at the station, in English, proclaiming: '(1) Be Indian. Buy Indian. (2) Kashmir to Kanniya Kumari, India is one. (3) Many religions, one nation. Let us be proud of it. (4) India is our country, let us help make it strong and prosperous.' Jaiselmer was left undisturbed by tourists until 1974 when a tourist bungalow was built; there are supposed to have been over 30,000 tourists there in 1988.

The attraction is the fort settlement, emerging out of a hillock in the desert like a phenomenon of nature until you are inside and see the intricate designs of balconies and doors wrought by skilled craftsmen over centuries. There are jeeps and auto-rickshaws to take rail passengers to the gates of the fort (expect to pay at least Rs 10 for an auto) and then it is a fascinating ramble through alleyways and alongside temples watched by hospitable and curious people. Actually many of the traders, street musicians and hangers-on are there for the pickings and don't come from Jaiselmer at all.

Chilled bottled mineral water is to be had at a reasonable price in the town square but for a beer wend your way through the alleys (or ask for directions) to the Hotel Jaisal Castle. (Fort Jaiselmer, Rajasthan. Tel: 2362, cable: JAISAL). It's the kind of place visitors like to keep secret and it has no sign outside. It is fashioned out of the walls of the fort, above the scrub and new buildings of the outer town. A narrow balcony with space for two hangs out over the fort wall and is a heady place on which to drink that ice cold beer. The hotel is the perfect desert guest house; cool, white-washed walls, low-ceilinged rooms with ornate hangings and rustic furniture, and clean, attached bathrooms with showers and western toilets with loo paper too. Although there is a tiny restaurant, dinner can be served on the roof under the stars. If you're lucky enough to meet Guman Singh who works there sometimes and lives deep in the carved clay fort walls close by, you will discover an excellent companion to show you around. The hotel's jeep meets every train, and camel safaris can be arranged. A double room costs Rs 200.

JAMMU TAWI

This busy station is the best railhead for Kashmir, abounding in touts to help or confuse the traveller heading for the bus stand for transport to Srinagar. Since the station is on the 'new town' side of the Tawi River, you'll have to take a mini-bus to the bus stand on the other side. There are retiring rooms at the station; they cost Rs 90 for a double and Rs 6 for a dorm bed.

It can take between 10 and 15 hours to travel the 585 km to Jammu from Delhi, depending on which train you choose; all trains are overnight. The superfast 171 originating at Bombay Central twice a week goes via New Delhi from where it takes 10 hours to Jammu. There is also a direct train from Madras, the 131, via all three mainline Delhi stations three times a week, and from Pune the daily 177 Jhelum Express via Agra and New Delhi. The journey from Pune to Jammu takes 41 hours for 2180 km and provides a link with Goa since trains between Vasco da Gama/ Bombay VT stop at Pune. There are also direct trains from Calcutta (1967 km) via Lucknow and these bypass Delhi; the journey is about 45 hours.

The real train nut may want to try the longest haul of all, from the Cape to Kashmir, the 907/908 Himsagar Express. This runs the length of India between Kanniya Kumari (KK) and Jammu Tawi (JT), a distance of 3,726 km, via Trivandrum, Madras, Agra and New Delhi. The departure days of this once a week trip change according to the season, so I dare not quote them, but it means four nights on the train. Fares quoted in KK for the trip to JT are: AC Sleeper (2 tier) Rs 1049,

1st Class Rs 967, 2nd Class (3 tier) Rs 506 and ordinary 2nd Class (no sleeper!) Rs 145.

However you travel to JT by train, advance reservations are essential, especially in the season (summer) and are best done through your Indrail Pass GSA before going to India, or at the ITB in New Delhi station. For return reservations, make them at Jammu Tawi on your way to Kashmir or contact the Railway Booking Office at Srinagar to avoid having to hang around Jammu while waiting for a berth on the way back.

JHANSI

You would only want to get out at this station if you're going to see the erotic temples at Khajuraho, and that's 176 km (five hours) away by bus. The list of trains that stop at Jhansi is long (see Chapter 9) because of its location at the centre of lines running north, east, south and west. Not many people stay, though, and there is only one, rather nasty, retiring room (Rs 46 for two) and a dormitory for six (Rs 14 each) adjoining platform 1. Both are controlled by formidable ladies who lock you in on arrival and only let you out on demand. The restaurant (open 0600–1900) is small and gloomy; behind it is a major, modernized base kitchen with capacity for 3,000 meals a day. The dinner that is served (included in the fare) on the evening run of the Shatabdi Express from Jhansi to Gwalior, Agra and New Delhi is prepared here. The Shatabdi Express is the best train to take to get to Jhansi, leaving New Delhi at 0630 and arriving at Jhansi, 414 km distant, at 1100, averaging 92 kph (see Chapter 11).

The station has two tourist bureaux; the one for Madhya Pradesh is very helpful with lots of leaflets; the one for Uttar Pradesh was closed whenever I visited. There is a rash of electronics here: digital clocks in the retiring and waiting rooms, and a display board that flashes when a train comes in. The gents upperclass waiting room has taped music. If you have to stay at Jhansi, escape from the station and try what is called 'the oldest western style hotel of Bundelkhand', the Jhansi Hotel (Shastri Marg, Jhansi, UP. Tel: 1360) a short auto ride away, where tea is served in silver pots left over from British days and there are some remarkable oil paintings of colonial gents above the bar and in the TV room. There is a full range of accommodation at Khajuraho which is actually closer (65 km) to Mahoba station than to Jhansi but the train links are impossible for same-day onward travel.

JODHPUR

When I saw the booking counter at Jodhpur station had a notice saying 'Foreign' in English above it, I was pleased this small station had a counter dedicated to foreign tourists. I was wrong. On this notice, 'foreign' means the counter sells tickets to 'foreign' stations, those outside the Northern Railway zone, not to foreigners. However, the station does have more signs in English than most, including several saying 'Foreign tourists beware of touts. Tourist Bureau Platform 2.'

Platform 2, which is also platform 1 and 3 at different points along its length, is the main platform and the Tourist Bureau is next to the 2nd Class booking hall. It is open 0500–2300 daily especially to help foreign tourists with reservations, ticket purchase and information, and it also serves as a waiting room, a temporary left luggage office and it even has a toilet. Run by Northern Railway, it is a facility that other stations frequented by foreigners could copy. An illustrated tourist map is in the station's booking lobby and a notice saying the city booking office is situated in Metha Market where booking and reservation facilities are available.

Retiring rooms are on the first floor with two twin bedded rooms (at Rs 60) and four four-bedded (at Rs 25 per bed). A pleasant refreshment room (V and NV) open 0600–2200 is on the same floor. Downstairs a counter is open 0800–2000 for AC and 1st Class reservations with the current booking office open 0445–2300. The station is on the MG line and is the junction for trains to Jaiselmer (qv) to which the 1st Class fare is Rs 140 for non AC sleeper and Rs 37 for 2nd Class 3-tier sleeper. There are two overnight trains to Jodhpur from Delhi; the fastest being the 61 Mandore Express which leaves Delhi (626 km distant) at 1810 and arrives at 0545. From Jaipur, which is where most visitors stop before coming to Jodhpur, there is one day-time train, the 513 Marudhar Express (leaves Jaipur at 1405, arrives Jodhpur at 2115) and four overnight trains. You can get to Jodhpur from Bombay by changing trains at Ahmadabad.

The city isn't just a transit stop on the way to Jaiselmer but worth a longer visit for its grand palaces, 15th century fort and the bazaar atmosphere of the old town. Another reason for staying is to check into the fabulous Umaid Bhawan Palace (Jodhpur 342006. Tel: 22316), six km from the station, which is a museum and a maharaja's home as well as an unusual and very stately hotel, actually built 1929–42. If its hallowed marble halls, filled with western classical music, are too intimidating, dive down to the basement for a swim in its subterranean pool reminiscent of the pool on the old *Queen Mary* liner and open to non-residents. Room rates, quoted in US dollars, start at $55 for a single, $78 for a Royal Chamber double and $178 for the Regal Suite.

KANNIYA KUMARI

You go to Kanniya Kumari (KK), Cape Cormorin, because it's there – at the tip of India where the Indian Ocean and the Arabian Sea meet the Bay of Bengal – and to see the sun rise. It is the Land's End of India and has probably the only station in the world with a specially-built sunrise observation roof and sunset and sunrise times posted in an information booth. The SS wears green epaulettes with gold stripes on his smart white uniform and proudly shows visitors around the station. There are two single retiring rooms (at Rs 20 each), two doubles (at Rs 30 per room) and one dormitory with eight beds (Rs 10 each); all are basic but convenient for the early-morning stint at the viewing platform. Since that faces east, for sunset and simultaneous moon rise on full moon days, head for the sea shore, within walking distance. September to January is the best time; March 15 to July 15 is the period of summer vacation so KK, which is really rather seedy, is packed then.

Separate counters cater for ladies and gents bookings in the station lobby. The reservation counter is open 0800–1200 and 1400–1600 but it is advisable to fix up your reservations before coming here because of limitations, or check with the SS. Not many trains come to KK because it is the absolute terminus, but every afternoon the 81 KK express completes the 2149 km journey from Bombay. It leaves for the return trip before sunrise and takes almost 48 hours to reach Bombay VT. There are three other daily arrivals/departures, all passenger trains, from/to Nagercoil Jn, Tirunelveli Jn and Trivandrum Central. Once a week the superfast 907 Jammu Tawi Express comes from Kashmir and starts its return the same day (see *Jammu Tawi* entry for details).

LONAVLA

Situated 127 km out of Bombay on the line to Pune and beyond (to Madras or Goa), Lonavla is a small station you may not notice except when the train stops for an extra engine to be added for the haul through the hills. At 625 m above sea level, it is a hill resort popular as an escape from Bombay's heat; it gets chilly in winter. You alight here for the 2,000 year-old Buddhist caves at Karla (10 km). The station forecourt is small and the station building barely seems to be a station at all. There is a booking office inside but the main platform is the centre island platform, number 2. There are no retiring rooms and few facilities. The 1st Class waiting room has a fine dressing table from the British period which looks out of place in its drab surroundings. Foreigners are rare at this station and should seek out the SS (his office is on platform 2) for any special requirements.

Trains from Bombay VT and Dadar stop here and so does the 301 Deccan Queen every evening from VT station, taking just over two hours for the journey. As well as being well-served by commuter trains, there are direct trains from Bangalore City (130 Udyan Express), Hyderabad (number 32), Secunderabad (102 Minar Express), Kanniya Kumari (82 KK Express) and from Madras and Miraj (with connections from Vasco da Gama).

Lonavla has some lively eateries, and is famous for its sweet confection, *chikki*. A tourist information bureau is near the station, and there are several places to stay at reasonable rates within its vicinity. The Fariyas Holiday Resort (PO Box 8, Frichley Hill, Lonavla 410401. Tel: 2701) is four km from the station set in landscaped gardens. There are no TVs in the rooms 'to encourage guests to use the public areas' and there are two restaurants, a club-style bar and a coffee shop gallery overlooking the interior swimming pool. Suites are exotically decorated, one has a swing seat in its parlour, but rooms are small. Rates are from Rs 850 for a double.

Lonavla station enquiries: Tel: 2215.

LUCKNOW

There are two stations at Lucknow (at Charbagh, three km from down town), both in the same compound but otherwise quite different in facilities and atmosphere. The main one is the stone building with dozens of turrets that symbolizes Lucknow for the visitor. A stone set into the wall of the station proclaims: 'Within this turret wall was laid on the first day of August, 1925, by G.I. Colvin, Esq. CB, CMG, DSO, agent of the East Indian Railway, a casket containing current coin with newspapers of the day to commemorate the successful completion of the foundations of the building'.

That is one of the few signs in English. The lobby of the station is hung with signs in Hindi, including one saying enquiry office, so you'll have to ask for it unless you can read Hindi. There is no special counter to deal with foreign tourist reservations but the reservation officer has a counter next to the enquiry office (by the grand staircase leading to platforms 2 to 7). The reservation office, on the left of the lobby, is open 0800–1400 and 1430–1930 daily; you pick your way over sleeping bodies to get to it. The platforms of this station are notable for their filth. There is an Uttar Pradesh tourist bureau in the lobby which might be open 0730–1930 but wasn't when I visited. The station staff say not many foreign tourists come to this station so they don't cater for them. There are retiring rooms up a grim, lavatorial staircase, where bed, tea, four biscuits, a newpaper, towel and soap are included in the price of Rs 60 a double.

The waiting rooms, off platform 1 (which is where the retiring room booking office is located) have retained their original ornate green wall tiles. A dormitory close by has 35 beds, another (upstairs) has 16 (Rs 20 each). The Tarana self-service restaurant (open 0600–2200) has a wall of 1930s mirrors; it also has a private dining room furnished like an Indian stereotype with couches, hukka water-pipe and fringed lamp shades. The menu says: 'Enjoy the traditional hospitality of OUDH at our air-conditioned de luxe dining room. Pay Rs 3 extra per passenger and have a spicy bite in a luxurious musical environment. The

Northern Railway Station, Lucknow, brings the ultimate convenience'. Chicken curry costs Rs 12 here (that's less than a US dollar).

Lucknow's other station, run by North Eastern Railway, is called **Lucknow Jn** and used to be exclusively MG, now three platforms are BG. It is situated on the left of the forecourt of the main station and has had a face-lift and false turrets added to make it a scaled-down version of its neighbour. It is compact and neat, and is being upgraded to a model station. This includes solar hot water heaters installed to serve the retiring rooms which are on the first floor; Rs 20 for a dorm bed rising to Rs 150 for a double AC room. Also on this floor are the waiting rooms and veg restaurant. The non-veg one, called Coffee Corner by its Hindi sign, is at the end of the MG platforms (4, 5 & 6). It is like a coffee bar and a pleasant place to watch the station parade. Potted plants have been placed on the platforms and in the forecourt to give the station a pleasing appearance.

There is a tourist assistance counter in the concourse which also serves as a complaint and enquiry desk. Tourists should start there since there is no counter for tourist reservations in the lobby where the booking office is located. The SS will personally help with any problems travellers have. Despite the presence of people asleep during the day on most available floor space, this station is cleaner and more efficient than its grand neighbour.

There is also a station called **Lucknow City**, about six km away. No trains originate there and only some halt there on the way to and from the main Lucknow stations. Since it is served by trains of Northern and North Eastern Railways, Lucknow has many direct connections with northern India. It is on the line from New Delhi (507 km) and trains stop here on the way to/from Gorakhpur (276 km), New Jalpaiguri (1118 km) and Guwahati (1541 km). The fastest from New Delhi is the 510 Avadh Assam Express which leaves ND at 0900 and arrives at 1740. From Bombay VT there is a superfast express (number 933) which takes 26 hours for the 1414 km trip via Bhopal and Jhansi.

Several trains a day link Lucknow with Varanasi (302 km). The 9/10 Doon Express stops here on its run between Howrah and Dehra Dun, as do the 173/174 Himgiri Expresses (three times a week) and the daily 51 Express between Howrah and Jammu Tawi. There is a nightly MG service between Agra Fort and Lucknow (486 km/13 hrs) by the 513/514 Marudhar Express, while the Ganga Yamuna Express serves Agra Cantt and Lucknow every night too.

Lucknow station, NR enquiries: Tel. 51234. NER enquiries: Tel. 51433.

MADGAON (GOA)

Madgaon is the official name for this station but people refer to it as Margao. It used to be recommended as the railhead for Goa's capital,

Panaji, but now its bus station has been moved 5 km from the station, it is best to stay on the train to Vasco da Gama (qv) and get a bus there. You're near the tourist area at Madgaon station, obvious from its signs warning passengers 'not to entertain touts'.

MADURAI

The sigh of steam is often heard at Madurai station as 24 of its 42 trains a day are steam hauled. They are the local passenger trains; all the 18 expresses are diesel. Madurai is an MG station but buildings are being put up for the day when it will be served by BG trains. The present station, remodelled in 1979, was being re-remodelled at the end of 1988. On the left of the large entrance lobby are the 2nd Class booking counters, with upper class in a separate section on the right, open 0930–1300 and 1400–1700. Foreign tourists should begin their enquiries at the Rail Tourist Information Counter (open 0600–1800) since there is no special counter for them. This is opposite the lobby entrance, next to the Tamil Nadu information office (0700–2000).

The facelift to Madurai station includes improvements to the retiring rooms which are reached by a flight of stairs from platform 1. (There are four platforms.) Ten double rooms (Rs 50 each, AC room Rs 80), two family rooms and two dormitories (Rs 10 a bed) are here. There is no water available from 2200 to 0500. The rooms open onto a long gallery overlooking the station forecourt, with the bathrooms (western style) backing onto the station roof.

Station facilities include a large 2nd Class waiting hall, a vegetarian restaurant with a 'Tiffin and Coffee Section' (open 0430–1000, 1700–2130) and a 'Meals Section' (open 1830–2130). The booking hall has drawings of trains above the reservation charts so that passengers can identify their carriages. There is also a diagram of the station showing its facilities. Madurai itself, for all its bustle, has a certain raffish charm. It is dominated by the Meenakshi Temple complex with its orange and black vertical striped walls around which traffic swirls. It is a determined shopper's haven, as well as a focal point for pilgrims.

The best hotel in town is the 20 year-old Pandyan Hotel (Race Course, Madurai 625002. Tel: 42470) at five km from the station. The ceilings of its corridors are low, its rooms large and centrally air-conditioned with local style bathrooms and western toilets. Doubles cost from Rs 500. There is a 'permit room' but this would appeal only to the desperate drinker.

The hill resort of Kodaikanal is 120 km by road from Madurai station and a tourist leaflet advises visitors to wear 'tweed and flannel' during the day. The closest rail access is Kodaikanal Road, but that's actually 80 km from it. There is a rail booking office at Kodaikanal run

by a licensee. A jaunt for steam fanatics is the 3 hrs 40 mins daily run by passenger train to Bodinayakkanur, famous as a cardamom centre. Important trains serving Madurai are listed in Chapter 9.
Madurai station: Tel. 24535.

MALDA TOWN

Clinging to the edge of West Bengal, above Bangladesh, Malda Town is the last major station in the Eastern Railway zone before the Northeast Frontier zone station of New Jaipalguri. Its attraction is that it is small and friendly with ticket collectors who wear ties and uniform jackets and smile, and a passenger information centre that actually helps instead of staff merely repeating train times by rote.

My regard for Malda Town began when, having sent a message ahead for soda water, I was met at the carriage door by the SS and his traffic inspector who both apologized for there being none available. At another station, my message would probably have been ignored. Since I was feeling pretty rotten, I decided to stay.

The station was built in the 1960s and is in the process of being modernized. On the first floor there are two non AC retiring rooms with two beds (Rs 36 per room) and one AC room (Rs 70) and two dormitories of four beds in each, at Rs 11 per bed. The roof of the station at the end of the corridor has been converted to a terraced garden with a forest of plants in pots. Access to the rooms is by stairs alongside the passenger information counter and the reservations office. Since my stay at Malda Town was unscheduled, unannounced and on impulse, and it was a Sunday night, I was very impressed by the help I received.

The reservation office opens 0900–1330 and 1600–1930 and is on the right of the small entrance lobby. The 2nd Class waiting hall, not very comfortable, is on the left; the 1st Class waiting room shows its need for modernization. There are signs in English as well as Hindi and Bengali for the various facilities. The station is two km from downtown where there is the West Bengal Tourist Development Corporation operated Malda Tourist Lodge (Malda, West Bengal. Tel: 2213). A non AC double room, of retiring room standard, costs Rs 70, and Rs 130 for AC double. A sign in reception says 'Lunch/dinner compulsory'.

The town is also called English Bazaar, a name derived from Englezabad; it dates from 1680. The station is on the line between Calcutta and New Jalpaiguri, and between Delhi and Guwahati as well as Howrah and Guwahati. On a gruesome note, look down out of the window as the train approaches the next station of New Farakka and you'll see the bloated bodies of the dead bobbing against the sluice gates where the railway bridge spans the holy Ganga river.

MANGALORE

There are three retiring rooms at Mangalore, on the first floor gallery overlooking the booking hall. The rooms are compact and clean with twin beds, a western style bathroom and hot shower, Rs 50 for 24 hours. There are also eight beds in a large, well ventilated room at Rs 15 each. The station has lots of reading matter on its noticeboards with one advising on 'Guidelines for passenger grievances'. The booking office is open 0200–2210, with separate queues for ladies and gents, and the advance reservations office opens 0900–1300, 1400–1700. There is no special desk for foreigners but instructions are that they should have priority; if no berths are available efforts are made to accommodate them through the emergency quota.

The station is the terminus for both broad gauge (two platforms) and metre gauge (one platform). The BG line follows the Malabar coast northwards from Shoranur (see Chapter 11) and is linked with Madras by the daily 27/28 West Coast Express and the 1/2 Madras Mail. The MG line, sometimes closed through landslides, provides a spectacular ride through the western ghats to Hassan. Access to the town at Mangalore station is easier from the end of platform 2 or 3 than from the main entrance/exit.

A note on **Hassan**, a small country station where you can make a connection by steam passenger train to Mysore and Bangalore. Hassan has an advance reservation counter nominally open from 0900–1200, 1400–1900 but general tickets are only on sale 30 minutes before a train's departure. Hassan is 189 km from Mangalore and 119 km from Mysore and the station has few facilities. However, a short walk (100 m) to the left outside it, and you'll find the Navarang Bar Restaurant. It's very much a local dive with six private cubicles and an amazing range of chilled beers at low prices and plates of mutton, chicken or fish at Rs 6 each. Foreigners are rare and made especially welcome.

A bell is rung on the station 30 minutes before the train is due to arrive and the sight of the engine puffing steam as it approaches the platform is an exciting one. The 2nd Class compartments have wooden seats, and a toilet at both ends of the carriage. The two 1st Class compartments are colonial parlours and each has an attached private toilet with a wooden seat. When I took the Arsikere to Mysore passenger train, number 861, which left Hassan at 1605 it stopped frequently in the middle of paddy fields to pick up workers who flagged it down. The engine driver waved back at children greeting us as we steamed through hamlets. At Mandagere the train stopped for the engine to take on water and the driver descended with his oil can to lubricate the pistons. We arrived at Mysore 35 minutes late, but it didn't seem to matter.

Puri, Orissa, with Jaganath temple, one of the four holiest cities in India, and the centre for the Car Festival held each June/July to celebrate the journey of Krishna from Goleul to Mathura. (Anthony J. Lambert)

Sunrise on the Taj Mahal, as seen from across the Yamuna River, Agra. (Hugh Ballantyne)

Pilgrims at the Ganga River, Varanasi. (Hugh Ballantyne)

MIRAJ

The signs at Miraj station give an idea of the place: 'This way to the Railway Police Station', 'Do not exhibit your valuables and ornaments while sleeping or sitting near the window', and 'To be safe from pickpockets, take care of your luggage'. There is a disturbing atmosphere about the place and the 30 minute wait here while changing trains to/from Vasco da Gama and Bombay will be ample for most travellers. If you want something else to look at, there are some attractive ceramic tiles fronting the counter selling soft drinks. The metre gauge and broad gauge tracks serve different sides of the same platform. There are retiring rooms here but the less said about them the better.

MYSORE

From the outside it is difficult to know that Mysore station really is a station. Built during the days of maharajas it is on palatial lines with a domed clock tower and wide verandahs on its first floor. The platforms barely rise above the level of the metre gauge track and a road used to run onto the main platform to allow the maharaja to drive right up to his private carriage. The main lobby has the booking office (open 0400–2300) and a pay toilet (.25p). A separate lobby leads to the advance reservations counters (0730–1330, 1400–2000) with an enquiry desk where the needs of foreign travellers are attended to promptly. A display cabinet shows photos of the stunning Western Ghat rail journey – the Emerald Route – from Hassan to Mangalore.

The main platform is wide and clean with Victorian cast iron pillars (down the inside of which the rain runs) supporting the roof and adding to its period appearance. Zinc-topped tea counters do a brisk business alongside the V and NV restaurants which are only open during train departures. A wheelchair and self-help trolleys are available, and there is a bathing cubicle on the island platform. A dormitory of 10 beds, each with its own locker (bring your own padlock) is at platform level.

The retiring rooms are on the first floor and are rated the best in the Southern Railway zone. They have high ceilings and a walk-around verandah with a view of the pretty station forecourt on one side and steam trains shunting on the other. Number 1 has been air-conditioned yet it was built with high arched doors and windows that, pre-AC, could be opened to catch the breeze from different directions. A private staircase leads to the forecourt or into the station. The rooms cost Rs 50 and Rs 75 (AC) a double, and a dorm bed is Rs 15.

Mysore is renowned as a leisurely city, famous for its jasmine, maharaja's palace, zoo, and government sandalwood oil and silk factories. The Brindavian Gardens and Krishnarajasagar Dam are 19 km distant by road. The main way to get to Mysore by rail is via Bangalore (139 km) from where there are daily expresses taking about 3½ hours. Other routes are from Mangalore (qv) via Hassan or from Arsikere (also via Hassan). You can get to Mysore from Goa via Arsikere instead of via Bangalore. The station is also linked by MG passenger train to Chamarajanagar (61 km/2 hrs 20 mins). There is only a road link with Ooty (Udagamandalam).

Mysore station enquiries: Tel. 20100.

Rail museum

Walk to the end of the platform at Mysore station, cross the track to the Krishnarajasagar Road and follow the curve of the road northwards for about 100 metres and you will find the entrance on your right to the Regional Rail Museum. It's open every day, except Monday, from 1000 to 1300, then 1500 to 1900. Admission tickets are sold from a guard's brake van that came from an old goods train; camera permits cost Rs 5, and Rs 15 for a movie camera. The museum was set up in 1980 as the first (so far there are no others) regional display of India's railway heritage. It is small and seems somewhat neglected although its gardens are well maintained and it is a fascinating place to visit. A guide booklet is available.

The Chamundi Gallery houses a series of paintings and photographs about the history of the railways. The adjacent Sriranga Pavilion is home to two coaches which formed part of the royal train of the Maharaja of Mysore; the Maharani's saloon, built in 1899, and the kitchen/dining car, built in 1914. (The Maharaja's saloon is at the Rail Museum in Delhi.) These coaches are adjustable to BG or MG track. The saloon is complete with platform and brass railings, bedroom, bath and lavatory, luggage room and servants quarters. Rail bygones in the gallery include a Theobold's Block instrument used before 1929 between Dodjala and Devanahalli stations on the NG line, and a Mysore State Railway clock, made in New York in 1889. Wooden pillars, doors and balustrades from the old Srirangapatna railway station were used in the construction of the gallery itself.

In the grounds are various MG and NG steam engines and a coach, built in 1927, from the Bangalore to Bangarapet NG line with bench type seating facing the sides, not forwards, and its special dog box. The oddity is an Austin motor car, adapted to run on rails as an inspection vehicle. A battery operated electric mini-train, built at the Mysore Railway Workshop mostly out of scrap metal, runs on a small circular track to provide a joy ride for children.

The Mysore Rail Museum, K.R.S. Road, Mysore, 570001.

PATNA

Patna Jn station is one where foreign tourists have to go to the office of the CRS if they want help in securing reservations since there are neither counters, nor signs, for foreigners. This is odd since for foreigners arriving from Nepal this can be their first major railway station. The advance reservation building is at the side of the main entrance and is rather gloomy. The main lobby has counters for 1st Class reservations for that day, and for platform tickets. There is an enquiry stage with clerks standing on it and shouting information like auctioneers to the crowd below them. A novel feature is the noticeboard displaying photos of the station employees of the month; the best employee wins Rs 500.

The original station was built in the 19th century but the current ugly building dates from 1939 with extensions added in the 1960s. As a junction its importance stems from the meeting of the Patna–Gaya branch line with the main and chord lines of Eastern Railway; trains both terminate and transit here. It has seven platforms and a combined veg/non-veg restaurant with a base kitchen that can prepare 1,000 casserole meals a day.

The retiring rooms are upstairs from platform 1. They are small, airless cells, some with AC, at Rs 100 a double. Two dormitories have 10 beds in each, at Rs 20 a bed. A notice, which you can disbelieve, says 'Check out is at 1200 am'. A roof garden is opposite rooms 1 to 7 with the 2nd Class waiting hall (like an underground car park for human bodies) below. There is a Bihar Department of Tourism kiosk in the station with useful maps of Patna and information on the town's sights. The 7.5 km road bridge, opened in 1983 linking north with south Bihar over the Ganga, is one of them.

Buses to Raxaul, four km from the Nepal border, cross this bridge at the start of their six hour journey from Patna. It is possible to get to Raxaul by train via Muzaffapur from where the 51 Express leaves at 0815 and arrives at Raxaul at 1245 daily. From Patna, via Barauni and Muzaffapur to Raxaul, the fare is Rs 168, 1st Class, and Rs 47 for 2nd Class. It's a complicated journey and actually there are direct trains to Muzaffapur from Delhi, such as the 510 Avadh Assam Express.

Patna is on the main New Delhi to Calcutta line and is served by the trains (except Rajdhani Express) linking those cities. It is 992 km from Delhi (about 15 hours train time) and 545 km from Calcutta (about nine hours). The superfast 922 North East Express from New Delhi to Guwahati stops at Patna as does the 156 Tinsukia Mail from Delhi and the 945 Bombay–Guwahati Express. The 914 Chhapra/Bombay and the 169 Bhagalpur/Bombay Expresses also call here. From Madras there is a once a week service by 943 Madras/Patna Express (2147 km/42 hrs). Patna is also served by trains from Amritsar, Bokaro Steel City, Dehra Dun, Dhanbad, Gwalior, Hatia, Jammu Tawi,

Ranchi, Samastipur, Tatanagar and Vijayawada. Patna's other station is Patna Saheb, the old City station, at which most trains to and from Patna stop. A tip for non-smokers: the 87/88 South Bihar Express linking Patna and Tata is unusual in having a non-smoking carriage for 2nd Class (3 tier) passengers.

Patna is popular with Buddhist tourists, especially Japanese and many Japanese groups stay at the Welcomgroup Maurya-Patna Hotel (South Gandhi Maiden, Patna 800001. Tel: 22067). A basic, Indian-style 5 star hotel for guests who don't stay very long, the hotel has a bank with a foreign exchange counter. Rooms start at Rs 610.

Patna Jn station enquiries: Tel. 22012.

PONDICHERRY

The Union Territory of Pondicherry comprises four enclaves in three South Indian states: the seaside towns of Pondicherry and Karaikal in Tamil Nadu, Yanam in Andhra Pradesh and Mahe (see Chapter 11) in Kerala. From 1814 the territory was French, merging with the rest of independent India in 1954. The new town of Auroville is 10 km from Pondicherry station. The station building is being remodelled, in keeping with the development of the town as a cultural and industrial centre.

Only two trains a day go to Pondicherry, both steam from Villupuram (38 km). The 631 leaves Villupuram at 0500 and arrives at 0700, and the 633 leaves Villupuram at 1805 arriving at 1915. These trains depart from Pondicherry at 0815 (632) and 2030 (634). Getting to Pondicherry from Madras Egmore by train is possible, but it's a long journey via Villupurum (leave Madras by 109 at 2140, arrive Pondicherry at 0700) and the only sleepers are in 1st Class. However, buses leave Madras Egmore bus station every half hour for the 160 km journey by good, broad road. As Villupuram has rail links with towns in the south which are worth visiting (such as Trichy and Madurai) it would be possible to make a side trip to Pondicherry when you pass through Villupuram on the way to Madras Egmore, instead of from it.

PUNE

The approach to Pune by rail with its shanties close to the track doesn't prepare you for the spacious sweep of the station building, extravagantly designed and built in 1925. The black, marble-faced columns of the entrance lobby sparkle in the sodium lights at night. The station has won the Central Railway shield for General Appearance, Cleanliness and Tidiness nine times since it was first awarded in 1946;

the most recent was in 1987. A statue of the unmistakable figure of Ghandi seen from the rear greets the traveller emerging from the station. Buses to the city and suburbs are available a few minutes walk to the right of the forecourt.

The 2nd Class reservations office and waiting hall are in a separate building to the side of the forecourt. 1st Class reservations are dealt with at a counter off the entrance lobby, open 0900 to 1630. The waiting rooms, with showers, are on the first floor. The non-veg restaurant has cowboy movie style swing doors, and antique wood and glass fronted almirahs serving as crockery cupboards. There is a dormitory ('Janata Room') on the same floor with hot water showers and eight beds at Rs 15 each. Included in the cost (Rs 70) of a twin bed room are afternoon tea, shoe-shine and morning paper.

Pune (don't pronounce it to rhyme with prune; it's Poona still) is an agreeable town at 549 m above sea level. There is a tourist information centre at the station. Express and commuter passenger trains link it with Bombay VT. Fast trains such as the superb Deccan Queen (see Chapter 11) do the 192 km journey in 3½ hours, others like the Sinhagad or the Deccan Expresses take over four hours. A separate service of EMU trains runs between Pune and Lonavla and there is also a Pune/Daund shuttle service. The 178 Jhelum Express from Jammu Tawi (qv) terminates here, and the station is served by regular trains from Bangalore, Kanniya Kumari, Kolhapur, Madras, Nagpur, New Delhi, Secunderabad, Trivandrum and Vasco da Gama (via Miraj).

Pune station enquiries: Tel. 67333.

PURI

Puri is known for its annual chariot festival and as a seaside temple city lapped by the waters of the Bay of Bengal. Peak periods are during the winter months, and the summer and autumn vacations. The South Eastern Railway Hotel (Chakratirtha Rd, Puri. Tel: 2063) was established in 1925 and its traditional style has its admirers; single rooms start at Rs 285. Retiring rooms at the station cost Rs 46, double, Rs 12 for a dorm bed. The sun temple at Konark is 28 km from the station, reached by road.

Trains originating and terminating at Puri include the 915/916 superfast Puri/New Delhi (Nizamuddin) Express four times a week, the 175 Puri/ Nizamuddin Neelachal Express (three times a week) and the daily 77/78 Kalinga Utkal Express also between Puri and Nizamuddin (2,142 km). There are daily expresses from/to Howrah. Connections to Madras are made at Bhubaneswar (qv).

Puri station enquiries: Tel. 2065.

QUILON

People come to Quilon Jn to get away from it, either by backwaters' boat to Alleppey or by MG train (No. 762) to Madurai. The station has a long main platform with a variety of unattractive rest and refreshment rooms. There are six single (at Rs 20) and two double (at Rs 30) retiring rooms. An air of neglect hangs over the station. It is a compulsory stop for BG expresses to/from Trivandrum and the beginning of the single track MG line that cuts inland to Sengottai. You can get here direct from many stations (see Chapter 9) and terminating trains include the 105 Quilon MG Mail from Madras Egmore and the 761 Quilon MG Express which wends its way overnight across the south via Madurai (qv) from Tiruchchirappalli (qv).

RAMESWARAM

Although this station on an island at the tip of India was remodelled in 1986, the sea air, sand, dust and pilgrim traffic have given it a sad appearance. A passenger arriving here by ferry (currently suspended) from Sri Lanka would find it a depressing sight and unlike other stations of Southern Railway. There are 12 retiring rooms built in a block alongside the station and, according to the SS, they are the only rooms for tourists in Rameswaram which have water 24 hours a day. They cost Rs 30 a double with fan and basic bathroom facilities. There is a waiting room for ladies on the station, kept locked and opened on request, and a large room for upperclass passengers. A combined fruit and non-veg stall sells quick meal packets and there is also a veg refreshment room.

There are four reservation counters (0700–1300, 1330–1800) on the right of the entrance lobby and a notice saying the Indrail Pass is on sale. When the ferry brings passengers from Sri Lanka, the SS reckons to sell 150 passes a year. There is a tourist office here with details of trips around Rameswaram. A devout Hindu who visits Benares (Varanasi) is expected to visit Rameswaram also for the culmination of his quest for salvation, hence its popularity with pilgrims. Buses are available from the railway station to various places on the island. Until the road bridge opened recently (and it is a magnificent sight from the rail crossing), train or boat was the only means of getting to Rameswaram. Direct train links are from Coimbatore and Madras Egmore, via MG stations in the south.

Although the ferry is suspended, I was able to hitch a ride on a shunting steam engine to Rameswaram Port station. This is a cluster of sheds and palm-thatched huts which on ferry days handles about 800 passengers. They can spend up to six hours in squalid conditions, watched by desperate-eyed residents, waiting to be processed for either the train or the boat to depart. Even when the ferry is operating again, I would advise foreign tourists to continue to fly between Sri Lanka and India instead.

RANCHI

Ranchi station, originally exclusively narrow gauge, had BG added in 1961 and is now subject to a 'modelization' programme. Fortunately, the one-storey Lego-like façade from the early years of this century is being retained, as are the candy-striped awnings of wood over the cages within which are the sole retiring room (two beds; Rs 50), the dormitory (four beds; Rs 12 each) and the ladies waiting room, all with bathroom facilities. The veg and non-veg refreshment rooms which have an ancient look are to go and there will be new reservation and ticket offices. The present ones are open 0800–1330, 1430–2000.

It is worth a visit to Ranchi station for its narrow gauge, miniature wooden carriages pulled by steam engines (see Chapter 11) and to see the Highline Transhipment system of transferring freight from NG to BG. NG wagons loaded with bauxite are shunted up a ramp and onto a track built over a BG line. The BG wagons are shunted underneath then the floors of the NG wagons are opened and the bauxite falls into the BG wagons below. There is a steam loco shed here housing 16 NG steam engines of the ZE type (see Chapter 8). The oldest (No. 95) in operation entered service in 1931; the others in the 1950s. As well as pulling the two passenger trains a day which go to Lohardaga, they haul goods trains on the same line. Hatia station (seven km away) is the main depot for Ranchi's BG trains.

There are direct services to Ranchi from Madras by the 89 Bokaro Steel City Express which takes nearly 37 hours for the approximately 1670 km journey northwards, and from Howrah by the 15 Hatia Express which leaves at 2115 and arrives the next day at 0645. There are also trains from Patna, the 23 Patna/Hatia Express (11 hrs) and the daytime 93 Patna/Hatia Express (9 hrs). From Gorakhpur, the 28 Maurya Express takes just over 24 hours for the 929 km journey.

At Ranchi station there is a noticeboard with a list of places of interest in and around Ranchi, mostly hills, lakes and falls. A tourist bureau is soon to open at the station and the tourist literature describes Ranchi as a 'popular hill station'. Whatever it may have been in the past, it is hardly that now. It has become an industrial centre without much charm, the change being wrought by bauxite and iron ore.

However, the hill station atmosphere (it's 629 m above sea level) is retained in the South Eastern Railway Hotel (Station Road, Ranchi, Bihar. Tel: 21945), one of only two railway hotels in India (the other is at Puri). It is reached by crossing the NG line and strolling through a garden of healthy lawns and shade trees to its bungalow verandah entrance. 22 rooms are grouped in cottage units with red tiled roofs and wide galleries, built in 1915. They cost from Rs 210 single, AP. There are coal fires in the public rooms in winter. The bearers have resisted change and wear the uniform and brass cap badge of the Bengal Nagpur Railway.

SECUNDERABAD

Secunderabad is the HQ of the South Central Railway which serves six states: Andhra Pradesh, Maharashtra, Karnataka, Goa, Madhya Pradesh and Tamil Nadu (well, 8 route km of it). Its zone stretches from Kakinada in the east to Goa in the west, linking the Bay of Bengal with the Arabian Sea. The HQ building, Rail Nilayam, has a vintage 1905 NG locomotive called Sir Alec, on display outside it.

Secunderabad station has a tourist office run by the Andhra Pradesh Tourist Development Corporation on its main platform but most of the tourist attractions are in its twin city of Hyderabad (qv). To get a taxi at Secunderabad station for a tour, you must ask a traffic cop (they wear white shirts and khaki pants) since they are parked around a corner from the station entrance. An even more frustrating feature of this station is the location of its reservation office. From the station you turn right, walk to the bus station, then turn right again and enter a yard to find the building is close to the station platform, but there's no short cut. Don't try it with heavy luggage. However, once there, the token system cuts down queuing and computers process reservations speedily. Current bookings are made in the lobby of the station.

From the lobby a wooden staircase leads up to the first floor where there is the Kohinoor Restaurant, opened in 1978. It has fans and meals served on plates, not *thalis* or casseroles, but its atmosphere is gloomy and it seems a fancy name for a station restaurant. Adjacent are the retiring rooms off a flower-bedecked balcony. There is one AC suite (Rs 150) 13 double rooms (from Rs 50) and one single (Rs 30).

There are dozens of direct trains to Secunderabad from all parts of India, including Ahmadabad, Ajmer, Bhubaneswar, Cochin, Tirupati and Visakhapatnam. From Bombay VT, there is the daily 101 Minar Express, 14 hrs 20 mins for the 800 km journey, and from New Delhi, the fast (26 hrs 20 mins for 1665 km) daily 124 Andhra Pradesh Express. The fastest service from Madras (784 km) is by the 59 Charminar Express which takes 14 hours. From Howrah, the daily 45 East Coast Express completes the 1581 km trip via Bhubaneswar in just under 31 hours.

SHIMLA

Shimla station is located at 2,075 m above sea level and has a charm to match its breathtakingly beautiful setting. As well as the fascination of getting there (see Chapter 11), Shimla is a welcome destination after the hectic heat of Delhi. Citizens and visitors stroll through the town for the sheer pleasure of it, watched by monkeys who think they own the place, and by residents gazing from the balcony of the outside of the Amateur Dramatic Club's Victorian theatre. With snow-capped mountains of the Himalayas in the background and lush green valleys below, the town is not only spectacular but rich in a magical atmosphere. In his wonderful *Guide to Simla* (obtainable from his own Maria Brothers bookshop, straight out of *Kim*, on the town's Mall), Mr O.C. Sud, the author, speculates that the town's name, really pronounced Shimla despite its occasional spelling of Simla, comes from *Shamla*, meaning 'Blue Female' another name for the goddess Kali.

Shimla has almsot 150 hotels and guest houses but there is only one which captures its essence (and one of the few with a bar): the Oberoi Clarke's Hotel (The Mall, Shimla. Tel: 6091). The rooms have the comfortable feel of the 1930s with views of the forest-clad hills and the town. Rates are from Rs 650, single, and Rs 850, double, including all meals, which are superb. Since cars are not allowed, you will have to walk from the lift that takes you from the lower part of the town, near the station, to the Mall. The air always seems clean here despite the concentration of houses and people. The main season is April to June, September to October, and Christmas. But foreigners, drawn by Shimla's spell, visit year round.

An extra touch of the unexpected is provided by one of the drivers of the diesel locomotives on the Kalka/Shimla line. The beturbaned and bearded and meticulous Mr B.S. Gill is no ordinary engine driver; he is an accomplished artist who has had exhibitions throughout India and whose paintings, especially those of railways and landscapes, are much sought after. He lives at Beverley, Shimla 4, and has worked on the line since 1971. He carries colour slides of his paintings to show interested passengers and it is he who sketched the portrait of the author that appears in this book.

The ways to get to Shimla are shown in Chapter 9. As well as from New Delhi, it is also possible to reach Shimla from Jammu Tawi and from Howrah, via Ambala (qv) and Kalka.

Shimla station enquiries: Tel. 2915.

UDAGAMANDALAM

This station will always be known as Ooty, short for Ootacamund, by its fans. A summer resort since the days of the Raj and 'Queen of the Hill Stations', the town nestling in the Nilagiris, or Blue Mountains, may have lost its dignity (there are video games at the lake) but it is still relaxed and rural. You sense it on arrival at the station (for the journey there see Chapter 11) which, until its threatened moderniza-tion takes place, preserves a forgotten, leisurely style.

A spiral staircase leads to the retiring rooms (Rs 60 a double) furnished in the manner of a rustic boarding house with patterned sheets, thick red blankets, lived-in armchairs and hot water from a tap in the bathroom (no shower, only a plastic bin and a dipper). There are more rooms (Rs 25 a bed) adjoining the sole platform with access day or night since the station is always open. The popular veg restaurant can be entered from the platform or the forecourt. When I was having lunch there one day, a horse calmly trotted through one open door and out the other.

Although, at 2,203 m above sea level, the station is at the end of the line, its loco shed is only for stabling engines and carriages, the main yard being at Coonoor on the way up. Any reservation requirements should be discussed with the affable SS. The station has quotas to Madras, Cochin, New Delhi, Bilaspur and Ahmadabad. Ooty is 2,833 km, via Coimbatore, from New Delhi (1st Class fare is Rs 767, 2nd Class Rs 180), 1,924 km from Bombay VT (1st Class: Rs 557, 2nd Class: Rs 135), 394 km from Trichy (1st Class: Rs 171, 2nd Class: Rs 42) and 578 km from Trivandrum (1st Class: Rs 227, 2nd Class: Rs 58).

The town, bus station (for Mysore/Bangalore/Coimbatore) and race track are close to the station. Out of Ooty is better than in it, and what remains of the woods and downs can be enjoyed best by a stay (or at least a visit) to The Fernill Palace Hotel (Ootacamund. Tel: 3097 if it works).

It was formerly the summer palace of the Maharajah of Mysore and is now owned by his son. It is a rambling, dilapidated single-storey building dating from the 1880s with wonderful period furniture and carved teak decor, glass walled patios, flower gardens and vast lawns, and swarthy bearers wrapped in sweaters. All rooms are different reminders of a lost age and they all have hot water bathtubs or showers. Singles and doubles start at Rs 150 (Rs 300 in season April–June) up to Rs 800 (Rs 1200 in season) for the Maharajah's suite complete with swing. Bring warm woolies for the night although log fires are available in the bedrooms on demand. Camping is possible Rs 25 per person. From the hotel, you can walk the one kilometre to town along the railway line. In Commercial Road (take an auto from the station, 6 minutes) is Shinkows, a Chinese restaurant, where, in 1989, two of us had an enormous meal of steaming-hot meat and fish dishes with fresh Ooty cauliflowers and sweet peppers substituting for bean sprouts and bamboo shoots, plus piles of rice and noodles, for £2.00 (US$3.50).

UDAIPUR

The Udaipur City station building is nothing special to look at, especially when compared with the lavish beauty of the marble and crystal palaces of the city. It was built in 1963 but its drab exterior gives way to a station that's well run and a pleasure to visit. The large booking hall has counters well labelled in English with an enquiry window open daily 0500–1300 and 1400–2200, and a reservation window beside it, giving reservations on that day's trains until 1230. The CRS and the SS actively look for tourists in need of assistance.

There is an embankment of steps up from platform 1 to the exit and the booking office. Steps lead from the lobby to the retiring rooms. The dormitory has wooden screens around each of the ten beds but its (very clean) bathroom is next door; dorm beds cost Rs 12 each. A single room is Rs 18 and the sole twin-bedded room with attached bathroom and a terrace is Rs 35. Next to the rooms is a veg restaurant like an English tea room; it specializes in breakfast. Downstairs on platform 1 are snack bars which sell bottles of chilled mineral water.

The friendliness of Udaipur City station gives way to a city of magnificent palaces, at least two of which are extraordinary hotels. Photos of the Lake Palace Hotel (Pichola Lake, Udaipur. Tel: 23241) floating like a white marble wedding cake on the clear blue waters of Lake Pichola are instantly identifiable. Built on four acres of rock, in 1628, it was a royal retreat, converted by the Taj group in 1972 into a splendid hotel, reached by ferry five minutes drive from the station. It is a maze of courtyards, fountains, gardens, filigreed screens, marble pavilions, mirrors, inlaid ivory and pools. Rooms start at Rs 900 single, Rs 1,500 double up to Rs 5,000 for a suite and are worth every rupee, even if it's your last.

Even greater splendour is to be found on the mainland opposite, at the Shivniwas Palace Hotel (Udaipur, Rajasthan. Tel: 28239) which is still the residence of its maharana. The Imperial and Royal suites are only available by special approval but there are 14 rooms at Rs 600 a night. The priceless Crystal Room with its royal gallery and Belgian cutglass furniture is at the centre of this crescent shaped, fabulous palace.

This is Rajasthan, so choose your time to visit wisely; October to March is best. The easiest way to get to Udaipur by train is from Delhi (via Jaipur and Chittaurgarh), a distance of 739 km, by the 515 Garib Nawaz Express three times a week (as a portion of the 501 Pink City Express) or by the 15 Chetak Express which leaves Delhi every day at 1300 and arrives in Udaipur at 0915 the following morning. Other connections, such as from Bombay, are via Ahmadabad (297 km) from where the 44 Express leaves at 2315 and arrives at 0815, and the 86 Fast Passenger train leaves at 0640 and reaches Udaipur at 1635.

Udaipur station enquiries: Tel. 23471.

VARANASI

Considering the amount of foreign rail travellers who use Varanasi (formerly Benares), even arriving by charter flights from overseas, facilities at this station for tourists to make rail bookings are poor.

There is a counter (23) on the right after entering the booking hall with a sign that says 'Indrail Pass' and a list of destinations in Hindi. Do not be confused into thinking, as I did, that Indrail Pass holders can make reservations there. They can't, neither can foreign tourists buy a rail ticket, unless it is to one of the destinations listed in Hindi. Counter 23, open from 0800 to 1930 with lunch at 1400–1430, is for local reservations but during the hours of 1030–1600, the clerk will sell Indrail Passes. The sale is about two a month which shows the uselessness of the counter when every day there are foreign tourists queuing (frequently in the wrong line) to buy tickets or to make reservations. The CRS and the clerk at the Indrail counter claim to appreciate the problems foreigners have at Varanasi but say shortage of space and staff limit their ability to do anything about it. So the foreigner with an Indrail Pass or just wanting to buy a ticket, must join the long lines of people in front of the desired reservations counters.

In general, an air of indifference pervades Varanasi, a characteristic it shares with Lucknow, a station in the same Northern Railway division. However, there are bright features at the station. The Uttar Pradesh Tourist Centre, just by the office of the SS, has very helpful staff who not only dish out maps of Varanasi but also help foreigners with train reservations, which isn't their job. The retiring rooms are exceptional too, with 70 beds in doubles and dormitories from Rs 20 for a dorm bed to Rs 150 for a deluxe AC double with TV, fridge, morning tea and newspaper. The rooms, under the management of a dapper gentleman called Matron, are kept clean and have printed sheets which are changed after every occupant, even if only utilized for eight hours.

The station has four BG platforms and two MG (for trains of North Eastern Railway). Platform 3 is the main platform with BG on one side and MG on the other. The ladies waiting room there has an exquisitely tiled fireplace (not used); the gents is intolerable. The AC cafeteria above platform 1 seems to resent having customers during its 0600–2200 open hours; anyway it only serves snacks. People and dogs sleep unchallenged in areas reserved for ticket holders and cows wander through the booking hall and along platforms. If the sight of steam engines raises your spirits, Varanasi's MG services are operated by steam, as are 20 per cent of BG. How to get to Varanasi is detailed in Chapter 9. The other stations of Varanasi and Varanasi City are exclusively MG, run by NE Railway.

A hotel that advertises itself as 'within walking distance from the railway station' is the Taj Ganges (Nadesar Palace Compound, Varanasi. Tel: 42485), at least ten minutes walk from the station's back entrance. It does not have the luxury of major hotels but there is a swimming pool in a suburban garden setting, a tennis court and a jogging track; one restaurant. Rates are from Rs 800 for a double.

The most fascinating aspect of Varanasi is life on the river front at dawn. Hindu pilgrims inspired by their faith in life after death flock to the *ghats* (stepped embankments) on the river bank to perform ablution: a dip in the river and salutations to the sun. Sarnath, the venerated spot where Lord Buddha preached his first sermon after enlightenment, is 10 km by road from the station.

VASCO DA GAMA (GOA)

The main railway station from which to reach all parts of Goa is Vasco da Gama, known simply as Vasco and pronounced 'Barsco'. It's a mean looking station with few facilities although its atmosphere is friendly and the SS helpful. Its main neighbouring station is Madgaon (qv).

At Vasco there is a small reservation office with a counter for Indrail Pass holders and foreign tourists, shared with 1st class passengers. Tickets can be paid for in foreign currency and the day's exchange rate is displayed. The office is open from 0800 to 1200 and 1500 to 1700. The general booking office has opening hours of 0800 to 1400 and 1500 to 2300 and closes ten minutes before the departure of a train.

There are clean, if musty, retiring rooms in an annexe to the station, reached by climbing stairs from the end of the platform to a balcony that overlooks the station forecourt. The dorm has six beds. There is no restaurant at the station, only a tea counter, but since the town abounds in food kiosks, wine shops and restaurants with a western ambience, meals can easily be obtained.

Panaji is the capital of Goa, 30 km from Vasco which is the best station for reaching it since the bus park is opposite the railway station. Limited rail reservations can be made in Panaji at the Railway Out Agency.

Goa's airport is at Dabolim and although there is a station at Dabolim, it is a rural halt with no bus/taxi service so passengers bound for the airport should alight at Vasco. With more international flights going to Goa, Vasco Station is a good starting point to begin a rail journey. The Indrail Pass is sold at the station.

Vasco's rail access to the rest of India is by MG trains via Londa to Bangalore or, via Miraj, to Bombay. I prefer the link with Bangalore since no change of train is involved on the approximately 24 hour journey by the 201/202 Vasco/Bangalore Mail/Passenger train.

However, connections via Miraj for the change over from MG to BG trains are good and the complete trip between Bombay VT and Vasco takes around 21 hours. Trains serving Miraj and Bombay VT stop at Pune from where there is the daily Jhelum Express to/from Jammu Tawi via Agra Cantt and New Delhi.

Reports that the MG train is a boring/arduous way of getting to Goa are not to be believed if you enjoy mountain scenery and good company, but go 1st Class for comfort (there's no AC coach). The atmosphere livens up when the train crosses the Goa border and vendors swarm aboard selling beer and Goa's special tipple, *feni*, a cheesy smelling *eau de vie* made from the fruit of cashew nuts.

Goa is famous for its three fs: fish, football and, say the Goans, the third is left to your imagination. Actually, it's feni.

All trains going to Goa pass through Londa, and then the ghats begin: a range of magnificent green hills through which the train gropes along tunnels, or meanders over bridges with streams plunging below. After Caranajol station, you're in Goa and the hills soar into the distant clouds. Dudhsagar has a lookout tower to scan the lush depths of the valley and river below. Then after tunnel Number 11, the train emerges into heavy spray as it crosses perilously close to the Dudhsagar waterfalls. The track doubles back on itself giving a heart-wrenching glimpse of the moss covered railway bridge that spans the rush of the falls and seems so fragile beside the force of the water gushing under it.

The journey back through the ghats from Goa is, if anything, more spectacular, since an ancient steam engine is attached at Kalem to push the train up the hill. At Castle Rock it is detached while passengers have tea, if it's been ordered in advance.

In the season, a chair car is added on the daytime departure from Goa and the train makes a halt alongside the falls. You can spend the day there and return on the evening train. The shelter at the falls is 241 m above sea level with the falls plunging down from 100 m above that.

Although Vasco da Gama is the terminus of the line, there is a 4 km extension to Mormugao Harbour where a train goes every morning and evening. Accommodation at all rates is plentiful around Vasco. The nearest star-class hotel to the station and to the airport is the Oberoi Bogmalo Beach. Despite looking like a concrete monolith astride a sandy cove, it's comfortable and convenient.

Vasco da Gama station enquiries: Tel. 2398. Panaji Agency: Tel. 5620.

Chapter 11

Great Trips

Great trips by rail in India can be on the country's fastest train, by a maharaja's special, on a crack intercity express, on a trunk route, by a hill railway, in a private coach or on an ordinary 2nd Class passenger train chugging through magnificent scenery. Such is the diversity of Indian railways.

SHATABDI EXPRESS

This is India's equivalent of Japan's bullet train. It began service between New Delhi and Jhansi in July 1988 and has a speed potential of 140 km an hour, which makes it the fastest train in India. The train's electric loco, designated WAP-3, was made by the Chittaranjan Locomotive Workshop and the coaches by the Integral Coach Factory in Madras. The locomotives are of 4704 horse power fitted with six traction motors of 784 horse power each.

The Shatabdi Express was extended in 1989 to run on to Itarsi (instead of terminating at Jhansi). New timetable unknown at time of going to press. A non-stop train on the lines of the Shatabdi Express was planned in 1989 between New Delhi and Kanpur.

Timings:

No. 2002				No. 2001
0630	lv	New Delhi	ar	2215 ↑
0825	ar	Agra Cantt	lv	2010
0830	lv	Agra Cantt	ar	2000
0930	ar	Gwalior	lv	1850
0953	lv	Gwalior	ar	1847
↓1100	ar	Jhansi	lv	1745

Fares: (Rs)

	Adult	Child
New Delhi/Agra	110	55
New Delhi/Gwalior	140	70
New Delhi/Jhansi	165	85
Agra/Gwalior	70	35
Agra/Jhansi	95	50
Gwalior/Jhansi	65	35

Meals are included in the ticket price between New Delhi/Agra
Cantt/New Delhi. Reservation necessary. Indrail Pass (1st Class)
holders travel without extra charge but 2nd Class holders must pay a
supplement as the train is all AC Chair Car accommodation.

The seven royal blue coaches of the Shatabdi (Centenary) Express
wait every morning at New Delhi station for a full complement of 469
passengers. The train conductors in tailored light grey suits with blue
ties look smarter than their passengers. A notice on the platform
beside the train where a man stands with a bucket, reads 'Please
contact for free cleaning service'. He's there to clean any part of a
carriage that needs it, not to polish shoes.

Each coach has 69 grey rexine covered seats which recline by lever
control and have lots of leg room. There is a magazine pocket in the
back of the seat in front and a table which drops down for meal service.
You expect to be told to fasten your seat belt; instead Indian music
comes through the loudspeakers, and continues for the whole of the
journey.

Each seat is numbered. The layout is 3 × 2, three seats on one side
of the aisle and two on the other. The aisle links up with the other
carriages, but the passage between coaches has an awkward step up
and the doors are clumsy to open.

The coaches are air conditioned, often too cold, and also have fans.
Smoking is not permitted. A lighted sign in the coach indicates when
the toilets are occupied. These are western style with fan, toilet paper
and liquid soap, but no hand towel or tissues.

There is a galley in each coach, opposite the toilet, equipped with
gadgetry for boiling water, keeping food hot (meals are supplied by the
Delhi or Jhansi base kitchens), and for cooling drinks. Two bearers
serve in each carriage, with tea or coffee in individual flasks, on
demand.

On a trip to Agra, breakfast is included in the fare. Served from a
trolley, it is presented on a tray. The foil dish contains an omelette and
croquettes, or a potato patty with peas. There is also a plastic cup with
a tea bag, sachets of sugar and creamer, and of tomato ketchup, salt
and pepper, and a roll and butter. Plastic cutlery.

A veg or non-veg dinner, included in the fare, is served from Agra to
New Delhi; usually soup and two vegetable curries, dhal, rice and roti
with curd, or chicken masala. Snacks between Agra and Jhansi have to
be paid for.

The windows of the train are darkened so people can't see in and
this gives a brownish hue to the outside world as you speed through it.
The Shatabdi Express is a travel machine, an Indian land plane; clean,
fast and comfortable. It's a great trip that will impress you. Pity about
the music.

The Darjeeling Himalayan "toy train". (Anthony J. Lambert)

A Darjeeling Himalayan B Class 0-4-0ST, 779 with train, climbing near Gayabari. (Hugh Ballantyne)

The Palace on Wheels (M. D. Sharma)

Taj Express

For long the favourite way of getting from Delhi to Agra by train, the Taj Express has been downgraded to just another train in favour of the Shatabdi Express, even though it has kept its romantic name. It has no AC and is all chair seating. The 1st Class coach has 60 chair seats, in 2 × 2 layout. The other coaches are 2nd Class with 90 bench type seats in 2 × 3 format. There is a pantry car, with snacks and meals available from bearers passing along the aisle.

The Taj Express leaves New Delhi every day at 0705 and arrives at Agra Cantt at 0950, returning from Agra Cantt at 1845 and reaching New Delhi at 2200. Fares are 1st Class: Rs 95, and 2nd Class: Rs 32.

PALACE ON WHEELS

The romance of rail travel does still exist, for a price, in a train confusingly named *Palace On Wheels*. It's confusing because the name conjures up palatial luxury and that's not what passengers get for the fare of Rs 1,550 to Rs 2,800 per person per night. No, you can't use the Indrail Pass. Tickets must be purchased from a travel agent or as part of a holiday in India package, or from the Rajasthan Tourist Development Corporation (see page 158).

As a way of seeing the palaces of Rajasthan on wheels, this is the perfect train. Elephant, camel, bus rides and guided tours are included and for a week there is no need to change trains or worry about accommodation.

At 1900 hours every Wednesday evening from October to March, some 90 passengers gather at Delhi's Cantonment station and receive the first of many flower garlands at the beginning of an unforgettable week of touring by rail to some of the legendary sights of India. Two metre-gauge steam engines, one dubbed *Desert Queen*, both freshly hosed down and looking terrific, are waiting to haul the twenty cream coloured wooden coaches to Rajasthan. The passengers dine on board then retire to their cabins for the 2245 departure to Jaipur.

Inaugurated in 1981, this train has become renowned. Many people, usually those who have not been on it, speak in awe of its luxury, superb food and attentive service. Alas, the Palace On Wheels, whose passengers are described by station masters *en route* as POWs, does not live up to its name or fame even though it is composed of renovated coaches once used by maharajas as their palaces on wheels.

Each coach has been converted into sleeping accommodation and two bathrooms with western toilets and hand-held showers, which don't work when held high. Solution: fill the plastic bucket provided and use the plastic jug to pour water over yourself for a bath Indian style; don't worry about getting the floor wet, the water drains off.

Some of the cabins are called twin-bedded. In fact they have two lower berths and two upper ones which no amount of beautiful drapes

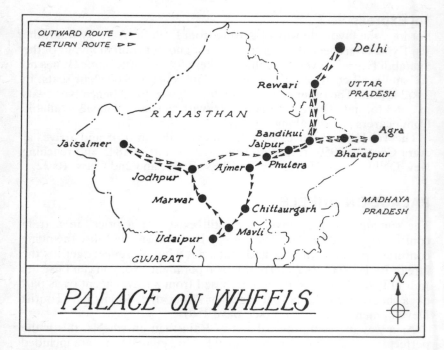

OUTWARD ROUTE ►►
RETURN ROUTE ▷▷

Delhi

Rewari

UTTAR
PRADESH

R A J A S T H A N

Bandikui

Agra

Jaisalmer

Jaipur

Bharatpur

Jodhpur

Ajmer

Phulera

Marwar

MADHAYA
PRADESH

Chittaurgarh

Udaipur

Mavli

GUJARAT

PALACE on WHEELS

N

The Desert Queen.

can convince are anything but cramped. The coupés, with lower berth and upper bunk, are small even for one person; two strangers sharing wouldn't be strangers for long.

There is no AC (except in the bar) and each cabin has fans and casement windows (without bars) that can be opened fully. There are reading lights, a call bell, piped music which can be switched off, and a shallow wardrobe for clothes. The mattresses are comfortable, the pillows hard. Because the coaches are old MG stock, they roll a bit at night so sleeping is not always easy.

There is a saloon/parlour/lounge in every coach where its occupants (sometimes as many as eight) take breakfast prepared in the coach's small galley. On the run through the desert to Jaiselmer, the saloon's windows have to be closed to stop the dust coming in. It still seeps through somehow.

There are two extravagantly refurbished restaurant cars with one even having a postage-stamp sized disco-lit dance floor. Lunch and dinner are served on the move or at isolated halts. Service is erratic with the courses coming in any order and all dished out by waiters onto the same plate instead of being served course by course. The food is good, but after the second night you realize it is the same all the time: a mishmash of rather bland Indian delicacies.

Because there is space only for 44 diners (20 in one car, 24 in another), there are two sittings. Meals can be served in the coaches if required. There is no corridor on the train so access to the restaurant (and to the bar) is possible only when the train stops. Beers and other drinks are available in each coach. The bar-cum-library car is a glorious creation of maroon curtains and plush velvet upholstery where the beer is served in souvenir tankards. This is the only train in India serving alcohol.

Each coach has a beturbaned captain and attendant who sleep in the galley to be on call at any time. Some have worked on the train since its first trip and know every trick. Perhaps that's why guests have to sign a chit for every biscuit and banana and piece of toast they consume. At the end of the tour, when it's time to leave tips, a box is placed in the library for them.

Once the tourists get over their disappointment of the train not being quite what they expected, they enjoy it. The steam engine is often replaced by diesel traction but that does not detract from the romantic adventure of travelling through desert landscape in coaches dating from the Edwardian days of the Raj. The coaches have been condemned as being too old to keep on running into the 1990s, so you'll have to hurry if you want to try this great trip.

The coaches
(All sleeping coaches have at least two bathrooms with shower and toilet.)

CT 3
The oldest carriage in the *Palace On Wheels* train is also the most sought after since it has the only four berth cabin with an *en suite* bathroom. It was originally built in 1889 for the Maharaja of Bikaner.

CT 34757, known as 814
One of the few carriages with a gallery, complete with polished brass rails. However, because of the gallery, the saloon is small, as are the three coupés. The tiny pantry has barely enough space for the fridge and carriage captain. It was built in 1907 for the Maharaja of Porbinder State.

CT 744
The lower berths in the three coupés of this carriage are divan beds with tapestry headboards but the upper berths are narrow. There is a large saloon with two settees. Originally built in 1910 for use by the Maharaja of Rajputana.

CT 7
Built in 1911 by Amjer workshop to form part of the Viceroy's train, this carriage has four small cabins; three are coupés and one has four berths.

CT 17
The saloon is large and regal in this carriage originally built in 1913. There are four small coupés.

CT 34756
The unusual feature of this carriage, built in 1917 for the Nizam State Railway for use by the Nizam of Hydrabad, is its lounge. It is in the centre of the carriage with two coupés on either side.

CT 9S
This coach also has a large lounge in its centre with coupés either side. It was built in 1922 in the Bhavnagar Works for use by the Maharaja of Nawanagar.

CT 10
Perhaps because it was rebuilt in 1953 from the original 1923 coach used by the Maharaja of Bikaner, this coach is spacious. The lounge has a big period mirror on one wall and two settees. The three coupés have lower beds with headboards.

CT 34755
Used by the Maharaja of Bhavnagar and built in 1929, this coach has a small gallery. There are four two berth cabins.

CT 20
Of 1930 vintage, this coach has a four berth cabin as well as three coupés, with headboards for the lower berths. It was used by the Maharaja of Rajputana.

CT 31R
Another coach of 1930s vintage built for the Maharaja of Udaipur. Now it has a small saloon and four coupés.

CT 2
Built in Ajmer for the Maharajas of Jaipur in 1936, the coach has a large lounge and doors that part in the middle to roll open and reveal the coupés, of which there are five.

CT 7S
This was built in 1935 at the Bhavnagar Workshop for the Maharaja of Bhavnagar. It has a large saloon with a glass fronted cocktail cabinet. There are three coupés and only one bathroom, but that's a large one.

CT 43
Built in 1937 for use by the Maharaja of Jodhpur, this is a favourite with the staff since the galley is large and there is a two berth cabin and a private toilet for them. The four coupés for passengers have headboards for the lower berths and this is the only carriage with blue tinted windows in its cabins. There is a narrow lounge but it has large period mirrors on opposite walls.

CT 99
The main restaurant car is a modern coach with a dining area for 24 passengers at four tables of four each, and four of two. There is an aisle between them leading to the service area and the galley. From the galley there is an enclosed tube linking it with the service area of the restaurant annex.

CT 33065
Built in 1910 for a maharaja's pilgrimage to Haridwar, this old coach has been converted into an annex to the restaurant car, with 20 covers. It is cramped but has a romantic atmosphere, as well as a disco-light set into the floor and a fridge and plate warmer by the door where there is a wide gallery overlooking the tracks. Food is passed to the coach through a tube connecting it with the pantry attached to the main restaurant car.

CT 16J
The library and bar coach was built in 1936 for the Maharaja of Jaipur and is hung with maroon velvet drapes. There are 25 seats in the bar

and 15 in the library. The two lounges are separated by the bar counter and a storeroom.

There are also two staff cars, converted from MG first class carriages, and two generator cars attached to the train.

RAJDHANI EXPRESS

The quickest way of travelling between Bombay or Calcutta and New Delhi by train is on one of the Rajdhani Expresses which reduces the journey time to under 18 hours. Fares are at least 25 per cent higher than on ordinary expresses, so you expect a great trip. But you are mainly paying extra for the speed which, together with the elimination of lots of stops, cuts several hours off the usual journey time.

The train is open only to passengers with reservations and no interlopers are allowed. There are three types of accommodation, all AC. Chair car consists of 70 seats in a 2 × 3 format. These are rexine covered and recline, with a foot rest, a table dropping down from the seat in front, and a magazine pocket. Ten chair cars are on the typical Rajdhani Express which testifies to their popularity. Personally, I would rather travel in a sleeper on an ordinary express than be confined to one of those seats for 18 hours.

Sleeper class on the Rajdhani Expresses is like the AC two tier coaches of ordinary expresses. The layout is the same although the outside berths have been designed with a table between facing seats. The carriages hold 45 passengers; their toilets are the same as on ordinary expresses.

There is a difference in 1st Class which have the most luxurious toilets of any long distance train in India: rubber tiled floors, real washbasins and liquid soap in a dispenser. There is even toilet paper in some. For sleeping, there are 18 berths in three cabins of four, and three of two. During the day, these are converted to sofa style seats with woven upholstery. There are flowers in the cabin and a small washbasin and mirror. At night, the beds are made up with crisp linen.

Music is piped throughout the train but in 1st Class this can be switched off. There is a stern announcement before departure warning that it is an offence to drink alcohol on the train and threatening 'detrainment' and prosecution for anyone caught doing so. Maybe that's why the service is so miserable. Lumbering, unshaven bearers are no surprise on an ordinary express, but they don't fit the image of speed and luxury that one pays for on the Rajdhani trains.

Service is non-existent from 2200 to 0600 when many of the crew (there are over 70 servicing the train) are to be found sleeping on the floor in the corridor. Meals and tea or coffee are included in the fare and only soft drinks have to be paid for.

So is the extra expense of travelling on the Rajdhani Express worth it? If you're in a hurry, yes; and it is a great trip when things go well. But you might have more fun on an ordinary express.

Rajdhani Express.

Fares for Rajdhani Express				
	Km	AC 1st	AC Slpr	AC Chair Car
			(In rupees)	
New Delhi to Howrah	1441	1320	710	355
New Delhi to Kanpur Cent.	439	585	315	175
New Delhi to Mughalsarai	782	890	485	255
New Delhi to Dhanbad	1182	1180	645	320
New Delhi to Bombay Cent.	1384	1295	700	350
New Delhi to Vadodara	993	1030	555	285
New Delhi to Ratlam	732	860	470	245
New Delhi to Kota	474	605	335	185
Bombay Cent. to Vadodara	392	540	295	160
Howrah to Dhanbad	259	405	230	125
Howrah to Mughalsarai	661	800	435	230
Howrah to Kanpur Cent.	1002	1060	590	295
Ratlam to Bombay Cent.	652	790	435	230
Kota to Bombay Cent.	910	970	535	275

DECCAN QUEEN

The Deccan Queen is known as the pride of Maharashtra State. As train number 302 it leaves Pune at 0715 every morning for Bombay VT where it arrives (after stops at Lonavla and Dadar) at 1040. Every evening, as the 301, it returns from Bombay VT at 1710, stopping at Karjat and Lonavla before arriving at Pune at 2035.

During weekdays, the Deccan Queen is packed with commuters so it is better to travel on a Sunday when the service is just as good. Although it operates on a reserved seat basis only, in 2nd Class the gangways can be jammed.

There is a supplement payable on top of the reservation fee and fare. This is Rs 18 in 1st Class and Rs 2 in 2nd Class; no extra for Indrail Pass holders.

1st Class accommodation is in reclining armchairs with woven upholstery. Seats are in a 2 × 2 pattern with an aisle between. 1st Class season ticket holders have compartments of their own which are less luxurious.

2nd Class has seats in a 2 × 3 format and these are hard upright bench style. In some carriages they are wooden, and cost the same price. There are 90 seats in a typical second class carriage. Both classes have fans, no AC, and the windows in 1st Class have curtains. A carriage, reserved for ladies, has two uniformed lady constables travelling in it. Armed railway security guards also ride the train.

What makes the train so special, as well as its decor, is being able to have breakfast or dinner in the 28-seat restaurant. Tea is served in real pots, not plastic flasks; meals are on china plates and some of the silver-type cutlery bears the crest of Air India. The menu is imaginative with such dishes as baked beans on toast for breakfast. The tiny pantry produces 10,000 items a day on its trip to Bombay and back. Snacks are also served to passengers at their seats.

The blue diesel engine of the train is emblazoned with its name and the coaches are painted white and grey with a bold red stripe along their length. Pictures and posters adorn the walls inside the coaches, and in the restaurant car there is a fish mobile hanging in a glass case used as a partition.

The Deccan Queen rides above the mist-filled valleys of the western ghats in the morning. Monkeys gambol around the train when it halts and scoop up food tossed to them by passengers. The train provides a gentle approach to the congestion of Bombay, as trees give way to forests of power pylons and rural shacks lead to tenement blocks. It is a great train in which to arrive, or leave, Bombay.

PARASURAM EXPRESS

This is another all chair car train. Although it doesn't have the charm of the Deccan Queen, it is the journey it makes during the day along the west coast of India from Trivandrum to Mangalore which gives it a special appeal. It leaves Trivandrum in the grey light of dawn at 0600 for the whole day run through 635 km of coastal scenery to Mangalore.

The 49/50 Parasuram Express is listed as having an AC Chair Car. When I travelled on it there was an ordinary 1st Class chair car and the wooden park bench type seats of 2nd Class. The fare in 1st Class is Rs 247; 2nd Class is Rs 67.

Bearers begin passing through the carriages with breakfast only 20 minutes after leaving Trivandrum, and they move up and down the aisle selling refreshments throughout the journey. After 75 minutes, the train creeps into Quilon, then begins a sortie through waterways and waterlogged paddy fields to the bright blue station of Kottayam, at present the nearest one for Alleppey, the destination of the waterway boats from Quilon.

At Ernakulam Town the crowds board and there is standing room only. A bearer takes orders for lunch and the scenery changes to lush groves of bananas and coconuts. Lunch, put on at Trichur from its base kitchen, is served in chrome *thali* trays to each passenger's seat, even in the packed 2nd Class. Brick kilns and tile factories tower like temples in the middle of paddy fields; the rich brown clay being used for building and the scooped out trenches for growing paddy.

The lushness of the littoral closes in on the track only to open up with a view of the sea at Kadalundi where coconut shells are laid out on the banks to dry. The logging lands of Calicut, rivers choked with timber, come next and the crowd on the train thins out.

The train takes on a new life, speeding along the Malabar coast past huge salt mountains and gashes in the forests of palm trees where broad rivers flow lazily to the sea. It slips into the Union Territory of Pondicherry with a breathless stop at Mahe, then out again. Mahe station seems no more than a tea stall and an awning under huge shade trees.

Suddenly the train bursts through the palm groves to the sea's edge, close to the beach and huts of plaited palm leaves. Then it's inland to the town of Tellicherry with glimpses of auto-rickshaws that are box shaped instead of conical like city ones. Onward to the sprawl of Cannanore then the sun is poised to set over the Viddalapatnam river mouth. The train crosses the wide river cautiously, no barriers between passengers watching from its open windows and the water far below.

The Parasuram Express speeds past the plains of Payangadi to Payyanur with its pretty station among the banyan trees. Hills ring the distant coast line as the day turns back to grey. Darkness closes in, revealing beacons of light shining through trees from hamlets by the track. Few people remain for the last two hours of the journey and excitement quickens as the express approaches Mangalore. An ordinary train, but a great ride.

PANDYAN EXPRESS

The Pandyan Express is a crack metre gauge overnight train linking Madras with Madurai. As number 117, it leaves Madras Egmore nightly at 1900 and arrives in Madurai, 556 km distant at 0615 the next morning. As the 118 it returns nightly at 1930 and arrives in Madras at 0645.

Apart from the charm of its name, recalling the ancient Pandyan kingdom whose capital over 2,000 years ago was Madurai, the Pandyan Express appeals to passengers for its dainty comfort. The track permits speeds of 100 km per hour and the train glides along smoothly at 75 kph. It comprises three carriages for 1st Class passengers and seven for 2nd Class. There are also three unreserved carriages (three tier berths) and one seat-only carriage as well as a ladies compartment as part of the guard's coach.

The train is an example of the better accommodation in some metre gauge expresses compared with broad gauge ones. Instead of the 46-berth AC dormitory carriage of a BG train, the Pandyan Express offers berths in cabins for two, three or four people. The 1st Class AC sleepers are comfortable cabins with a wash basin and serviced by attendants who make up the bed and bring tea in the morning.

RANCHI/LOHARDAGA PASSENGER TRAIN

The narrow gauge train trip on the Lohardaga line from Ranchi is not one that attracts tourists. Its destination is not a fashionable hill resort like Darjeeling but an industrial bauxite ore town called Lohardaga. Yet it is a fascinating ride on a railway of the past. Trains leave Ranchi at 0930 (the 1RL) and 1835 (the 3RL), arriving back at 1720 (as 2RL) and 0830 (as 4RL). They are frequently late, as this is a single line track and goods trains take preference.

The engines are ZE type, belching steam and looking sprightly despite their age (most were put into service in the 1950s). The passenger carriages they haul are made of wood, each having the air of an old barn. In the sole 1st Class compartment there are spacious, cushioned bench seats for nine passengers in a saloon bar layout with seats against the carriage walls. There are fans, lights and a toilet.

2nd Class seating is solid wooden benches facing each other, polished to a shine by countless *lungied* bottoms. There are fans, lights and a toilet in each too, and a jolly atmosphere. The 2nd Class fare from Ranchi to Lohardaga (a distance of 69 km) is Rs 8; 1st Class costs Rs 47.

Passengers cling happily to the outside of the carriages as the tiny steam engine negotiates the tangle of tracks out of Ranchi and passes its loco shed with a cheery whistle to the other engines. It ambles through industrial areas camouflaged with greenery, block buildings giving way to red tiled shanties.

The first stop is Argora, a country market station, then it rolls across vast plains of paddy and electricity pylons. Piska station, at 707 m above sea level, consists of the station master's office and a sward for a platform. Here is the place to disembark and take pre-arranged road transport back to Ranchi if the four hour slog to Lohardaga is too hard.

It's a relaxed, pointless train ride that stays in the memory, perhaps because of the sign in one of the carriages which reads: 'Keep doors and windows open during severe storms to prevent capsizing of coaches'.

DARJEELING TOY TRAIN

Considering the time it takes (nearly nine hours from New Jalpaiguri, plus 13½ hours overnight from Calcutta) together with the tiresome bureaucratic necessity of getting a permit, you might wonder if travelling on the Darjeeling toy train is worth the trouble.

Two guide books I consulted had different opinions. One calls the train ride 'a superb experience which shouldn't be missed'. The other says, almost sacreligiously for train fans, 'I really wonder about all the fuss made over it,' and advises travellers to go by bus. (But see Hugh Ballantyne's comments, page 96.)

An authority that should know, the North East Frontier Railway who run the train, says in its timetable: 'A journey over the Darjeeling Himalayan Railways by "toy trains" is an unforgettable experience. Starting from New Jalpaiguri or Siliguri Jn in the plains, the railway winds its way along mountains and valleys to reach Darjeeling. On the way, one can break the journey at Kurseong, another hill resort at an altitude of 1,458 metres. The Batasia loop and Tiger Hill on the way are favourite spots'.

The Darjeeling Himalayan Railway (DHR) began as a steam tramway in 1880 from Siliguri to Darjeeling following a cart road built by military engineers in 1861. It was the first hill railway to be built in India. The line consists of 82 km of narrow gauge (0.610 m or 2 feet wide) track which climbs to 2,135 m in 65 km. The gradient in one place is actually 1 in 19 and the ruling gradient is 1 in 25.

To cut down on having to build tunnels, a system of loops and reverses was devised. This has the track circling around and passing over a gradient by means of a bridge, thereby obtaining a higher elevation. The reverse part is when the track runs diagonally upwards for a short distance and later uses a parallel alignment to the original, higher up the mountain. No wonder it takes so long.

The tank engine which pulls the train, and locals strolling beside it as it dawdles alongside the road, make marvellous photos and contribute to the fame of this railway. It is unique. It is also frequently closed through bad weather, breakdowns and political problems. If it is operating, the best time to go is September to November, before it gets too cold, or in the spring of mid-April to mid-June.

The conventional way is to take the 43 Darjeeling Mail from Calcutta Sealdah station, daily departure at 1900, which arrives at New Jalpaiguri (NJ) station at 0830 the following morning. The train has 1st and Sleeper Class AC berths, AC Chair Car and ordinary 1st and 2nd Class berths. Bed rolls are available.

It connects with the 1D passenger train (1st and 2nd Class coaches) which leaves NJ station at 0900. The train stops at a dozen stations on the way, as well as elsewhere when it pauses for breath. It should arrive at Darjeeling at 1730 but it is often late. The permit for Darjeeling is checked at NJ station on the way up and on the way back.

The return journey to Calcutta is by the 2D, at 0845, or 4D, at 1000, from Darjeeling which arrive at NJ station at 1620 and 1745 respectively. The Darjeeling Mail leaves there at 1845 and arrives at Sealdah at 0845 the next day.

There is an earlier departure scheduled from NJ for Darjeeling at 0715 (the 3D). To catch that you will have to arrive at NJ the day before, by the 57 Kanchenjunga Express which leaves Calcutta Howrah at 0600 for Guwahati (but not on Saturdays) and gives a daylight journey to NJ, arriving there at 1630. It has ordinary 1st and 2nd Class. You could stay at NJ station where there are four double rooms and three dormitory beds.

To make the return journey from NJ to Calcutta (a distance of 566 km) there is the 58 Kanchenjunga Express (leaves at 0945, arrives Howrah at 2035). On certain days there are also the weekly expresses from Guwahati to Bangalore, Trivandrum or Cochin which leave NJ at 1052 and arrive at Howrah at 2215. They have AC sleepers as well as 1st and 2nd Class.

As another option, and instead of going back to Calcutta, you could catch the 2D toy train down from Darjeeling and leave it at Siliguri Jn at 1715 and wait for the 15 Guwahati/Varanasi Express. This is a metre gauge train which departs Siliguri Jn at 0100 and takes 29 hours to reach Varanasi. There are two retiring rooms at Siliguri Jn.

Check with railway sources before planning to visit Darjeeling by train to avoid disappointment in case the train isn't operating.

MATHERAN HILL RAILWAY

Less than two hours from Bombay there is a great rail trip by another toy train, the one that goes to Matheran. The name means 'jungle head' or 'forest on the top' and it still applies to this place, discovered in 1850. It is the nearest hill resort to Bombay, 108 km away, situated in the western ghats at 803 m above sea level.

The narrow gauge railway was opened to traffic in 1907 and was, until a few years ago when a road was built, the only way to reach Matheran. Motor traffic does not penetrate beyond the resort's car park from where walking, pony riding or rickshaw is the only means of getting around.

The toy train begins its 21 km journey from Neral, pulled by a cute diesel locomotive. Although the climb of 610 m is slow (it takes two hours) time passes quickly because of the breathtaking scenery. The ruling gradient is 1 in 20 as the track zigzags upwards gradually revealing the full beauty of Matheran Hill.

It is possible to visit Matheran on a day trip, but many people (especially Bombayites escaping from the city) stay longer in this lush, traffic free town. The railway is closed from mid-June during the monsoon season and only opens again at the end of September or early October. There are no retiring rooms at Matheran station, nor at Neral, but the town has lots of places to stay. The fare to Matheran from Neral is calculated on a distance of 126 km instead of the 21 km actually travelled.

The first train of the day, the 601 passenger, leaves Neral at 0840 and arrives at Matheran at 1040. There are other departures at 1100 (the 603) and 1700 (the 605) with an extra train (the 607) leaving at 1015 in the season of mid March to mid June. To connect with these departures the 305 Deccan Express leaves Bombay VT at 0645 and arrives at Neral at 0819 in time for the 601 departure. The 307 Koyna Express leaves VT at 0845 and arrives at Neral at 1032 in time for the 603 departure.

Trains from Matheran are the 602 leaving at 0545, arriving at Neral at 0745; the 604 at 1310 arriving at 1450; the 606 at 1435 arriving at 1620; and the 608 (season time only) at 1620, arriving at 1803. There is no convenient connection back to Bombay unless you try a suburban train on the Karjat to Bombay line such as the S24 leaving Neral at 1645 and reaching VT at 1840. Another option is to leave Matheran at 0545 so you can catch the Deccan Express at 0819 to Lonavla or Pune.

NILAGIRI MOUNTAIN RAILWAY

The broad gauge Nilagiri Express from Madras terminates at Mettupalaiyam station and passengers change over during the 30 minute wait before the fabled Blue Mountain train departs for Ooty.

During the wait, vendors pass along the platform selling coffee and breakfast snacks, and the 1920s steam engine shunts into position at the back of the train. The station has the look of a frontier with the modern overnight Nilagiri Express, hauled by a huge diesel and with AC sleeper and 3 tier carriages, on one side of the platform, and the old wooden coaches of the metre gauge mountain train on the other.

Although the idea for a railway from Mettupalaiyam to Coonoor, a distance of 27 km, was first mooted in 1854, it wasn't in operation until 1899. The problem had been how to get the train up the steep gradients of the mountains and how to stop it running too fast on the way down.

The rack and pinion system was devised. Special rack bars were laid between the track rails where the line slopes to form a kind of elongated ladder. The train pinions itself onto the rack for the climb up, pushed by the engine. The rack section commences just after Kallar and continues up to Coonoor. Maximum speed on that section is 13 kph. The line was extended to Ooty in 1908.

The train is pushed by one of the eight X class steam locos remaining out of seven introduced in 1925 and five put on the line in 1952. One of those eight has recently retired to the Rail Museum in Delhi.

The train's coaches are as old as the engines. Made of wood, they are painted dark blue and a grubby yellow on the outside and pale blue inside. There are two 1st Class cabins at the front of the train, furnished with coconut fibre and foam bench cushions covered in green rexine. Both cabins seat eight passengers, or more, with the best seats on the way up being in the front cabin facing the way the train is going. Since the engine pushes from behind passengers have a glorious view of the jungle, mountains and valleys. Sit on the left side facing the window for the best views.

2nd Class carriages with wooden bench seats form the rest of the train, with a guards van and luggage box at the rear. Each of the coaches and wagons is crewed by a brakesman who stands on the open gallery at the front of the carriage and independently operates the wheel and rack brakes on whistle codes from the driver.

After the train leaves Mettupalaiyam, its first stop is at Kallar, a phantom station since it is not in the SR timetable, but this is where the rack and pinion system is engaged. The next stop is at the entrance to tunnel number 3, for the engine to take on water. At every tunnel the kids on the train erupt with hoots of excitement as the train passes through it, and look down aghast when the train emerges to cross vast chasms on spindly bridges.

Elephants and rock-falls are hazards on this run. At Hillgrove station where the train stops to take on water again, passengers flock to the refreshment stall. Wild monkeys perform on the station's roof for bananas. There are no toilets on the train but those at Hillgrove are new and good.

Coonoor, a little over half the way to Ooty, is surrounded by mountains and fringed with buildings. Its station was built in 1897 out of granite blocks and is painted bright blue and pale yellow. There are three retiring rooms, a refreshment stall, newly built and clean toilets, a fountain, and a pretty umbrella shaped shelter.

An attraction at Coonoor is the loco shed, the base for all the locomotives on this line. It is close to the station and has a hand-painted scene of a steam engine as its signboard. The engines are maintained and overhauled here with the oldest (number 37384, built in 1920) still in operation. The station bell is an old metal toothed wheel of the pinion system which is hammered with an iron bar to announce the last five minutes before a train's departure. It is possible to break the journey at Coonoor and catch a train later, or another day, up to Ooty. If you do stay in Coonoor (which many people prefer to Ooty because its scenery and charm are less spoiled) spend time at Hampton Manor, one kilometre from the station. Since 1977 this hotel (Originally a 19th century Briton's private residence) has been owned by Mrs Das, a tireless promoter for Coonoor's delights. The hotel has 31 bedrooms, all different, most with attached sitting rooms as well as vast bathrooms, in a pretty cottage-style setting. It is immaculately kept with beautiful gardens and priceless furniture. The service is traditional with shuffling bearers in turbans and white gloves, and a wood-panelled bar abrim with convivial atmosphere even when it's empty. Out of season, April–June, guests are few and Mrs Das despairs of having to sell to a chain, so visit soon before its ruined. Singles from Rs 125, doubles Rs 180–Rs 500.

The military base station of Wellington comes soon after, with an occasional glimpse of soldiers practising on the target range beside the track. At Aravankadu there is a cordite factory opposite the station and the railway retiring room has a view over it. The climb to Ooty broadens as the train chugs gently through forests and hills. On the evening run from Coonoor, skeins of mist hang in the valleys below the track and men wander along the line wrapped in blankets. It is chilly in Ooty in the summer, and cold in winter.

Four kilometres before reaching Ooty is a station named Lovedale, at 2,192 m above sea level. It is set in the forest and has a post office for neighbour, so there must be some residents but they are not to be seen. Lovedale lives up to its name; peaceful and romantic. The station, like an English country cottage, has two retiring rooms at Rs 30 for a double.

The train crosses 250 bridges on its way to Ooty and passes through 16 tunnels. The average gradient is about 1 in 24.50 but it is 1 in 12.28 from Kallar to Coonoor. The total length of the line is 45.88 km and the journey time is 4 hrs 25 mins going up and 3 hrs 20 mins coming down.

The line is subject to landslides and is often closed for weeks during the monsoon season. Every day the track is inspected and the train only leaves Kallar when it is safe to proceed. Elephants have attacked station buildings which is why some have been closed.

'Travel by rail and spend longer among the hills' reads a slogan painted on a retaining wall close to the tea growing area before Runnymeade, one of the closed stations.

After its arrival at Udagamandalam, as Ooty is now called, the train is shunted over a service trench where an engineer examines it underneath. For its descent, the loco leads (but in reverse) with the brakesman of each coach watching carefully to prevent too fast a run down hill.

The usual itinerary for independent travellers involves taking a bus from Ooty to Mysore since Ooty is the end of the line. It's a shame to do this and miss the descent, which is just as dramatic as the ride up.

The conventional way of getting to Ooty by train is from Madras on the 5 Nilagiri Express which departs nightly at 2105, arriving at Mettupalaiyam at 0715 the next day. This connects with the 564 leaving Mettupalaiyam at 0745, arriving Coonoor at 1045 and at Ooty at 1210. An additional train, (562) operates during periods of extra demand, such as the April/June season. There are also departures from Coonoor for Ooty at 0800 and 1730.

For the return, the 561 leaves Ooty at 1455 and arrives at Mettupalaiyam at 1825 to connect with the 6 Nilagiri Express, departing at 1915 and arriving in Madras at 0555 the next day. That train gets to Coimbatore at 2000 from where there are many connections to other parts of Southern India.

Fares on the Blue Mountain Railway are charged according to a calculated distance rather than actual distance. From Madras the basic fare is Rs 537 for 1st Class AC sleeper, Rs 322 for AC 2 tier, Rs 245 for 1st Class and Rs 62 for 2nd Class. From Mettupalaiyam, the fare is Rs 65 for 1st Class and Rs 10 for 2nd Class. Coonoor to Ooty is Rs 35 in 1st Class and Rs 4 in 2nd.

The Nilagiri Passenger Train.

Riding the Matheran Hill Railway. (Anthony J. Lambert)

The Himalayan Queen. (Philip Ferguson)

The Deccan Queen passing Karjat from Pune to Bombay. (Hugh Ballantyne)

Diesel operated locomotive on Northern Railway's Pathankot-Jogindarnagar line, the most northerly narrow gauge track in India. (Philip Ferguson)

Distances:

Station	Remarks	Actual km	Charged km	Elevation Metres
Mettupalaiyam	Rooms	0		326
Kallar		7.46		404
Allderly	Closed	12.27		731
Hillgrove	Snacks	17.26	50	1092
Runneymede	Closed	21.97		1407
Kateri Road	Closed	24.35		1547
Coonoor	Rooms	27.03	77	1711
Wellington	Rooms	28.54	80	1769
Aravankadu	Rooms	31.34	86	1812
Ketti		37.19	98	2092
Lovedale	Rooms	41.76	108	2192
Udagamandalam	Rooms	45.88	116	2203

KALKA SHIMLA RAILWAY

The best way to appreciate the grandeur of the 96 km of 0.762 m narrow gauge track as it climbs through the foothills of the Himalayas, is by Rail Motor Car. It makes you aware of the extraordinary feats of engineering that created this line with great arched viaducts spanning chasms, and over a hundred tunnels bored through the mountains.

The Rail Motor Car (No. 251) leaves Kalka at 0615. It's possible to take an overnight train, the 1 Howrah/Kalka Mail, from Delhi station at 2245, and arrive at Kalka at 0600. The Rail Car waits at the end of the platform where the Kalka Mail terminates. The sight of it, like a light blue 1920s Ford truck that's escaped from a museum, will make you rub your eyes in disbelief. There are actually four cars in service, built in 1927 and reconditioned in 1982.

The car has space for two next to the driver's cab and behind are four bench seats, all comfortably upholstered, for five passengers each. Upgrading of tickets to ride in this extraordinary vehicle, which has been in operation for over 60 years, is done by a ticket inspector at the empty, marble-topped snack bar counter close to where the Car is parked. It costs Rs 110 for the 4 hr 20 min run to Shimla and is worth every paise. 1st Class Indrail Pass holders pay Rs 10.

The driver engages gear and the Car leaps forward for the journey through 103 tunnels (the longest is number 33 at Barog, at a height of 1144 m) and over 869 bridges, climbing from 656 m above sea level at Kalka to 2,075 m at Shimla. The views are stunning and, seated in the Rail Car, you miss nothing.

The Car will stop at any station en route, if the request is made at Kalka or to the driver himself, but usually it sails right through the tiny picturesque stations. There is no toilet in the Car but the driver will stop if your need is great and even reverse if he passes your station and you forget to tell him.

A 15 minute halt is made at Barog where the restaurant is one of the nicest of any station in India. It is above the platform with a flower-bedecked verandah, a hillside view, service that is friendly and fast, and food that is freshly prepared. You should order meals in advance through the railway staff before leaving Kalka or Shimla.

Every one of the 18 stations on the journey to Shimla seems an attractive spot to linger, but none has retiring rooms. Above Solan station there is something called a 'Relieving Lodge' and Solan Brewery station is actually in the middle of a heady-smelling brewery. Shimla station has five retiring rooms, with plans for more. The rooms are on the first floor over the station and all have attached bathrooms with hot water. A deluxe room (Rs 100 in season) has a TV and fridge.

Shimla station has a magnificent view down the mountains and is kept clean (lots of blue paintwork) and well run. There is no foreign tourist quota for reservations at the station (which seems strange in view of Shimla's popularity with foreign tourists) but the SS and his staff try their best to arrange bookings. There are two waiting rooms, a tea stall and a restaurant.

The line was built in 1903 on a rising gradient meandering through the Shivalik Range, the steepest one being 1 in 33. Average rise works out to 1 in 67. About 70 per cent of the track is on curves. The Rail Car is permitted a maximum speed of 29 kph, and the diesel hauled passenger train is restricted to a maximum of 25 kph.

One of the passenger trains (no. 253) leaves Kalka at 0700 and there are also departures at 0845 (tourist season only) and at 1150 (no. 257). The 1150 departure waits for the 195 daytime Himalayan Queen which leaves New Delhi at 0600 and arrives at Kalka at 1125.

On the Kalka to Shimla train, 1st Class seats are in a chair car with one seat on one side of the aisle and a pair of seats on the other, total 18. The seats are reversible to face whichever end of the train is the front. Another type of 1st Class carriage has a coupé and a lounge with seats along the side of the carriage. Fare is Rs 98.

Seats in 2nd Class are wooden, with slats, and are rather hard for the journey which usually takes between five and six hours. Fare is Rs 25. Departures from Shimla are at 0940, 1255, 1500 (in season only), 1645 (rail car) and 1730.

The 1645 Rail Car gets to Kalka in time for the 2330 departure of the 2 Kalka/Howrah Mail. The 254 Shimla Queen train leaves Shimla at 0940 and arrives at Kalka at 1555 in time for the 196 Himalayan Queen's departure at 1635 for New Delhi. Other trains leave Shimla at 1255 (the 2KS), at 1500 (the in season only 256) and the 258 mail at 1730. On arrival at Kalka, there are connections to Ambala and from there to Jammu Tawi or eastwards.

BUTTERFIELD'S INDIAN RAILWAY TOUR

'I was pretty apprehensive about India and spending so much time on a train with a group of unknowns,' wrote Australian Lynne Barraclough to Jane and Ashley Butterfield. 'But thanks to you both I would happily return to India for another trip.'

Jane and Ashley Butterfield run rail tours in India from August to March by a specially converted railway carriage which is attached to scheduled trains. From their HQ in Yorkshire, they send out fact-filled brochures describing their tours so that potential passengers have a good idea of what's in store. Then they personally accompany every tour in India to look after their guests. The cost (around £600) includes train travel and train meals and some hotel accommodation and some excursions. Air fares to India are extra.

Their brochure states: 'Our carriage accommodates up to 26 people and comprises two large sitting rooms, a small dining room/library, a pantry, a kitchen, two wash rooms with showers and four Asian style toilets. It is equipped with electric lights and fans . . . At night the sitting rooms convert into dormitories, and then you can choose between sleeping on benches, upper berths or camp beds'.

The Butterfields have been running the only comprehensive railway tour of India using a private railway carriage for 15 years. Their experience of getting around India by rail is unique and their tours are ideal for those who want to try train travel but not alone. Londoner Barry, 25, wrote in the Butterfield comments book: 'If I had tried to do India on my own, I suspect that I would still be in Delhi arguing about seat reservations'.

A Butterfields' tour lasts for 18, 26 or 29 days and begins in Delhi with the 'bogie', the private carriage, being attached to a train to Haridwar. Then it is eastwards to Lucknow and Varanasi, south to Hyderabad and Bangalore, some independent touring in the south, and then by bogie to Bombay from Madras and on to Agra before getting back to Delhi. A new tour has been introduced utilizing an AC coach attached to metre gauge trains for a three week trip through Southern India.

The Butterfields tell passengers: 'Although we live together on board, when we stop you are free to be as independent as you please'. It is a formula people enjoy, as they can travel safely by rail in convivial company without having to worry about the arrangements, and yet can wander off on their own to explore when they want.

Address: Burton Fleming, Driffield, Yorkshire, YO24 OPQ. Tel: 0262 87230

Chapter 12

Super Trains

India has some trains that really are super: fast, comfortable and with a pantry car and bearer service. The best are the Superfast Trains, although they do not all share the same standards of accommodation and service. Some are exclusively 2nd Class and some have no refreshment facilities at all. In this section I have included a list of the main superfast trains, indicating with 'R' where a pantry car or on-board refreshment is available. However, even where there is no 'R', meals/refreshments could still be obtainable through station halts.

Express and mail trains are also good; a separate list of those having 1st Class AC sleepers is given here. There are over 200 express and mail trains with AC 2 tier (2nd Class) sleeper accommodation and the number is increasing; too many to include accurately here. However, unless it is an all 2nd Class (3 tier) 'Janata' train, most expresses will have a non-AC 1st Class carriage if there is no AC 2 tier sleeper. A separate list is given of trains which have AC Chair Car coaches.

Superfast express and mail trains
A supplementary charge (see Chapter 3) is levied for travel on the trains listed here. Not all are daily. 2 = all 2nd Class; ND = New Delhi; MG = Metre Gauge.

Number	Express	Service between
1/2	Howrah/Kalka Mail	R
3/4	Frontier Mail	ND/Bombay Central R
15/16	Grand Trunk Exp.	ND/Madras Central R
17/18	Prayag Raj Exp.	ND/Allahabad
19/20	Konark Exp.	Bhubaneswar/Secunderabad/ Bombay
21/22	Agra Fort/Jaipur Exp.	MG
25/26	Paschim Exp.	Amritsar/Bombay Central R
39/40	Brindavan Exp. (ACCC & 2 only)	Madras Central/Bangalore City R
49/50	Visakhapatnam/ND	link express
57/58	Kunchenjunga Exp.	Howrah/Guwahati R
59/60	Gitanjali Exp.	Howrah/Bombay R
61/62	Mandore Exp.	Delhi/Jodhpur MG
75/76	Kovai Exp.	Madras/Coimbatore R
79/80	Taj Exp.	ND/Agra Cantt/Gwalior R
81/82	Deluxe Exp.	Amritsar/Howrah R

Number	Express	Service between
101/102	Minar Exp.	Bombay/Scunderabad
103/104	Deluxe Exp.	Amritsar/Howrah R
115/116	Pallavan Exp.	Madras Egmore/Trichy R·MG·2
119/120	Gomti Exp.	ND/Lucknow R
121/122	Tamil Nadu Exp.	ND/Madras Cent. R
123/124	Andhra Pradesh Exp.	ND/Secunderabad R
125/126	Kerala Exp.	ND/Trivandrum R
127/128	Karnataka Exp.	ND/Bangalore City R
135/136	Vaigai Exp.	Madras Egmore/Madurai R·MG·2
141/142	Coromandel Exp.	Howrah/Madras Central R
153/154	Vaishali	ND/Mazaffarpur R
155/156	Tinsukia Mail	ND/Guwahati R
167/168	Malwa Exp.	ND/Indore R
171/172	Jammu Tawi/Bombay Central Exp.	R
173/174	Himgiri Exp.	Jammu Tawi/Howrah R
181/182	Sarvodaya Exp.	ND/Ahmadabad R
191/192	Magadh Exp.	ND/Patna R
301/302	Deccan Queen	Bombay VT/Pune R
405/406	ND/Ludhiana Exp.	
415/416	Ganga/Gomti Exp.	Lucknow/Allahabad
501/502	Pink City Exp.	Delhi/Jaipur MG R
505/506	Ashram Exp.	Delhi/Ahmadabad MG
507/508	Marwar Exp.	Jodhpur/Ahmadabad MG
515/516	Garib/Nawaz Exp.	Delhi/Udaipur MG R
901/902	Trivandrum/Guwahati Exp.	R
903/904	Trivandrum/Ahmadabad Exp.	R
905/906	Karnataka Exp. ND/ Bangalore City	R
915/916	Neelachal Exp.	ND/Puri
921/922	North East Exp.	ND/Guwahati R
925/926	Mahanadi Exp.	Bilaspur/Bhopal
927/928	ND/Bangalore Exp.	R
929/930	Cochin/Hyderabad Exp.	R
931/932	Ahmadabad/Hyderabad Exp.	R
933/934	Bombay VT/Lucknow Exp.	
935/936	Cochin Harbour/Bombay VT Exp.	
937/938	Cochin Harbour/Ahmadabad Exp.	
939/940	Cochin Harbour/Guwahati Exp.	R
941/942	Navijivan Exp.	Ahmadabad/Madras Cent. R
949/950	ND/Varanasi Exp.	
951/952	Cochin Harbour/Howrah Exp.	
953/954	Amarkantak Exp.	Durg/Bhopal
959/960	Gwalior/Howrah Exp.	
961/962	Lashkar Exp.	Gwalior/Dadar
963/964	Dadar/Madras Exp.	
965/966	Bombay/Varanasi Exp.	

First Class AC Sleeper Trains

Trains with 1st Class Air Conditioned Sleeper coaches are listed here. Usually there is one coach per train, sometimes combined with other accommodation. 1st Class AC berths are not necessarily provided daily, even though the train may run daily.

Number	Express	Service between
1/2	Bombay VT/Howrah Mail	
1/2	Howrah/Kalka Mail	via Delhi R
1/2	Gujarat Mail	Bombay Central/Ahmadabad
1/2	Delhi Mail	Delhi/Jaipur MG
1/2	Delhi Mail	Delhi/Ahmadabad MG
3/4	Frontier Mail	Bombay Central/Amritsar R
3/4	Howrah/Bombay VT Mail	via Allahabad
3/4	Howrah/Madras Mail	
5/6	Punjab Mail	Bombay VT/Firozpur
5/6	Howrah/Amritsar Mail	
5/6	Nilagiri Exp.	Madras/Mettupalaiyam
5/6	Howrah/Sambalpur Exp.	
7/8	Godavari Exp.	Hyderabad/Visakhapatnam
7/8	Nainital Exp.	Lucknow/Kathgodam MG
7/8	Howrah/Puri Exp.	
11/12	Ispat Exp.	Howrah/Raurkela
11/12	Howrah/Delhi Exp.	Kanpur/Delhi
13/14	Steel Exp.	Howrah/Tatanagar
15/16	Howrah/Hatia Exp.	via Ranchi
17/18	Prayag Raj Exp.	ND/Allahabad
19/20	Dehra Dun Exp.	ND/Kota
25/26	Paschim Exp.	ND/Bombay Central R
25/28	AC Exp.	ND/Amritsar R
27/28	Exp.	Bombay Central/Vadodara
29/30	Lucknow Mail	ND/Lucknow
31/32	Howrah/Danapur Exp.	
33/34	Jammu Mails	Delhi/Jammu Tawi
41/42	Mussorie Exp.	Delhi/Dehra Dun
43/44	Darjeeling Mail	Sealdah/New Jalpaiguri
81/82	AC Exp.	ND/Amritsar
81/82	AC Exp.	ND/Howrah R
101/102	Rajdhani Exp.	ND/Howrah R
103/104	AC Exp.	ND/Amritsar R
103/104	AC Exp.	ND/Howrah R
117/118	Pandyan Exp.	Madras Egmore/Madurai MG
119/120	Gomti Exp.	ND/Lucknow R
121/122	Tamil Nadu Exp.	ND/Madras R
123/124	Andhra Pradesh Exp.	ND/Secunderabad R
151/152	Rajdhani Exp.	ND/Bombay Central R
157/158	Kashivishvanath Exp.	ND/Varanasi
191/192	Magadh/Vikramshila Exp.	ND/Patna R

Number	Express	Service between
307/308	Black Diamond Exp.	Howrah/Dhanbad R
309/310	Coal Field Exp.	Howrah/Dhanbad R
415/416	Ganga Gomti Exp.	Lucknow/Allahabad
507/508	Marwar Exp.	Jodhpur/Ahmadabad MG

AC Chair Car

In this list of trains that have air conditioned carriages with seating accommodation, some only have a few seats available in carriages combined with 1st Class AC Sleepers.

Number	Train	Service between
1/2	Golconda Exp.	Secunderabad/Guntur R
15/16	Shanti Niketan Exp.	Howrah/Bulpur
25/26	Paschim Exp. R	ND/Bombay Central
25/26	AC Exp. R	ND/Amritsar
39/40	Brindavan Exp.	Madras/Bangalore R
43/44	Darjeeling Mail	Sealdah/New Jalpaiguri
47/48	Flying Mails	ND/Amritsar
49/50	Parasuram Exp.	Trivandrum/Mangalore R
75/76	Kovai Exp.	Madras/Coimbatore R
81/82	AC Exp.	ND/Amritsar
81/82	AC Exp.	ND/Howrah R
101/102	Rajdhani Exp.	ND/Howrah R
103/104	AC Exp.	ND/Howrah R
103/104	AC Exp.	ND/Amritsar R
119/120	Gomti Exp.	ND/Lucknow R
121/122	Tamil Nadu Exp.	ND/Madras R
123/124	A.P. Express	ND/Secunderabad R
151/152	Rajdhani Exp.	ND/Bombay Central R
195/196	Himalayan Queen	ND/Kalka
197/198	Shane Punjab Exp.	ND/Amritsar R
309/310	Coal Field Exp.	Howrah/Dhanbad
313/314	Indrayani Exp.	Bombay VT/Pune
415/416	Ganga Gomti Exp.	Lucknow/Allahabad
2001/2002	Shatabdi Exp.	ND/Jhansi R

Some trains with pantry or refreshment cars

(in addition to those indicated with "R" in train lists)

5/6	Kamrup Exp. (MG)	Guwahati/Dibrugarh Town
11/12	Gujarat Exp.	Bombay Cent/Ahmadabad
15/16	Sauhashtra Exp.	Bombay Cent/Ahmadabad
15/16	Guwahati and Varansi Exp. (MG)	
21/22	Flying Ranee Exp.	Bombay Cent/Surat

23/24	Ferozpur Janata Exp.	Bombay Cent/Ferozpur
31/32	Aravali Exp.	Ahmadabad/Delhi
59/60	Kamrup Exp.	Howrah/Guwahati
89/90	Bikaner Exp.	Delhi/Bikaner (MG)
93/94	Jodhpur Mail	Jodhpur/Ratangarh (MG)
131/132	Jayanti Janti Exp.	ND/Cochin
139/140	Ganga Kaveri Exp.	Madras/Varanasi
153/154	Jayanti Janti Exp.	ND/Samastipur
177/178	Jhelum Exp.	ND/Pune
201/202	Panchavati Exp.	Bombay VT/Manmad
231/232	Jayanti Janta Exp.	Delhi/Ahmadabad (MG)
265/266	Jodhpur Bhildi (MG)	
301/302	Venad Exp.	Shoranur/Trivandrum
303/304	Vanchinad Exp.	Trivandrum/Ernakulam
305/306	Deccan Exp.	Bombay VT/Pune
309/310	Sinhagad Exp.	Bombay VT/Pune
501A/502A	Gharib Nawar Exp.	Delhi/Ajmer/Udaipur
503/504	Marudha Exp.	Jodhpur/Lucknow (MG)
509/510	Avadh Assam Exp.	ND/Guwahati
801/802	Muri Amritsar Exp.	Amritsar/Ranchi
911/912	Cochin Harbour Gorakhpur Exp.	
943/944	Madras Central Patna Exp.	
945/946	North East Exp.	Guwahati/Bombay VT

Chapter 13

Help

Onboard emergencies
For health and security problems contact the train superintendent or conductor immediately. There are emergency cords in every compartment to stop the train. Trains carry books in which complaints can be made.

At the station
Contact the Station Superintendent in person, or if the station is too small to have one, then the station master, if you experience problems at his station. Many stations have police posts at which reports can be made, and public grievance booths. There are also complaints books available on demand; complaints are taken seriously and investigated. The SS will have a list of doctors who can be called on in an emergency.

Consul
The UK Foreign & Commonwealth Office have a leaflet available called *Consular Assistance Abroad* which contains invaluable advice that applies to travellers of all nationalities. Don't expect your consul to get better treatment for you in hospital (or prison) than is provided for local nationals, or to interfere in local judicial procedures. However, the consul can provide a list of lawyers, interpreters, and doctors, and sometimes arrange for messages to be sent to relatives or friends if you are arrested.

The leaflet recommends that, as soon as you arrive, you jot down the address and telephone number of your local embassy, high commissioner or consul to carry with you; check the local telephone directory for it. Carry your passport with you at all times in India.

Mail/Messages
Holders of American Express travellers cheques or credit cards can use the local American Express office as a mail drop. If you have a reservation to stay at a reputable hotel at some stage during your tour of India, have your mail sent there, with arrival date marked on the envelope. Mail can be sent to stations (see Chapter 2) but you might never get it. Telegrams can also be sent to you at stations.

Homesick

If you are feeling homesick, or perhaps simply overwhelmed by India and too much travelling, don't bottle up your misery. Talking to fellow passengers can help. In a town, turn to the telephone directory, or hotel management, or even the SS, for addresses of social organizations or professional associations with which you have some connection at home, such as Lions, Rotary, trade unions, sports clubs, hobby groups.

Foreigners who have an interest shared by Indians are likely to be given a splendid welcome which banishes feelings of loneliness. Some towns have clubs where visitors can become temporary members. If the club has a western style menu, that can help cure homesickness.

Elephant shunting; Rajgangpu station cement factory.

Chapter 14

Endpiece

A summary of how to get the best out of travelling in India by rail.

- Travel on an Indrail Pass, preferably bought from an overseas GSA so he can make your first reservation in advance.

- Go for at least 21 days.

- September to March is the best time.

- Make full use of the facilities for foreigners by booking your subsequent reservations through the ITB at New Delhi station, or through the Foreign Tourist Cells at the other main stations.

- If you intend buying rail tickets in India from the Foreign Tourist Quota, have foreign currency or travellers cheques to do this; especially as it saves a trip to the bank to change them.

- Make train reservations well in advance and allow time to do so; if you have problems, ask the CRS or the SS for advice and help.

- Travel 1st non-AC or AC 2 tier sleeper class.

- Sleeping on trains and in station retiring rooms saves money for memorable nights in classic hotels in Rajasthan and major cities.

- Use *Trains At A Glance* to plot your own itinerary.

- Choose trains which arrive/depart during daylight.

- Avoid tight connections.

- Allow days in your itinerary for doing nothing; you might need spare days in the event of delay.

- Take your full quota of duty-free liquor into India.

- On long distance trains, let the bearer be your friend since he can be a source of advice and extra comforts.

- Drink lots of liquid but not station water unless you've purified it yourself.

- Travel light but include a padlock (to secure your luggage to something in the train or waiting room and to lock the retiring room door), a pocket knife/bottle opener, a hand towel, a water bottle and purifying tablets.

- Wear loose cotton clothing and underwear; buy plastic sandals in India to wear in train or station toilets and showers.

- Keep travellers cheques and travel documents on you, never in your luggage; have change handy for purchases from platform vendors.

- When alighting from a moving train, face the way it's going; always check up and down a track before you cross it.

- When dealing with railway people, be patient and polite; know what you want and ask for it intelligibly.

FOR YOUR OWN SAFETY **BE CAUTIOUS** WHEN NEGOTIATING A RAILWAY LEVEL CROSSING.

CENTRAL RAILWAY SAFETY ORGANIZATION

Remember AGAINST A RAILWAY ENGINE YOU STAND **NO CHANCE**

Appendices

FURTHER READING

Since this book is intended as a guide to India by rail and not as a general guide to India, you will need maps and books that tell you about the places and ways of the country as well. There is no point in travelling by train to, say, Madurai unless you know something about all those temples you'll be gazing at.

Maps

India (Hildebrand) 1 : 4,255,000 – £2.95.
A general road map with shaded relief, railways, brief historical descriptions of major sites, and other tourist information.

Nelles Verlag Maps 1 : 1,500,000 – £4.95
A newly published series of five regional road maps of the Indian subcontinent, with shaded relief, railways, tourist information, and insets of city plans. The most comprehensive coverage of India at a consistent scale.

Guide books

India: a travel survival kit (Lonely Planet). £11.95.
The book I, and thousands of other visitors to India, depend on. Very comprehensive (over 800 pages).

The Best of India (Pilot Books USA, distributed in Europe by Bradt Publications). £7.95.
Concise guide to the best value in Indian travel, with an emphasis on "hard information".

Handbook for Travellers in India, Pakistan, Nepal, Bangladesh and Sri Lanka. (John Murray). £25.00.
The classic guide to the subcontinent, now in its 22nd edition.

Other guides to India include:

Into India (John Murray). £6.95.

India (Hildebrand). £5.95.

The Cadogan Guide to India (Cadogan Books). £8.95.

India, Nepal and Sri Lanka: the Travellers Guide (Springfield Books). £8.95.

India Discovered (Collins). £8.95.

Indian Subcontinent at Cost (Little Hills Press). £6.95.

Local guides are available at bookshops or railway book stalls in India including the newly published booklet, *Passenger Handbook*, from Indian Railways.

SPELLING

Many stations and train names have two or more ways of spelling them in English, such as Hardwar/Haridwar, Nilgiri/Nilagiri, and Shimla/Simla. I have tried to use the spelling which appears in the zonal timetables although sometimes even those sources are not consistent.

GLOSSARY

Indian Railway bureaucracy is riddled with initials and abbreviations used freely in conversation among railway men as well as in signs intended for foreign tourists. For instance, at Agra Fort there is a sign which tells tourists to contact 'the CRS'. You'll frequently be asked for your 'PNR'. Above a door at a station I saw a sign which said VLRRMTP. I pushed it open to find it meant 'Vegetarian Light Refreshment Room, Mettupalaiyam'.

Terms used in this book are as follows:

AC	Air conditioned
ACC	Air conditioned chair
BG	Broad gauge
CCTV	Closed Circuit TeleVision
CRS	Chief Reservations Supervisor
CRS	Computer Reservations System
Crore	100 lakhs, ie: 10,000,000
DHR	Darjeeling Hill Railway
Direct	'Without any change of train'
DRM	Divisional Railway Manager
EMU	Electric Motor Unit
ETA	Estimated Time of Arrival
GRP	Government Railway Police
GSA	General Sales Agent (for Indrail Passes)
ITB	International Tourist Bureau
Jn	Junction
Lakh	100,000
MG	Metre Gauge
ND	New Delhi

NER	North Eastern Railway
NG	Narrow Gauge
NJ	New Jalpaiguri station
NR	Northern Railway
NV	Non-vegetarian (restaurant/meal)
PNR	Passenger Name Record (ie: number on a computer generated reservation coupon)
R	Refreshments available
RAC	Reservation Against Cancellation
Rexine	Artificial leather
RPF	Railway Protection Force
SER	South Eastern Railway
SM	Station Master
SR	Southern Region
SS	Station Superintendent
TAG	*Trains At A Glance*
TC	Ticket Collector
TS	Train Superintendent
TTE	Travelling Ticket Examiner
V	Vegetarian (restaurant/meal)
VT	Bombay Victoria Terminus station

UPDATE

For this book to maintain its value for travellers, it needs to be updated. As much as I would like to spend a few months each year travelling in India by rail, it would take me a long time to ride every train, visit every station, and discover every change. So if you have any new information, tips for other rail travellers or reports on new developments which could be included in the next edition of *India by Rail*, please send them to me:

Royston Ellis,
INDIA BY RAIL,
c/o Bradt Publications,
41 Nortoft Road,
Chalfont St Peter,
Bucks SL9 0LA,
England.

Contributions which are used will be acknowledged in the next edition, as well as being of great help to other rail travellers.

Index of Place Names

(for other subjects see *Contents*)